Crochet

Crochet

The complete step-by-step guide

Essential techniques ✿ More than 80 crochet patterns

**LONDON, NEW YORK, MUNICH,
MELBOURNE, DELHI**

DK UK
Senior Editor May Corfield
Senior Art Editor Glenda Fisher
Editor Katharine Goddard
Managing Editor Penny Smith
Managing Art Editor Marianne Markham
Jacket Designer Rosie Levine
Producer, Pre-Production Sarah Isle
Producer Che Creasey
Creative Technical Support Sonia Charbonnier
Photography Ruth Jenkinson
Art Director/Stylist for Photography Isabel de Cordova
Art Director Jane Bull
Publisher Mary Ling

DK US
Senior Editor Shannon Beatty
US Editor Margaret Parrish
US Consultant Jennifer Wendell

DK INDIA
Senior Editor Dorothy Kikon
Art Editors Zaurin Thoidingjam, Neha Wahi
Assistant Editor Aditi Batra
Assistant Art Editor Pooja Verma
Managing Editor Alicia Ingty
Managing Art Editor Navidita Thapa
Pre-Production Manager Sunil Sharma
Production Manager Pankaj Sharma
DTP Designers Neeraj Bhatia, Rajdeep Singh

First American Edition, 2014
Published in the United States by DK Publishing
4th floor, 345 Hudson Street
New York, New York 10014

14 15 16 17 18 10 9 8 7 6 5 4 3 2 1
001—192555—Feb/2014

A catalog record for this book is available from the Library of Congress.
ISBN 978-1-4654-1591-2
DK books are available at special discounts when purchased in bulk for
sales promotions, premiums, fund-raising, or educational use. For details,
contact: DK Publishing Special Markets, 345 Hudson Street, New York,
New York 10014 or SpecialSales@dk.com.

Printed and bound in China by South China Printing Co. Ltd

Discover more at www.dk.com/crafts

Contents

Introduction

This book is suitable for all crocheters—beginners with no previous experience, as well as those with more advanced skills. If you have never held a crochet hook before, but want to learn, this book will take you through all the basic crochet stitches to enable you to make beautiful items, both small and large. If you already know how to crochet, you will find a wonderful collection of unique and attractive, good-value patterns to try out.

Crochet guides you through the basic techniques and stitches—presented clearly and simply with step-by-step photographs—covering the relevant abbreviations and symbols on the way. Beginners can work through the comprehensive and easy-to-follow techniques section in the first part of the book, stopping along the way to try out a mini project to practice the stitch they have just learned. More experienced crocheters can dip into this section to revisit stitches they already know. The mini projects include items ranging from a simple chain stitch bracelet (pp. 30–31) to a stylish intarsia pillow (pp. 122–123).

Once you are confident with all the crochet stitches, you can launch into the projects chapter and begin making crocheted items as diverse as a traditional granny blanket (pp. 148–151) for a baby, a tiny flower pin cushion (pp. 184–185), and a little girl's summer tunic dress (pp. 246–249).

With more than 80 projects to choose from, there is something for everyone: from blankets and pillows, to hats and scarves; gloves, socks, and slippers; items for the home; garments and bags; plus a range of charming toys to make. *Crochet* will enable you to make your own unique, custom-made crocheted pieces for yourself, your home, and your family and friends.

Crochet know-how

Each project shows the yarn and stitch gauge used (if relevant), but the main yarn recommendation is a generic one, to enable you to make an item in a yarn that is easily available to you. For example, the simple beaded necklace on pages 28–29 is made with DMC Petra Crochet Cotton Perle No. 3 yarn, but you can use any yarn that you have for this, as long as you ensure that the thread you are using will fit through the holes of the beads. Similarly, for the chunky rug on pages 186–187, we have used an acrylic yarn for its durable properties, but you could use another super-chunky weight yarn with a synthetic content to get a similar effect; just bear in mind that the size might be slightly different, depending on the yarn weight.

A note about yarn and hooks

It is also important to consider the fact that for some projects, for example, the filigree bookmarks (see pp. 178–179), and the jungle finger puppets (pp. 282–285), you will only need a certain proportion of the ball of yarn recommended for each color, and you will have yarn left over. However, look on this as an opportunity to make more of the same, or use it for a new project!

When making items such as garments, or other projects for which gauge is important, it is always advisable to crochet a gauge swatch first in the yarn you intend to use; if your gauge swatch is smaller than that recommended, you may need to use a larger hook; if it is larger, use a

smaller hook. With many projects, the gauge is not a vital element, for example, the coasters on pages 58–59, and the cat basket on pages 174–175, do not need to be an exact size.

Make sure that you calculate the amount of yarn needed for a project by yardage/meterage, since the amount needed may vary and different weights of yarn have different yardage/meterage lengths. Check your hook size, too. As you become more experienced as a crocheter, so you will become accustomed to which hook sizes are appropriate for the different types of yarn.

A note about crocheted toys

When making crocheted toys for babies or very young children, it is always safest either to embroider the eyes onto the toy or use special safety eyes. Never use buttons on a toy that is for a baby or very young child, since there is the risk that the child could choke on the buttons if they become detached. If you are using safety eyes on toys, always make sure that they comply with current safety regulations.

Extend your skills

In addition to a comprehensive guide to basic stitches and techniques, *Crochet* provides an extensive gallery of stitch textures, crocheted edgings, openwork, and colorwork, as well as a guide to making granny squares and stunning flowers, all with patterns. Use these to build on your basic crocheting skills, before embarking on more adventurous and impressive crochet patterns, and you will find yourself equipped to create any project in the book!

Size chart

Women's sizes	To fit bust (approx)
S (small)	32in (80cm)
M (medium)	36in (91cm)
L (large)	41in (102cm)

Slipper/sock sizes	Sole length (approx)
Baby 3–6 months	4–4½in (10–11cm)
Child 2–7 years	4½–6in (11–15cm)
Women's 5½–9½	8¾–10¼in (22½–26cm)
Men's 9–12	10¾–11½in (27½–29½cm)

Tools and techniques

Yarns

There are many types of yarn, allowing crocheters to enjoy a variety of sensory experiences as they express themselves through the medium. Yarn may be made of different fibers and have a range of textures, as shown here.

Fibers

Yarns, like fabrics, are made from fibers. A fiber may be the hair from an animal, man-made (synthetics), or derived from a plant. The fibers are processed and spun to make yarn. Yarn may be made from a single fiber, such as wool, or mixed with other fibers to enhance its attributes (for example, to affect its durability or softness). Different blends are also created for aesthetic reasons, such as mixing soft, luxurious cashmere with a rougher wool. As a result, all yarns have different properties, so it is important to choose an appropriate blend for the project in hand.

Merino wool

This is wool from the merino sheep, which is said to have one of the softest wools of any sheep breed. The bouncy, smooth-surfaced fiber is just as warm as a more wiry, coarse wool. Merino is a fantastic choice for wearing against the skin, and is often treated to make it suitable for machine-washing. It is good for soft scarves, arm warmers, and children's garments.

Wool

The hair, or wool, of a variety of breeds of sheep, such as the Shetland Moorit or Bluefaced Leicester, is made into pure wool yarns, or blended with other fibers. It is very warm and durable, and great for winter wear such as jackets, cardigans, hats, and gloves. Some wool is rough, but it will soften with wear and washing. Wool sold as "organic" contains a high proportion of lanolin, making a strong, waterproof yarn.

Cotton crochet threads

Traditionally, crochet was worked in cotton threads that were suitable for lace. Today, cotton threads are still used for lace edgings and filet crochet (see pp. 90–95 and pp. 108–115).

Fine-weight cotton yarns

This yarn is a good weight for garments and accessories and will show the texture of stitch patterns clearly.

Acrylic

Acrylic fibers are produced from ethylene, which is derived from oil, and they are very cheap to manufacture. Acrylic yarn feels slightly rougher than other synthetics, and often comes in very bright and luminous shades that are hard to create with natural fibers. Robust and resistant to moths, acrylic yarn is ideal for toys, novelty pieces, and budget projects. The yarn tends to accumulate static electricity.

Natural and synthetic mixes

Man-made fibers are often blended with natural fibers to bring structure, strength, and washability; also to alter their appearance, such as to add a sheen. They help bind other yarns, such as mohair and wool, together and prevent shedding; they also prevent animal fibers from shrinking. The strength of such blends makes them perfect for socks and gloves.

Fabric

Traditionally, fabric from old clothes and other textiles was often made into doormats and rugs by tying strips together. Think about using fabric strips to crochet with, too. The hook size will depend on how thick the strips are.

String

Ideal for crocheting practical household items such as bowls and boxes, string is available in a range of colors and weights. Experiment on relatively small hooks, such as H/8 US (5mm), to create a very stiff fabric capable of holding its shape. Coat finished household items with diluted craft glue to waterproof them and make future cleaning easy: just wipe with a damp cloth.

Wire

This unusual medium is often used for crocheting jewelry: buy beading wire, which is available in a range of colors, and crochet it into chokers, necklaces, and bracelets. Try stranding beads on the wire before you work and place them in the crochet as you go along. For a really unusual project, strand the wire with another yarn to crochet a malleable fabric that holds its shape and make three-dimensional sculptures.

Plastic bags

Recycle plastic bags by cutting them into strips and joining these together with tight knots to form yarn. Create interesting textures by mixing colored and clear bags; the knots will add further texture. Crochet with a large hook, depending on the width of the strips you have cut—N/15 US (10mm) upward is recommended; also choose the size according to whether you want a very tight or a floppy plastic fabric. Use this technique to make bags, mats, and waterproof items such as toiletry bags or garden seat covers.

Buying yarn

Yarns are packaged for sale in specific quantities and sold by yardage or weight. Common yarn measures for crochet are balls, hanks, and skeins, and standard weights are 25g, 50g, and 100g.

Hank

A twisted ring of yarn, a hank (also called a skein) needs to be wound into a ball before it can be used. You can do this by hand, or by using a ball-winder. This gives you the opportunity to check that there are no knots or faults in the yarn as you wind it. Some yarns avaliable as hanks consist of soft, delicate fibers, and these are unsuitable for certain industrial ball-winding machines.

Donut

The stock in a yarn store may include balls that look like "donuts". These are ready to use: just pull the yarn from the center to start crocheting.

Ball

A ball of yarn is ready to use without any preparation. Keep the label in place as you work to ensure that it doesn't unravel and pull the yarn from the center to start crocheting.

Cone

This is often too heavy to carry around in a project bag and the yarn is best wound into balls before you start crocheting.

Yarn weights

The yarn "weight" refers to the thickness of a yarn. Some yarns are spun by manufacturers to fall into what are considered as "standard" yarn weights, such as sport or worsted. These standard weights have long histories and will probably be around for some time to come. However, even within these "standard" weights there is slight variation in thickness, and textured novelty yarns are not easy to categorize by thickness alone.

When defining yarn weight, visual yarn thickness is only one indicator of a yarn-weight category. A yarn can look thicker than another yarn purely because of its loft—the air between the fibers—and the springiness of the strands. By pulling a strand between your two hands you can see how much loft it has by how much the thickness diminishes when the yarn is stretched.

The ply of a yarn is also not an indication of yarn thickness. Plies are the number of strands twisted together around each other in the opposite direction from which they were spun to form a strong, balanced yarn (the most common yarn plies used in crochet are 3-ply and 4-ply). A yarn with four plies can be very thick or very thin, depending on the thickness of each individual ply.

Standard yarn-weight system

Yarn weight symbol & category names	**0** Lace	**1** Superfine	**2** Fine	**3** Light	**4** Medium	**5** Bulky	**6** Super bulky
Crochet gauge ranges in sc to 4in/10cm	32-42 dc	21-32 sts	16-20 sts	12-17 sts	11-14 sts	8-11 sts	5-9 sts
Recommended hook in metric size range	1.6-2.25mm	2.25-3.5mm	3.5-4.5mm	4.5-5.5mm	5.5-6.5mm	6.5-9mm	9mm and larger
Recommended hook in US size range	6 steel, 7 steel, 8 steel, B/1	B/1 to E/4	E/4 to 7	7 to I/9	I/9 to K/10½	K/10½ to M/13	M/13 and larger

Guidelines only
The above reflect the most commonly used gauges and hook sizes for specific yarn categories. The categories of yarn, gauge ranges, and recommended hook sizes have been devised by the Craft Yarn Council of America (YarnStandards.com).

Yarn labels

Everything you need to know about a yarn is on its label. It will include symbols that tell you how to crochet with it and how to clean it. Here is just a selection of the most common symbols. Always keep the labels—they are vital for identifying the yarn if you run short and need more. New yarn needs to have the same dye lot number as the original purchase in order to prevent a slight difference in color in the finished item.

Ball band

A yarn label is also known as a ball band. It features information on the yarn's weight and thickness as well as washing guidelines. Yarns range from the fingering and light to the thick, chunky, and super bulky.

Symbols

Yarn manufacturers may use a system of symbols to give details of a yarn. These include descriptions of suitable hooks and the required gauge.

Yarn weight and thickness

US G/6 (4mm)
Recommended hook size

Gauge over a 4in (10cm) test square

SHADE/ COLOR
520
Shade/color number

DYE LOT NUMBER
313
Dye lot number

50g
NETT AT STANDARD CONDITION IN ACCORDANCE WITH BS984
Weight of ball of yarn

100%
WOOL
Fiber content

Machine-wash cold

Machine-wash cold, gentle cycle

Hand-wash cold

Hand-wash warm

Do not bleach

Dry-cleanable in any solvent

Dry-cleanable in certain solvents

Do not dry-clean

Do not tumble-dry

Do not iron

Iron on low heat

Iron on medium heat

Choosing yarn colors

When embarking on a new crocheting project, the choice of color is a very important decision. Even a simple design gains impact from good color choices. The color wheel is a useful tool that will introduce you to color theory.

The color wheel: The three primary colors—red, yellow, and blue—can be placed side by side to create a color wheel. When two adjacent colors are combined, they create "secondaries." Red and yellow make orange, yellow and blue make green, and blue and red make purple. Intermediate colors called tertiaries occur when a secondary is mixed with the nearest primary.

Complementary colors: Colors that lie opposite from one another on the wheel, such as red and green, or yellow and violet, are called complementaries. They provide contrasts that accent design elements and make both colors stand out. Don't forget black and white, the ultimate opposites.

Hue, shade, tone, and tint: Each segment shows the hue, shade, tone, and tint of a color. A hue is the pure, bright color; a shade is the color mixed with black; a tone is the color mixed with gray; and a tint is the color mixed with white (pastels). The use of color can affect the appearance of a project dramatically.

Monochromatic designs: These use different versions of the same color. So a project based on greens will not stray into the red section of the color wheel, but might have shades and tints of yellow and blue mixed in, which can then become "harmonious" combinations of colors that are next to each other on the color wheel. These "adjacent" colors can also be combined to great effect, as long as there are differences in value between them.

Color temperature: Color has a visual "temperature," with some colors being perceived as "warm" and others as "cool." Many people tend to think of blue and its adjacent colors as being cool, while the reds and yellows are warm, but, in fact, there are warmer and cooler versions of all the primaries; think, for example, of a warm, azure blue and a cold, icy blue. Color temperature is an important element in whether a color recedes or advances—that is, in whether it stands out from or blends in with the background and surrounding colors.

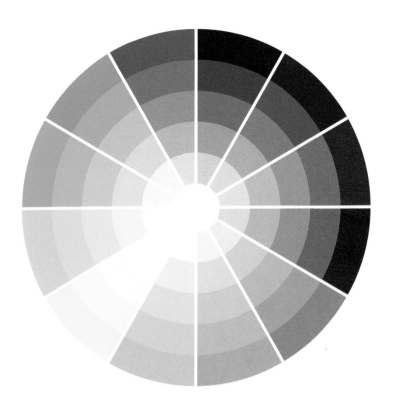

Black and white

Black and white are not included on the color wheel because they are not classified as colors. Black is an absence of all color and white is a combination of all colors in the spectrum. Keep in mind that when using black, not only is your work more difficult to see, but also that texture work will not be seen to its best effect in the final garment. White, however, guarantees that every stitch and detail will be clear; the drawback is that white shows smudges of dirt more quickly and therefore needs to be washed more frequently.

Warm shades

The warm end of the color spectrum consists mainly of red and yellow tones; browns, oranges, and purple are part of this group. Use these colors to add richness and depth. A blend of warm shades can be a very flattering mixture to use, depending on your coloring: hold yarn against your face to see what suits you.

Cool shades

Blue, green, and violet are at the cool end of the spectrum, and these can look very good used together. Cool colors are generally darker in tone than warm ones. If used with warm shades, their impact is lessened; if you need to balance a warm mixture in a project, you will need a higher proportion of cool to warm colors to do it.

Pastels

These very pale, often cool variations of deeper, darker colors are very popular for babies' and small children's garments; consequently, a variety of suitable synthetic yarns and blends are available. Pastels also feature strongly in spring/summer crochet patterns for adults; look for ice-cream colors in lightweight yarns and enjoy using a delicate color palette.

Brights

Vivid and fluorescent shades are fun to use in a project, and they often make particularly eye-catching accessories or color motifs. A great way to liven up a colorwork project that consists of muted shades is to add a bright edging or set of buttons. This burst of color can change the project's overall impact completely.

Seasonal mixtures

Nature can be a great source of inspiration. Think about sunsets, fall leaves, frosted winter berries, or vibrant spring flowers. Keep a record in a sketchbook or in photographs, and notice the proportion of each color in view. Most good yarn stores change their line of colors according to the season; in spring, for example, more pastels and brights will be available.

Hooks and other equipment

Crochet is probably one of the most economical needlework crafts there is, since it requires very little equipment. In addition to yarn, you will need a crochet hook of appropriate size for the project and a blunt needle for darning in ends. You will also need some essential pieces that you are likely to have in your sewing kit already.

Crochet hooks

If you are a beginner, start learning to crochet with a good-quality standard metal crochet hook. Once you know how to work the basic stitches with a lightweight wool yarn and a size G/6 or 7 US (4mm or 4.5mm) hook, branch out and try some other types of hook to find the one that suits you best.

Standard metal hook

Parts of a crochet hook
The hook lip grabs the yarn to form the loops and the shank determines the size of the loop. The crochet handle gives weight to the tool and provides a good grip.

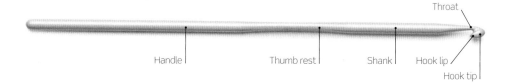

Throat

Handle   Thumb rest   Shank   Hook lip

Hook tip

Alternative hook handles

Comfort handle
Hook handles come in different shapes. If you find the standard crochet hook uncomfortable to hold because it is too narrow, investigate hooks with alternative handles. This is a high-quality Japanese hook designed and refined especially for comfort and good grip.

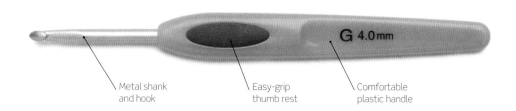

G 4.0 mm

Metal shank and hook   Easy-grip thumb rest   Comfortable plastic handle

Hook sizes

Crochet hooks are manufactured in the various sizes (diameters) listed in the hook conversion chart on the opposite page. The millimeter sizes are the diameters of the hook shank, which determines the size of the crochet stitches.

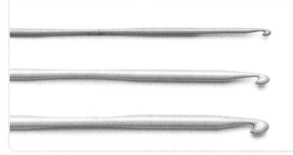

Although the middle range of hook sizes—from size B/1 US (2.25mm) to size M/13 US (9mm)—is the most commonly used, the finer and thicker hooks are also very popular for lace crochet and jumbo crochet. See page 14 to find which hook size to use with the different yarn weights.

Hook types

Point protector

Lace hooks

Because lace crochet hooks are so fine, ranging from size 14 steel US (0.6mm) to size 5 steel US (1.75mm), they are always manufactured in metal. Keep them with their metal point protectors in place to prevent accidents.

Plastic hooks

Plastic hooks are not as precisely made as metal and wooden hooks, but they come in great colors, so are enjoyable to work with.

Wooden hooks

Hardwood and bamboo hooks are very attractive and lighter in weight than metal hooks. They also provide a good grip to prevent your fingers from slipping when crocheting.

Metal hooks

Some ranges of aluminum hooks are available in bright colors—a different color for each size, which is handy for picking up the right size at a glance.

Jumbo hooks

The largest crochet hook sizes—from a size N/15 US (10mm) to a size S US (20mm)—are made in plastic. They are used for making thick crochet fabric very quickly.

Broomstick

A broomstick is a thick stick used in conjunction with a regular hook to create the lace loops in broomstick lace. It is best to use an oversized knitting needle such as this one.

Tunisian hooks

A Tunisian hook is longer than a regular hook, since you have to fit on many stitches, as opposed to only one stitch with a regular hook. These can be double-ended, like this one, or have a stopper on the end.

Conversion chart

This chart gives the conversions between the various hook-size systems. Where there are no exact conversions possible the nearest equivalent is given.

EU METRIC	US SIZES	OLD UK
0.6mm	14 steel	
0.75mm	12 steel	
1mm	11 steel	
1.25mm	7 steel	
1.5mm	6 steel	
1.75mm	5 steel	
2mm		14
2.25mm	B/1	
2.5mm		12
2.75mm	C/2	
3mm		10
3.25mm	D/3	
3.5mm	E/4	9
3.75mm	F/5	
4mm	G/6	8
4.5mm	7	7
5mm	H/8	6
5.5mm	I/9	5
6mm	J/10	4
6.5mm	K/10½	3
7mm		2
8mm	L/11	
9mm	M/13	
10mm	N/15	
12mm	P	
15mm	Q (16mm)	
20mm	S (19mm)	

Other equipment

In addition to a crochet hook, you will need a blunt-ended yarn needle for darning in yarn ends. Other essentials include scissors, pins, and a tape measure. Handy extras such as stitch markers and row counters will help keep track of stitches.

The essentials

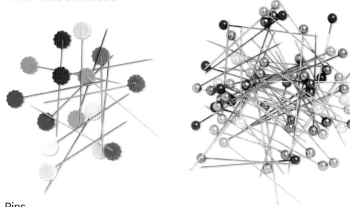

Pins
Use pins with glass heads or large heads (such as knitting pins), for seams and blocking (see p. 70).

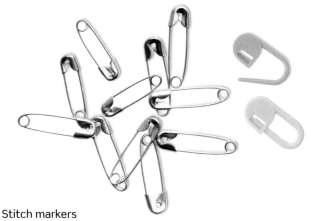

Stitch markers
Small safety pins and stitch markers can be hooked onto the crochet to mark a specific row or a specific stitch in the row, or to mark the right side of your crochet.

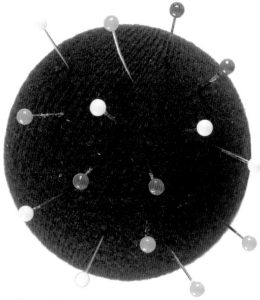

Pin cushion
A useful item to have by your side when working.

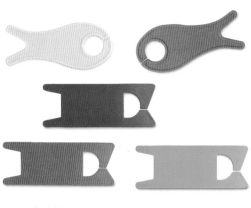

Yarn bobbins
Useful for holding short lengths of yarn for jacquard crochet (see p. 118).

Blunt-ended yarn needles
Use these for sewing seams and darning in yarn ends (make sure the eye of the needle is big enough for your chosen yarn).

Tape measure
Keep a tape measure on hand for checking your gauge and measuring your crochet.

Scissors
Keep a sharp pair of scissors on hand for cutting yarn and trimming off yarn ends.

Row counter
These are useful for keeping track of where you are in your crochet. String it on a length of cotton yarn and hang it around your neck—change it each time you complete a row.

Crochet bag
Bags for crocheters often have several compartments—perfect for storing equipment and materials for your current project and keeping everything in one place when you are not working on the crochet.

Basic stitches

Learning to crochet can take some time because there are several basic stitches to master. There is no need, however, to learn all the stitches at once. With only chain stitches and single crochet at your disposal, you can make attractive striped blankets and pillow covers in luscious yarns.

Getting started

Before making your first loop, the slipknot (see p. 23), get to know your hook and how to hold it. First, review the explanation of the parts of the hook on page 18. Then try out the various hook- and yarn-holding techniques below and on the following page when learning how to make chain stitches. If you learned to crochet as a child, you will automatically hold the hook the way you originally learned, and you should stick to the position you know, whether it is the pencil or knife position.

Holding the hook

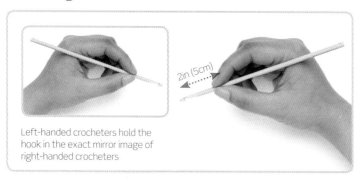

Left-handed crocheters hold the hook in the exact mirror image of right-handed crocheters

Pencil position: To hold the hook in this position, grip it as you would a pencil. If the hook has a shaped thumb rest, position this above your thumb and under your index finger. The center of your thumb will be about 2in (5cm) from the tip of the hook if the hook has a thumb rest, and this is where you should also hold a hook without a thumb rest.

Left-handed crocheters hold the hook in the exact mirror image of right-handed crocheters

Knife position: To hold a crochet hook in this position, grip it as you would when using a table knife to cut food. As for the pencil position, if the hook has a thumb rest, settle your thumb and index finger in this shaped section with the center of your thumb about 2in (5cm) from the hook tip. Grip a hook without a thumb rest the same distance from the tip.

Holding the yarn

To control the flow of the yarn to your hook, you need to lace it around the fingers of your free hand. Both of the techniques shown here are only suggestions, so feel free to develop your own.

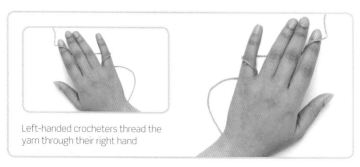

Left-handed crocheters thread the yarn through their right hand

Method one: Start by winding the yarn around your little finger, then pass it under your two middle fingers and over your index finger. With this method, the index finger is used to position the yarn.

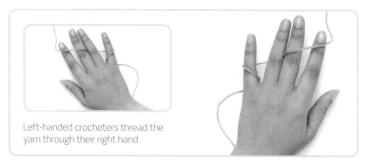

Left-handed crocheters thread the yarn through their right hand

Method two: Wrap the yarn around your little finger, then pass it behind the next finger and over the top of the middle finger and index finger. This method allows you to position the yarn with either the index finger or middle finger, whichever is more comfortable and gives you more control (see Tensioning your yarn, opposite).

Making a slipknot

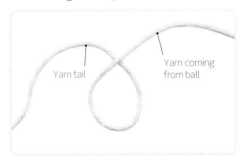

1 To make the first loop (called the slipknot) on your hook, begin by crossing the yarn coming from the ball over the yarn end (called the yarn tail) to form a circle of yarn.

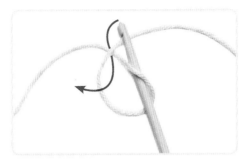

2 Insert the tip of the hook through the circle of yarn. Then use the hook to grab the ball end of the yarn and pull the yarn through the circle.

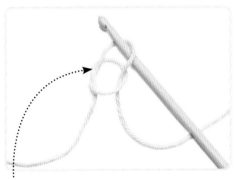

3 This forms a loop on the hook and a loose, open knot below the loop.

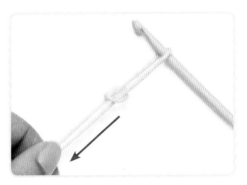

4 Pull both ends of the yarn firmly to tighten the knot and the loop around the shank of the hook.

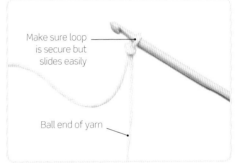

Make sure loop is secure but slides easily

Ball end of yarn

5 Make sure the completed slipknot is tight enough on the hook that it won't fall off, but not so tight that you can barely slide it along the hook's shank. The yarn tail on the slipknot should be at least 6in (15cm) long so it can be threaded onto a blunt-ended yarn needle and darned in later.

Tensioning your yarn

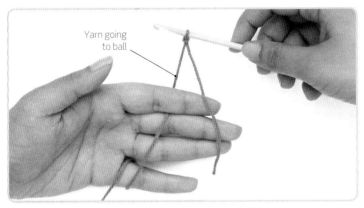

Yarn going to ball

1 With your slipknot on your hook, try out some yarn holding techniques. Wrap the yarn around your little finger and then lace it through your other fingers as desired, but so that it ends up over the tip of your index finger (or your index finger and middle finger).

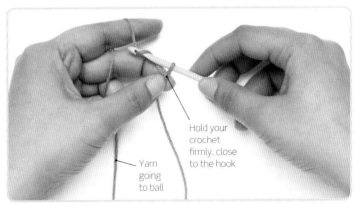

Hold your crochet firmly, close to the hook

Yarn going to ball

2 As you crochet, grip the yarn tightly with your little finger and ring finger and release it gently as you form the loops. Use either your index finger or your middle finger to position the yarn, and hold the base of the crochet close to the hook to keep it in place as the hook is drawn through the loops.

Chain stitches (Abbreviation = ch)

Chain stitches are the first crochet stitches you need to learn because they form the base for all other stitches—called a foundation chain—and for turning chains (see p. 68). They are used in combination with other basic stitches to create a vast array of crochet stitch patterns, both dense textured stitches and lacy ones. Practice chain stitches until you are comfortable holding a hook and releasing and tensioning yarn.

Making a foundation chain

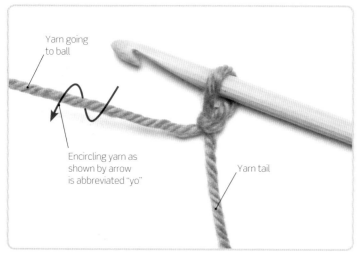

Yarn going to ball

Encircling yarn as shown by arrow is abbreviated "yo"

Yarn tail

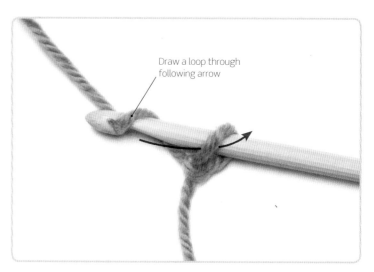

Draw a loop through following arrow

1 Start with a slipknot on your hook (see p. 23). Wrap the yarn around the hook; this action is called "yarn over hook" (abbreviated yo) in crochet patterns. When working a yo, move your hook under the yarn at the same time as you move the yarn slightly forward.

2 With the yarn gripped in the lip of the hook, draw a loop of yarn through the loop on the hook. (Hold the base of the slipknot with the free fingers of your yarn hand as you draw the loop through.)

1 chain made

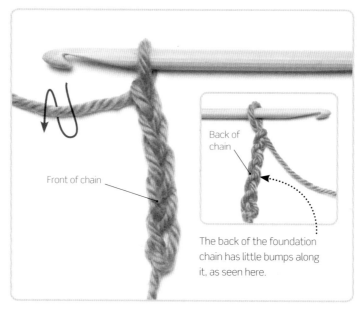

Front of chain

Back of chain

The back of the foundation chain has little bumps along it, as seen here.

3 This completes the first chain.

4 Yo and draw a loop through the loop on the hook for each new stitch. Continue making chains in the same way until you have the number specified in your crochet pattern.

Counting chain stitches

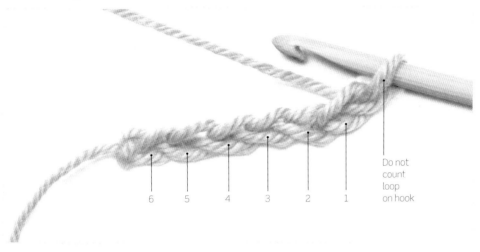

6   5   4   3   2   1   Do not
                            count
                            loop
                            on hook

Counting correctly: As you make chains for the foundation chain, count each stitch until you have made the required number. Then, before starting your crochet, recount the chains to check that you have the correct number. With the front of the chain facing you, start counting the stitches from the base of the hook and count leftward.

Fastening off chains and slip stitches

Stopping your crochet when it is complete is called fastening off. Since there is only one loop on your hook, the process is extremely simple and quick! Here is a visual aid for how to fasten off a length of chains or a row of slip stitches. The principle is the same for all stitches in crochet.

Fastening off a length of chains

1 Remove the loop from the hook. Pull out the loop to enlarge it so that it does not start to unravel.

2 Cut the yarn, pass the cut yarn end through the loop, and pull tightly to close the loop. Make sure you leave a long enough yarn end to darn invisibly into the chain later, if necessary.

Fastening off slip stitches

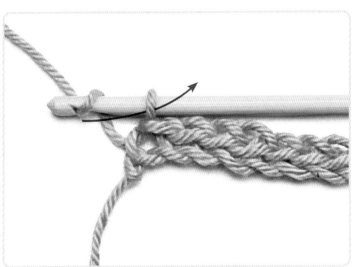

Securing ends: Fasten off in the same way as for the chain stitches. Alternatively, you can use the hook to draw the cut end through the remaining loop, as shown here by the large arrow.

Slip stitch (Abbreviation = ss)

Slip stitches are the shortest of all the crochet stitches. Although they can be worked in rows, the resulting fabric is so dense that it is only really suitable for crocheting bag handles. Slip stitches, however, appear very frequently in crochet instructions. They are used to join in new yarn (see p. 57), to work invisibly along the top of a row in order to move to a new position (see p. 53), and to join rounds in circular crochet.

Working slip stitch as a fabric

1 Make a foundation chain of the required length. To begin the first stitch, insert the hook through the second chain from the hook, passing the hook under only one strand of the chain. Then wrap the yarn around the hook (yo).

2 Holding the base of the chain firmly with the fingers of your left hand and tensioning the yarn (see p. 23), draw a loop back through the chain and through the loop on the hook, as shown by the large arrow.

3 Continue across the foundation chain, working a slip stitch into each chain in the same way. Always work slip stitches fairly loosely for whatever purpose you are using them.

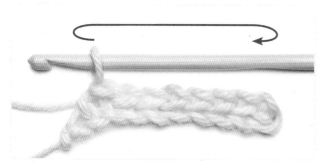 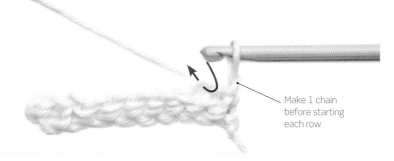

Make 1 chain before starting each row

4 After the last stitch of the row has been completed, and if you want to work another row, turn your crochet to position the yarn at the right edge of the piece of crochet ready to begin the second row.

5 To begin a second row of slip stitches, make one chain stitch. This chain is called the turning chain. For the second and following rows of slip stitch, work each stitch into the back loop only of the top of the stitches below. (It is not essential for a beginner to practice working slip stitch in rows, since it is rarely used this way.)

Using slip stitches to form a foundation ring

Making a ring: Slip stitches are also used to form the foundation rings for circular crochet (see p. 100). Make the required number of chains for the ring, then insert the hook through the first chain made, wrap the yarn around the hook, and draw a loop through the chain and the loop on the hook to close the ring.

These motifs are formed by first making a foundation ring. The technique, explained left, only requires basic crochet stitches. To practice making them, see pp. 104-107 for a selection of vibrant granny squares (also known as afghan squares) and flowers.

Beaded necklace

The most basic of stitches is used to stunning effect with this necklace, which is made with just chains and beads. This stylish piece of jewelry includes a series of long chains, but you can reduce the number of stitches to shorten its length.

PROJECTS
For more chain stitch patterns
>> *go to pages 180 and 212*

Essential information

DIFFICULTY LEVEL Easy

SIZE Approx 19in (48cm) long

YARN Use any yarn for this project—it requires only a very small amount so is perfect for using up scraps. The chain will simply be thicker or thinner— just make sure that the thread can fit through the holes of the beads you have chosen

x 1

CROCHET HOOK B/1 US (2mm) hook
1.5mm beading hook, or size needed to fit through your beads

NOTIONS Yarn needle
Selection of beads

GAUGE Exact gauge is not essential

NOTE To thread the beads onto the chain, you need to be sure that the beading hook can pass through the holes in the beads, so don't choose any beads with tiny holes.

Pattern
Make a chain of the desired length for your first bead placement.
Pull up the loop on the hook to make it larger and remove the hook from the loop.
Place a bead onto the shaft of the beading hook, then insert the hook into the elongated loop.
Pull the loop through the bead and work 1 ch to secure it, pulling on the yarn to make sure that the yarn is tight around the bead.
Repeat these actions at intervals to place all the beads desired.
Work a length of chain after the last bead has been placed, and join this with a ss to the first chain made on the necklace to form a ring and complete the necklace.
Fasten off yarn, weave in ends.

1 Make around 14 even chain stitches and then slide a bead up close to the hook.

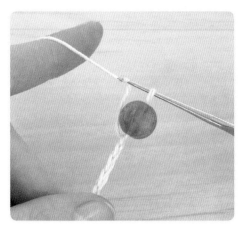

2 Thread the bead onto the yarn and make a chain stitch tightly around the bead to secure it in position on the necklace.

>> This necklace is made with DMC Petra No. 3, 306yds/280m/100g. in 53903.

Chunky bracelet

Create a bracelet with simple charm. Work the chain to a length that fits comfortably around your wrist once for a short bracelet, or multiply this by as many times as you want for a longer, thicker-looking bracelet.

PROJECTS

For more chain stitch patterns
>> go to pages 28 and 212

Essential information

DIFFICULTY LEVEL Easy

SIZE Approx 23½in (60cm) long

YARN Use any small amounts of DK yarn for this project, or try different weights—the chain will simply get thicker or thinner depending on the weight of the yarn

x 1

CROCHET HOOK E/4 US (3.5mm) hook

NOTIONS Yarn needle
Approx ½in (1cm) button or bead for fastening

GAUGE Exact gauge is not essential

NOTE Increasing the number of strands of yarn you hold together to crochet with will vary the bracelet's thickness.

Pattern

With a single strand of yarn, make a chain to your desired length, plus 5 ch. Ss into fifth ch from hook. Fasten off yarn, weave in ends.

2-strand variation

With 2 strands of yarn, make a chain to your desired length, plus 4 ch. Ss into fourth ch from hook. Fasten off yarn, weave in ends.

3-strand variation

With 3 strands of yarn, make a chain to your desired length, plus 3 ch. Ss into third ch from hook. Fasten off yarn, weave in ends.

Finishing

Sew a bead or button to the opposite end from the loop fastening.

>> This bracelet is made with Classic Elite Wool Bamboo DK, 118yds/108m/50g, in Shale (1677).

1 When the chain is the desired length, make a loop by working an extra 5 chains and then make a slip stitch into the fifth chain from the hook.

2 Attach a bead or button securely to the opposite end from the loop using the same yarn, and then weave in loose ends.

Single crochet (Abbreviation = sc)

Single crochet is the easiest crochet stitch to learn and the one that crocheters use the most frequently, either on its own or in combination with other stitches. Take your time and learn to single crochet confidently by practicing the stitch, because once you become proficient in single crochet the taller stitches will be much easier to master. Single crochet stitch creates a dense fabric that is well suited for many types of garment and accessory. It is also the stitch used for toys and containers because it can be worked tightly to form a stiff, firm textile that holds up well.

Working in rows: When single crochet is worked back and forth in rows, it looks identical on both sides. Worked in the round it looks different on the right and wrong sides, which you can see on page 100.

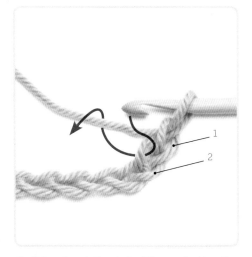

1 Make a foundation chain of the required length (see p. 24). Insert the hook through the second stitch from the hook and wrap the yarn around the hook (yo), following the large arrow. (You can insert the hook under one or two strands of the chain, but working under just one loop, as shown here, is easiest.)

2 Holding the base of the chain firmly with your left hand and tensioning the yarn (see p. 23), draw a loop back through the chain, as shown by the large arrow.

3 There are now 2 loops on the hook. Next, yo as shown by the large arrow.

4 Draw a loop through both loops on the hook in one smooth action. As you use the yarn, allow it to flow through the fingers of your left hand while still tensioning it softly.

Top of first completed single crochet

Skipped chain at beginning of foundation row

5 This completes the first single crochet. The skipped chain at the beginning of this first row does NOT count as a stitch on its own (in other words, it is not counted when you count how many stitches are in the row and it is not worked into in the next row).

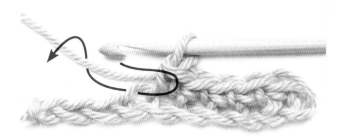

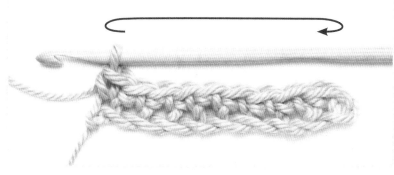

6 Continue across the foundation chain, working one single crochet into each chain in the same way.

7 At the end of the row, turn your crochet to position the yarn at the right edge of the piece of crochet, ready to begin the second row.

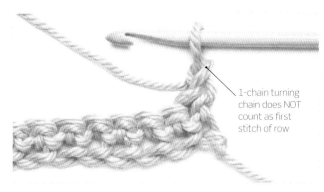

1-chain turning chain does NOT count as first stitch of row

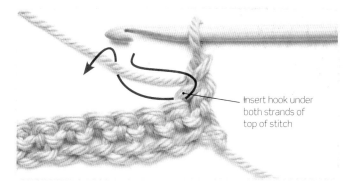

Insert hook under both strands of top of stitch

8 To begin the second row, make one chain stitch. This chain is called the turning chain, and it brings the work up to the height of the single crochet stitches that will follow.

9 Work the first single crochet into the top of the first stitch in the row below. Be sure to insert the hook under both legs of the "V" of the stitch. Work a single crochet into the top of each of the remaining single crochets in the row below.

10 At the end of the row, work the last stitch into the top of the last single crochet of the row below. Work following rows as for the second row.

11 When you have completed your crochet, cut the yarn, leaving a long loose end—at least 6in (15cm) long. Remove the hook from the remaining loop, pass the yarn end through the loop, and pull tightly to close it. Fastening off like this is done the same way for all crochet stitches.

Striped washcloths

These easy-to-make washcloths are constructed in single crochet, with a colorful stripe. They are an ideal practice project for beginners.

PROJECTS
For more single crochet patterns
>> go to pages 36 and 54

Essential information

DIFFICULTY LEVEL Easy

SIZE 8in (20cm) square

YARN Any fingering weight non-mercerized cotton would be an acceptable alternative

A x 2   B x 1   C x 1

CROCHET HOOK D/3 US (3mm) hook

NOTIONS Yarn needle

GAUGE 17 sc x 20 rows per 4in (10cm) square

NOTE When changing colors, always add new color on the last step of the last stitch of the previous row (see p.39 for instructions).

Ivory and geranium washcloth
With yarn A, work 35 ch.
ROW 1 1 sc in second ch from hook, *sc into next st, rep from * to end, turn. (34 sc)
ROW 2 1 ch, *sc into next st, rep from * to end, turn.
Continue to work in sc until piece measures 4³⁄₄in (12cm), changing to B on last yo of last row.
NEXT ROW (RS) With B, 1 ch, *sc into next st, rep from * to end, turn.
NEXT ROW (WS) Ch 1, *sc into next st, rep from * to end, change to A on last yo, turn.
Work two rows with A. Repeat stripe sequence twice more (three stripes worked in B).
Finish with two rows of sc with A.
Fasten off yarn. Weave in ends.

Edging
With yarn B and RS facing, rejoin yarn to any point along the edge of the washcloth with a ss, work a row of sc evenly around the entire edge of the washcloth, placing 3 sc into each corner stitch to turn the corners. When you are back at the first stitch, ss into first stitch to join round and fasten off yarn.
Weave in all ends.

Ivory and turquoise washcloth
Work as for first washcloth until piece measures 2³⁄₄in (7cm), change to C on last yo of final sc.
Work 4 rows with C, change to A.
Work 4 rows with A, change to C.
Work 4 rows with C, change to A.
Continue working sc with A for 2³⁄₄in (7cm).
Fasten off yarn. Work the edging in the same way as for the first washcloth.

>> These washcloths are made with DMC Natura Cotton, 169yds/155m/50g, in A: Ivory (N02), B: Geranium (N52), and C: Turquoise (N49).

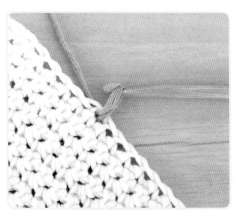

1 To make the edging, attach the new color to the top edge of the washcloth with the right side facing, and single crochet into each stitch all the way to the corner.

2 Work 3 sc into the corner stitch to turn, and continue to single crochet all the way up the row-end edge of the washcloth, making 3 sc at each corner. Join to first stitch of edging with a slip stitch.

Making these washcloths is a great way to practice single crochet and end up with a useful item when you're finished. Don't worry too much about the gauge of your square; it's fine for your washcloth to be slightly smaller or larger than the ones here.

Cell phone covers

Protect your phone from scratches with a rectangular cover made from single crochet. A speedy project to create, the crochet is simply sewn together to form a pouch.

PROJECTS
For another pattern with loops
>> go to page 60

Essential information

DIFFICULTY LEVEL Easy

SIZE Approx 2³⁄₄ x 5¹⁄₄in (7 x 13cm)

YARN Any DK weight yarn will work—try to use a durable yarn with some acrylic, since the cover will get a lot of use

A x 1   **B** x 1   **C** small amount

CROCHET HOOK J/10 US (4mm) hook

NOTIONS Yarn needle
³⁄₄in (18mm) button to fasten

GAUGE Exact gauge is not essential

Pattern

With yarn A or B, work 30 ch.
ROW 1 1 sc into second ch from hook, 1 sc into each ch to end. Turn. (29 sc)
ROW 2 Ch 1, 1 sc into each sc to end. Turn.

Plain cover
Repeat row 2 until the work is approx 5in (12.5cm).

Two-color cover
Repeat row 2 until work is approx 4in (10cm). Change to second color and repeat row 2 until work is approx 5in (12.5cm).

Both covers

BUTTON LOOP ROW Ch 1, 7 sc, 9 ch, sc back into last sc to form button loop, 1 sc in each sc to end.
Fasten off yarn, weave in ends.

Finishing
Block piece lightly.
Fold piece in half lengthwise with loop at top, and sew up bottom and side seam with a mattress stitch.
Sew button to corresponding point along opposite edge to button loop. Insert your phone and fasten button.

1 To make the button loop on the final row, sc across to placement of button loop, then chain 9 sts for the loop.

2 Work 1 sc into the same stitch at the bottom of the chain to close the loop, then sc to the end of the row.

>> This phone cover is made with Berroco Comfort, 179yds/165m/50g, in A: Crypto crystalline (2758), B: Purple (2722), and C: Teaberry (2730).

Button loops make great alternatives to buttonholes, and are ideal for phone covers where a single closure point is best. This loop uses just two crochet stitches—chain stitch and single crochet—worked into the final row of the phone cover.

Half double crochet (Abbreviation = hdc)

After single crochet, half double crochet comes next in order of stitch heights (see p. 68). It is firm like single crochet and is also fairly dense, but half double crochet produces a slightly softer texture, which makes it ideal for warm baby garments. The texture is also more interesting than single crochet, but not too lacy. Only learn to make half doubles once you can make single crochet stitches with confidence.

Working in rows: Half double crochet worked in rows, as here, looks the same on both sides, making it a totally reversible fabric, just like all basic stitches worked in rows.

1 Make a foundation chain of the required length (see p. 24). To begin the first stitch, wrap the yarn around the hook (yo).

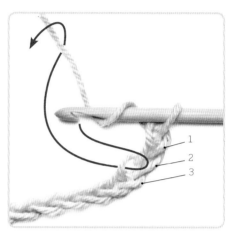

2 Insert the hook through the third chain from the hook, yo again (as shown by the large arrow) and draw a loop back through the chain.

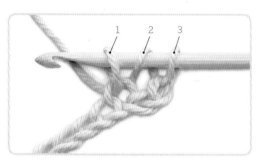

3 There are now 3 loops on the hook.

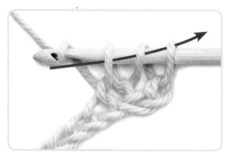

4 Yo and draw a loop through all 3 loops on the hook, as shown by the large arrow. (This motion becomes more fluid with practice.)

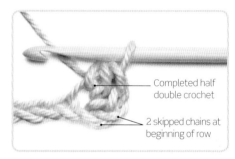

Completed half double crochet

2 skipped chains at beginning of row

5 This completes the first half double.

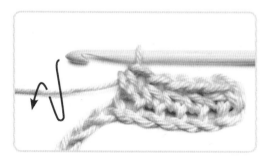

6 Work one half double crochet into each chain in the same way. Remember to start each half double by wrapping the yarn around the hook before inserting it through the chain.

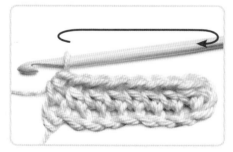

7 After working a half double crochet into the last chain, turn the work to position the yarn at the right edge of the piece of crochet ready to begin the second row.

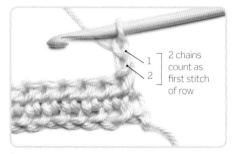

2 chains count as first stitch of row

8 Begin the second row by making 2 chains. This turning chain brings the work up to the height of the half doubles that follow.

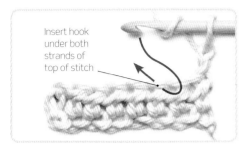

9 Yo and work the first half double into the top of the second stitch in the row below.

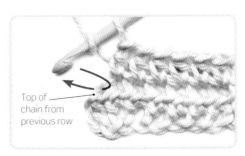

10 Work a half double into each of the remaining half double crochets in the row below. Work the following rows as for the second row.

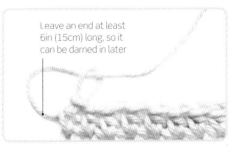

Leave an end at least 6in (15cm) long, so it can be darned in later

11 When the crochet is complete, cut the yarn. Remove the hook from the remaining loop, pass the yarn end through the loop, and pull tightly to close the loop and fasten off securely.

Joining on new yarn

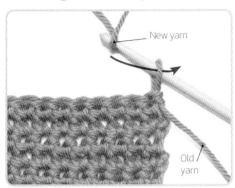

New yarn

Old yarn

Method one: Always join on a new yarn at the beginning of a row, if possible. Simply drop the old yarn and pull the new yarn through the loop on the hook, then begin the row in the usual way. Darn in the yarn tails later.

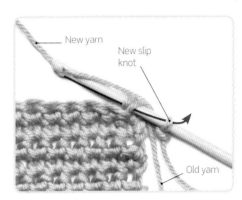

New yarn

New slip knot

Old yarn

Method two: This method is suitable for both stripes and solid crochet fabrics. First, fasten off the old yarn. Then place a slipknot on the hook, insert the hook through the first stitch of the row, and draw a loop through the top of the stitch and the loop on the hook.

Simple stripes

Stripes worked in basic stitches offer more potential for creativity than most crocheters realize. The only techniques you need to learn are how and when to change colors to start a new stripe and how to carry the yarns up the side edge of the crochet.

Changing colors

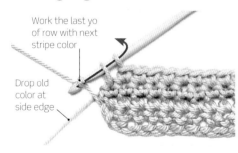

Work the last yo of row with next stripe color

Drop old color at side edge

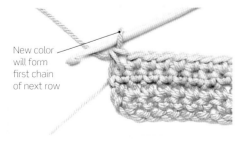

New color will form first chain of next row

1 When working stripes in any stitch, always change to the next color on the last yo of the last row before the next stripe color is started.

2 Drawing through the last yo of the row completes the last stitch. The new color is now on the hook ready to start the next stripe on the next row; this is so that the first turning chain in the next stripe is in the correct color.

Carrying colors up side edge

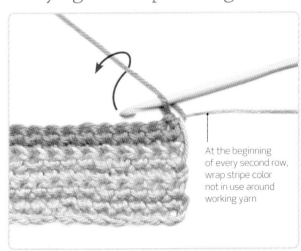

At the beginning of every second row, wrap stripe color not in use around working yarn

Wrapping yarn: If a color is not needed for more than 2 rows, wrap it around the other color to secure it. If it is not needed for more than 8 rows, cut it off and rejoin it later.

Self-fringing scarf

This comfortable scarf is made in simple half double crochet. Beginners will love how quickly this works up, and the color changes in each row add interest for more experienced crocheters.

PROJECTS

For more half double crochet patterns
>> go to pages 197 and 206

Essential information

DIFFICULTY LEVEL Easy

SIZE 5½ x 71in (14 x 180cm)

YARN You can use any aran weight 100% wool or wool/alpaca blend to achieve a similar effect

A x 1   **B** x 1

CROCHET HOOK G/6 US (4.5mm) hook

NOTIONS Yarn needle

GAUGE 11 sts x 10 rows per 4in (10cm)

NOTE Change yarn at the end of each row, leave a 6in (15cm) long tail when joining and cutting yarn to make the fringe.

Pattern

With yarn A, work 182 ch, turn.

ROW 1 1 hdc into third ch from hook, *1 hdc into next ch, rep from * to end, fasten off A. (180sts)

ROW 2 With yarn B, 2 ch, *1 hdc into each st, rep from * to end, 2 ch, fasten off B, leaving a long tail for fringe.

Continue to work a further 10 rows as row 2, changing colors at the end of each row, alternating A and B.

ROW 13 With A, 2 ch, *1 hdc into each st, rep from * to end, turn (do not cut yarn).

ROW 14 1 ch, 1 ss into top of each hdc to end, fasten off A.

Making the fringing

Knot long tails in pairs at both ends of scarf; add extra fringing if required (see p.74). Trim to desired length.

This scarf pattern cleverly uses tassels that are an integral part of the whole piece. They are made by leaving a long yarn tail each time you change color at the end of a row, and knotting them together in pairs.

>> This scarf is made with Rowan Creative Focus Worsted, 220yds/200m/100g, in A: Chocolate (03249) and B: Deep rose (02755).

Use contrasting colors to accentuate the stitch pattern.

TOP TIP

Double crochet (Abbreviation = dc)

Double crochet produces a more open and softer crochet fabric than the denser single and half double crochet stitches. Because double crochet is a tall stitch, the fabric grows quickly as you proceed, which makes it the most popular of all crochet stitches.

Working in rows: As you work double crochet in rows, you will see that it looks identical on the front and the back.

Make foundation chain of any length to practice doubles

1 Make as many chains as required (see p. 24). To begin the first stitch, wrap the yarn around the hook (yo).

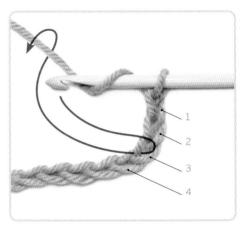

2 Insert the hook through the fourth chain from the hook, yo again (as shown by the large arrow), and draw a loop back through the chain.

3 There are now 3 loops on the hook.

4 Yo and draw a loop through the first 2 loops on the hook.

5 There are now 2 loops left on the hook. Yo and draw a loop through the remaining 2 loops.

Completed double crochet

3 skipped chains at beginning of row

6 This completes the first double. In double crochet the 3 skipped chains at the beginning of the chain count as the first stitch of the foundation row.

7 Work one double crochet into each chain in the same way. Remember to start each stitch with a yo before inserting the hook through the chain.

8 After the last stitch of the row has been completed, turn the work to position the yarn at the right edge of the piece of crochet ready to begin the second row.

1
2
3 } 3 chains count as first stitch of row

9 To begin the second row of double crochet, make 3 chain stitches. This brings the work up to the height of these tall stitches.

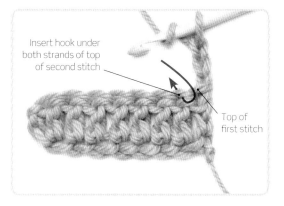

Insert hook under both strands of top of second stitch

Top of first stitch

10 Yo, then, skipping the top of the first double in the row below, work the first double into the top of the second stitch.

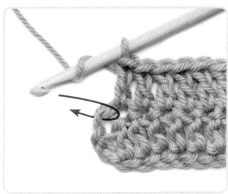

11 Work a double into each stitch, working the last stitch into the top of the 3 chains. Work the following rows in the same way.

Counting crochet stitches

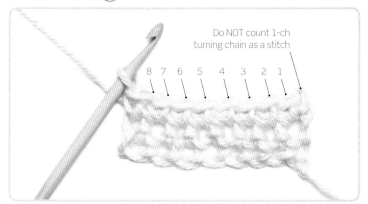

Do NOT count 1-ch turning chain as a stitch

8 7 6 5 4 3 2 1

8 7 6 5 4 3 2 1

Count 3-ch turning chain as first stitch

Counting single crochet stitches: With the front of the last row facing, count the top of each stitch. If you are losing stitches as your crochet grows, then you are probably failing to work into the last stitch in the row below; if you are gaining stitches, you may have worked twice into the same stitch.

Counting doubles: With the front of the last row facing, count the turning chain as the first stitch, then count the top of each double. If you are losing stitches as your crochet grows, you are probably failing to work into the top of the turning chain; if you are gaining stitches, you may be working into the first double of the row, instead of skipping it.

Textured pillow

Using a stylish yarn in a modern colorway, this simple but effective double stitch pillow adds a touch of style to any room and can easily be completed by a beginner with minimal sewing skills.

PROJECTS
For more double crochet patterns
>> go to pages 60 and 234

Essential information

DIFFICULTY LEVEL Easy

SIZE 16in (40cm) square

YARN Any "homespun," aran-weight, wool-rich yarn will work. You will need about 95 yds (90m)

x 1

CROCHET HOOK H/8 US (5mm) hook

NOTIONS Yarn needle
16in (40cm) square pillow form and cover
Sewing needle and matching thread

GAUGE 9 dc per 4in (10cm)

Pattern
Work 40 ch.
ROW 1 1 dc into fourth ch from hook, 1 dc in each st to end, turn. (36 dc)
ROW 2 Ch 3, 1 dc in each dc to end, turn.
Repeat row 3 until work measures 16in (40cm).
Fasten off yarn, weave in ends.
Block the crocheted square carefully to 16in (40cm) square. Then sew it on to the front of the pillow form with a sewing needle and the same yarn, using running or whipstitch. Finally, insert the pillow form.

>> This pillow is made with Erika Knight Vintage Wool, 95yds/90m/50g, in Bambi (34).

With the same yarn, sew the square on to the front of the pillow using running stitch or whipstitch. Keep the stitches as close to the edge of the square as possible, so that they are invisible.

The striking texture of this pillow is created by the height of the double stitches. Refer to pages 42–43 for more information on double crochet.

Pretty headbands

These simple yet attractive bands are perfect for keeping your ears warm. The child's size is given first, followed by two adult sizes to fit all.

PROJECTS
For more double crochet patterns
>> *go to pages 44 and 206*

Essential information

DIFFICULTY LEVEL Easy

SIZE Child size with bow: 18 x 2in (46 x 5cm)
Adult (small:medium) without bow:
19$\frac{1}{2}$(21$\frac{1}{4}$) x 2(2$\frac{1}{4}$)in/50(54) x 5(5.5)cm

YARN Any DK weight yarn will work here. Use a warm, comfortable yarn such as wool or alpaca. You will need approx 100yds (90m)

A x 1   **B** x 1

CROCHET HOOK G/6 US (4mm) hook

NOTIONS Yarn needle

GAUGE 17 dc per 4in (10cm)

Pattern
Ch 11(12:14).

Band
ROW 1 1 dc in fourth ch from hook and into each ch to end. Turn. (8(9:11)sts)
ROW 2 Ch 3, 1 dc in each dc to end of row. Turn.
Rep last row until work measures (18(19$\frac{1}{2}$:21$\frac{1}{4}$)in)/46(50:54)cm long or until desired length—enough to fit comfortably around your head.
Fasten off yarn.
Sew strip together at short ends to form a ring.

Tie
Continuing in same yarn, work 11 ch.
ROW 1 1 dc in fourth ch from hook and into each ch to end. Turn. (8sts)
ROW 2 Ch 3, 1 dc in each dc to end of row. Turn.
Rep last row 5 times more. (7 rows)
Fasten off yarn.
Wrap short strip around band at the seam to hide the seam. Sew strip together at short ends to form a ring around the band.

Bow
Continuing in same yarn, work 24(28) ch.
ROW 1 1 dc in fourth ch from hook and into each ch to end. Turn. (21(25)sts)
ROW 2 Ch 3, 1 dc in each dc to end of row. Turn.
Rep last row 3(5) further times. (5(7) rows)

Finishing
Fasten off yarn, weave in ends.
Slip bow under the tie and secure with a few holding stitches.

1 Wrap the short band around the seam of the headband to hide the seam, then sew or crochet the two short ends together.

2 Weave in loose ends and make sure that the seam is positioned at the back of the band so that it does not show.

>> The woman's band is made with Classic Elite Yarns Inca Alpaca. 109yds/100m/50g, in A: Fern (1141): the child's headband is made with B: Sweet pea (1164).

A pretty bow transforms this simple headband into a child's hair accessory. The bow measures approx 5(6) x 2(2¾)in/12(15) x 5(7)cm.

Treble crochet (Abbreviation = tr)

Worked in a very similar way to double crochet, treble crochet stitches are approximately one chain length taller because the stitch is begun by wrapping the yarn around the hook twice instead of only once (see p. 69).

Trebles are often used in lace crochet (see pp. 113-115) and in crochet medallions (see pp. 102-105), and in other fine crochet patterns that require an open-textured result.

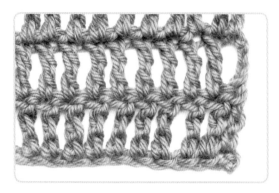

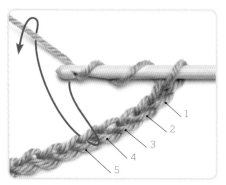

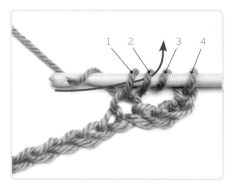

Treble stitch: Producing a double-sided fabric, either side can be used as the right side. The stitch worked in rows grows quickly because the stitches are taller but not that much slower to work.

1 Make a foundation chain, then wrap the yarn twice around the hook (yo) and insert the hook through the fifth chain from the hook.

2 Yo and draw a loop through the chain. There are now 4 loops on the hook. Yo and draw a loop through the first 2 loops on the hook.

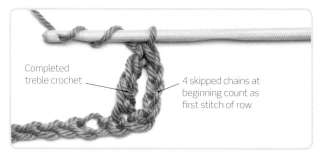

Completed treble crochet

4 skipped chains at beginning count as first stitch of row

3 There are now 3 loops remaining. Yo and draw a loop through the first 2 loops on the hook.

4 There are 2 loops remaining. Yo and draw a loop through these 2 loops.

5 This completes the first treble. As for all tall crochet stitches, the skipped chain stitches at the beginning of the foundation chain count as the first stitch of the foundation row.

Turning chain counts as first stitch of row

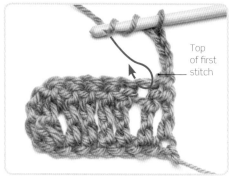

Top of first stitch

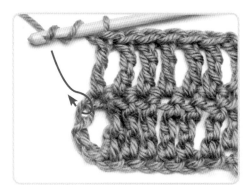

6 Work one treble into each chain in the same way. Then turn the crochet and begin the second row with a 4-chain turning chain.

7 Skip the top of the first treble in the row below and work the first treble into the top of the second stitch.

8 Work a treble into each of the remaining trebles in the row below. Work the last stitch of the row into the top of the 4 chains. Work following rows as for the second row.

Double treble crochet (Abbreviation = dtr)

Stitches taller than trebles are all worked in the same way as trebles, except that the yarn is wrapped around the hook more times before the stitch is begun and they require taller turning chains. Once you can work double trebles easily, you will also be able to work triple and quadruple trebles without much effort. The double treble crochet is a useful addition to your crochet repertoire.

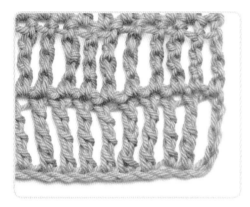

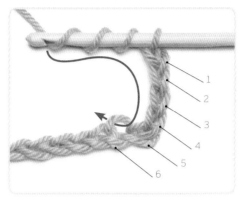

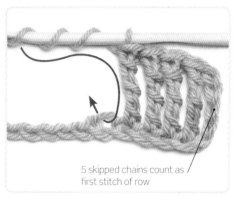

5 skipped chains count as first stitch of row

Double treble stitch: Worked in rows, double treble crochet looks the same on both sides of the fabric. Notice how airy the crochet texture becomes as the basic stitches get taller.

1 Wrap the yarn 3 times around the hook and insert the hook through the sixth stitch from the hook.

2 Work the loops off the hook two at a time as for trebles. Remember to wrap the yarn three times around the hook before starting each stitch. Start following rows with 5 chains.

Triple treble crochet (Abbreviation = trtr)

This stitch works in the same way as double treble, except that the yarn is wound around the hook 4 times, and the hook is then inserted into the seventh stitch from the hook. The loops are then worked off two at a time, and following rows start with 6 chains.

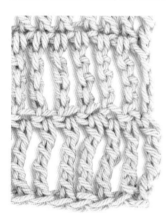

Triple treble stitch: This stitch is noticeably taller than double treble and also looks the same on both sides.

1 Once you know how to work the double treble stitch, you can begin to see how each following stitch is worked. So, as a double treble wraps the yarn around the hook twice, so a triple treble wraps the yarn around 3 times. Therefore, a quadruple treble means you wrap the yarn around 4 times, and so on.

2 You work the loops off the hook in the same way as the treble and double treble, in pairs, until there is only the working loop left. Now that you know the pattern, you can create a stitch as tall as you like.

Stitch heights

Each of the next stitches gets taller progressively and is worked by wrapping the yarn around the hook once more than the previous stitch, before inserting the hook. See page 68 for a diagram with basic stitch symbols.

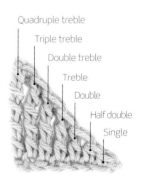

Quadruple treble
Triple treble
Double treble
Treble
Double
Half double
Single

Shaping crochet

To move from making simple squares and rectangles, a crocheter needs to know how to increase and decrease the number of stitches in the row to make a variety of shaped pieces. The most commonly used simple shaping techniques are illustrated here.

Single crochet increases

Paired increases: Increases on garment pieces are most frequently worked as "paired increases"—an increase of one stitch at the beginning of the row and one at the end.

3 At the end of the row, work 1 sc into the last sc of the row in the usual way. Insert the hook again into the last sc of the row and work a second sc into it.

1 To increase one stitch at the beginning of a row of single crochet, work 1 sc into the first sc in the usual way. Next, insert the hook again into the first sc and work a second sc in the same stitch.

2 This completes the increase. Continue across the row, working 1 sc into each sc in the usual way.

4 This increases one stitch at the end of the row.

Double crochet increases

End of row: Increases on garment pieces made using double crochet are worked using the same techniques as for single crochet. Again, these increases are most frequently worked as "paired increases"—one stitch is increased at each end of the row.

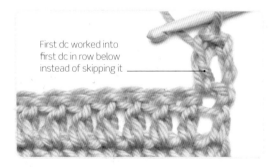

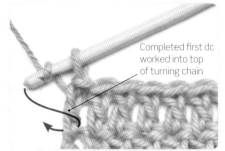

1 To increase one stitch at the beginning of a row of double crochet, first work the turning chain, then work 1 dc into the first dc in the row below. Because the first double in the row below is usually missed, this creates an increase at the beginning of the row.

2 Continue across the row, working 1 dc into each dc in the usual way. At the end of the row, work 1 dc into the top of the turning chain in the row below in the usual way. Then work a second dc into the same turning chain.

3 This completes the one stitch increase at the end of the row, as shown.

Step increase at beginning of row

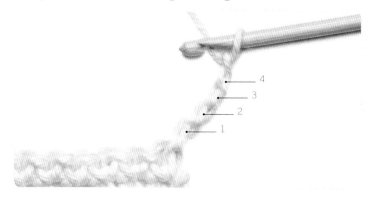

1 Increases are also frequently worked in crochet so that they form little steps at the edge. As an example, to add a 3-stitch step increase at the beginning of a row of single crochet, begin by making 4 chains as shown here. (Always make one chain more than the number of extra single crochets required.)

2 Work the first sc into the second chain from the hook. Then work 1 sc into each of the remaining 2 chains. This creates a 3-sc increase at the beginning of the row.

3 Continue the row in the usual way, working 1 sc into each sc in the row below. Any number of stitches can be added in this way and the same technique can be used for taller stitches.

Step increase at end of row

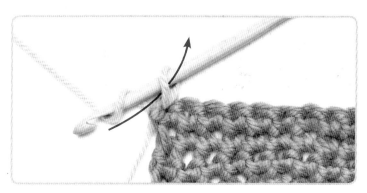

1 Before starting the row with the step increase at the end, remove the hook from the loop at the beginning of the row. Then, using a short length of matching yarn, place a slipknot on a spare hook and draw this loop through the last stitch in the row.

2 There is now one loop on the hook—this forms the first extra chain at the end of the row. Continue making chains until you have made as many as the required number of extra stitches.

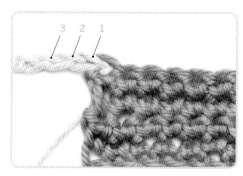

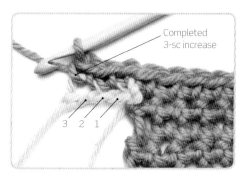

3 For a 3-stitch step increase, make a total of 3 chains. Then fasten off.

4 Return to the beginning of the row, slip the loop back onto the hook and tighten it, then work to the end of the row in the usual way until you reach the added chains.

5 Work 1 sc into each of the 3 added chains. This creates a 3-sc increase. Any number of stitches can be added in this way and the same technique can be used for taller stitches.

Single crochet decreases (Abbreviation = sc2tog)

Decreases on garment pieces, like increases, are most frequently worked as "paired decreases"—a decrease of one stitch at the beginning of the row and another at the end.

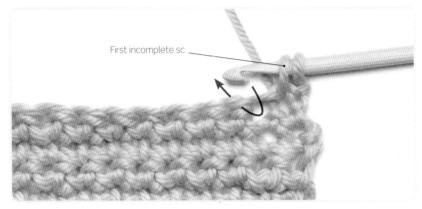

First incomplete sc

1 To decrease one stitch at the beginning of a row of single crochet, work up to the last yo of the first sc in the usual way, but do not complete the stitch—there are now 2 loops on the hook. Insert the hook through the next stitch as shown and draw a loop through.

Second incomplete sc

2 There are now 3 loops on the hook. Wrap the yarn around the hook and draw a loop through all 3 loops at once, as shown.

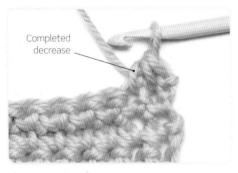

Completed decrease

3 This completes the decrease—where there were 2 stitches, there is now only one.

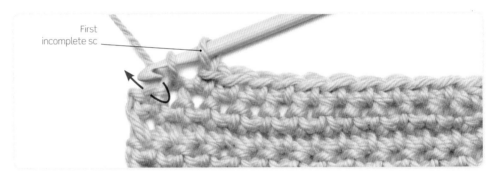

First incomplete sc

4 Continue across the row, working 1 sc into each sc in the usual way up to the last 2 stitches of the row. At the end of the row, insert the hook through the top of the second to last stitch and draw a loop through—there are now 2 loops on the hook.

5 Insert the hook through the last stitch in the row below as shown by the large arrow and draw a loop through.

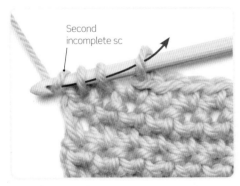

Second incomplete sc

6 There are now 3 loops on the hook. Wrap the yarn around the hook and draw a loop through all 3 loops at once, as shown.

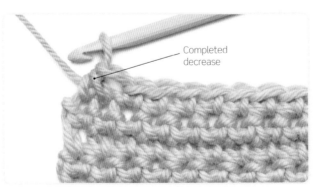

Completed decrease

7 This completes the decrease at the end of the row. (The same principle can be used for a "double decrease," where 2 stitches are decreased at once. For this, work 3 incomplete sc and join them together at the top with the last yo—this is called sc3tog.)

Double crochet decreases (Abbreviation = dc2tog)

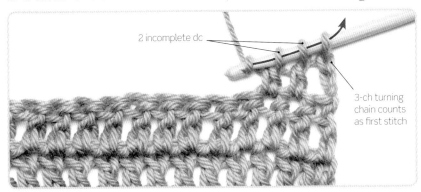

2 incomplete dc

3-ch turning chain counts as first stitch

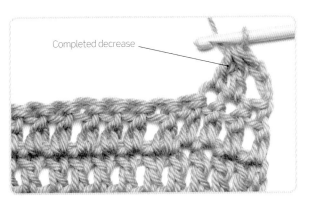

Completed decrease

1 To decrease one stitch at the beginning of a row of double crochet, first work the turning chain. Skip the first dc and work 1 dc in each of the next 2 dc but only up to the last yo of each stitch. Draw a loop through all 3 loops at once, as shown.

2 This completes the decrease—where there were 2 stitches, there is now only one.

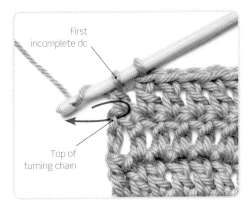

First incomplete dc

Top of turning chain

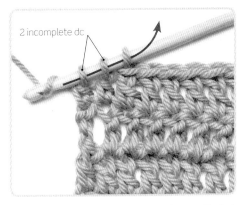

2 incomplete dc

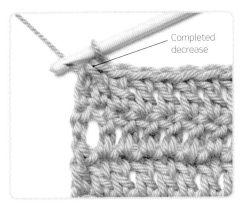

Completed decrease

3 Continue across the row in the usual way up to the last dc in the row below. Now work a dc into the last dc but only up to the last yo. Wrap the yarn around the hook and insert the hook into the top of the turning chain in the row below, as shown.

4 Work the dc in the top of the chain up to the last yo of the stitch. There are now 3 loops on the hook. Wrap the yarn around the hook and draw a loop through all 3 loops at once, as shown.

5 This completes the decrease at the end of the row. (The same principle can be used for a "double decrease," where 2 stitches are decreased at once. For this, work 3 incomplete dc and join them together at the top with the last yo—this is called dc3tog.)

Step decreases

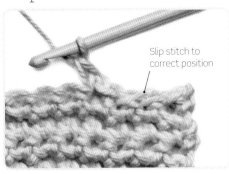

Slip stitch to correct position

At beginning of row: Decreases, like increases, can also be worked so that they form little steps at the edge. As an example, to decrease 3 stitches at the beginning of a row of single crochet, work 1 chain and then 1 slip stitch into each of the first 4 sc. Next, work 1 chain, then work the first sc in the same place that the last slip stitch was worked. Continue along the row in the usual way.

Turn before end

At end of row: For a 3-stitch step decrease at the end of the row, simply work up to the last 3 stitches at the end of the row and turn, leaving the last 3 stitches unworked. This technique can be used for all crochet stitches.

Party bunting

Making triangles is a great way to practice single crochet increases. Begin with a small number of stitches, then increase at each end until you have the desired triangle shape. Bunting is a super project for utilizing the resulting shapes.

PROJECTS

For more single crochet patterns
>> go to pages 170 and 210

Essential information

DIFFICULTY LEVEL Easy

SIZE Approx 5½ x 5½in (14 x 14cm) at the widest and longest points. Using 16 evenly spaced triangles, the bunting measures approx 138in (3.5m) long

YARN Any DK weight yarn will create the same effect, but you can use different weights to create different-sized triangles

A x 1   **B** x 1   **C** x 1   **D** x 1

CROCHET HOOK F/5 US (4mm) hook

NOTIONS Yarn needle

GAUGE Exact gauge is not essential

Triangles

Make 6 triangles in yarn A and 5 triangles each of B and C. Work 2 ch.

ROW 1 1 sc into second ch from hook.

ROW 2 Ch 1, 3 sc into next sc. (3sts)

ROW 3 Ch 1, sc in each sc to end.

ROW 4 Ch 1, 2 sc in first sc, sc to last sc, 2 sc in last sc. (5sts)

Rep last 2 rows until you have 25 sts. Work straight on these 25 sts for 6 rows, do not turn, but work 2 further stitches into the last sc, then work evenly in sc down the edge of the point, work 3 sc into the point of the triangle, work up other side of the point evenly in sc, join to the top row of sc with a ss. Fasten off yarn, weave in ends.

Finishing

With yarn D, work a chain of 13¾in (35cm) long, then work evenly in sc along the top of one yarn A triangle, then work 10 ch and work in sc along a yarn B triangle; now work 10 ch and then work in sc along a yarn C triangle. Continue in this way, joining the triangles in this color pattern, and finish with a red triangle.

Work a ch of 14in (36cm) long, turn. Skip 10 ch, sc into next ch, then into each ch to first triangle.

Work along the triangles and chains in sc to final 6 ch, work 5 ch, skip next 5 ch, then work 1 sc into last ch.

Fasten off yarn, weave in ends.

>> This bunting is made with Cascade Yarns Ultra Pima DK, 220yds/201m/100g, in A: Wine (3713), B: Jade (3735), C: Gold (3747), and D: White (3728).

1 Crochet a length of chain stitches, 13¾in (35cm) long. Starting at one corner of a triangle, insert the hook through the first stitch to work the first sc.

2 Work a row of single crochet stitches along the top of the first triangle. Work 10 more chains before attaching the next triangle with sc stitches.

Using a neutral yarn, such as white, for the single crochet chain helps to emphasize the colorful triangles and makes for a neat and attractive finish.

Flat circles

Making a simple circle is a good example for how other flat medallion shapes are started and then worked around and around from the center. The circle is also used in conjunction with the crochet tube to make containers (see p. 126) or the parts of toys, so it is worthwhile practicing.

1 Follow these steps when working the simple circle for the first time. The circle is worked from the center outward. Start with 4 chains. Then work a slip stitch into the first chain as shown by the large arrow.

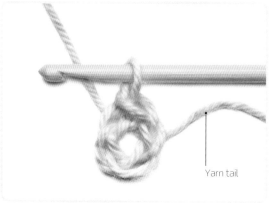

Yarn tail

2 This forms the foundation ring, which is the base for the first round of stitches.

Work stitches over yarn tail

3 For a single crochet circle, start the first round with 1 chain. Then lay the yarn end around the top of the chain and start working the single crochet stitches of the first round through the center of the ring and around the yarn tail.

Move marker to last stitch at end of every round

4 When all 8 single crochet stitches of the first round are complete, mark the last stitch of the round with a stitch marker as shown. Then pull the yarn tail to close the center hole and clip it off close to the crochet.

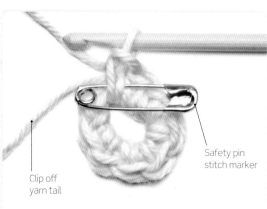

Clip off yarn tail

Safety pin stitch marker

5 Work 2 sc into each sc in the second round as explained in the pattern, working the last 2 sc into the top of the marked stitch in the last round. Then count your stitches to make sure there are 16 in total. Continue the pattern until the circle is the required size.

Tips for motifs

The principle for starting any motif shape and working it in rounds is the same as for the simple circle, and many simple crochet flowers are also worked using these techniques (see pp. 106–107). If you find it awkward to fit all the stitches of the first round into a tiny foundation ring (see previous page), try the simple adjustable ring below. Two other useful tips are the techniques for starting new colors and for joining motifs together (see below).

Making a simple adjustable ring

Pull to close ring

1 Making the simple adjustable ring is a quick way to start working a flat shape in the round, and it allows you to make the center hole as tight as desired, or as open as desired. Start as if you are making a slipknot (see p. 23), by forming a circle of yarn and drawing the yarn through the center of it.

2 Leave the circle of yarn open. Then, to start a round of single crochet stitches, make 1 chain.

3 Work the first round of single crochet stitches, working them into the ring and over the yarn tail as shown by the large arrow.

4 When all the required stitches are worked into the ring, pull the yarn tail to close the ring. Then continue as explained in the pattern instructions.

Joining on a new color

When starting a new color at the beginning of a motif round, you can either change to the new color with the last yo of the previous round or fasten off the old color and join on a new color with a slip stitch.

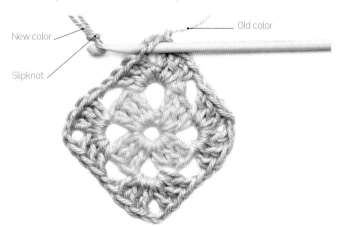

New color

Old color

Slipknot

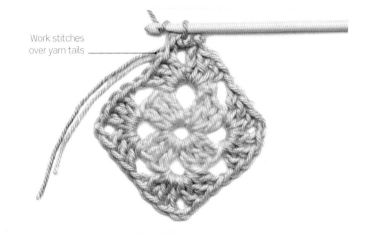

Work stitches over yarn tails

1 Joining on the new color with a slip stitch makes a firm attachment. Make a slipknot with the new color and remove it from the hook. Then insert the hook at the specified position and draw the slipknot through.

2 Start the new round with the specified number of chains, drawing the first chain through the slipknot. Work the stitches of the round over both yarn tails (the new color and the old color) so that there aren't so many ends to darn in later.

Coaster set

Cotton is lightweight and a good insulator, which makes these coasters ideal table protectors all year round. Work each coaster in rounds of simple doubles.

PROJECTS
For more double crochet patterns
>> *go to pages 148 and 236*

Essential information

DIFFICULTY LEVEL Easy

SIZE Approx 4¼in (11cm) diameter

YARN Any DK weight non-mercerized cotton would be a good substitute for this project

A x 1   **B** x 1   **C** x 1   **D** x 1   **E** x 1

CROCHET HOOK F/5 US (3.75mm) hook

NOTIONS Yarn needle

GAUGE Exact gauge is not essential

NOTE This pattern uses two shades in any combination of A, B, C, D for the main part, with the trim crocheted in E.

Pattern
With yarn A, work 4 ch, ss in first chain to form a ring.
ROUND 1 Ch 3, 1 dc, *1 ch, 2 dc, rep from * four times, (6 dc pairs made). Fasten off A.
ROUND 2 Join B into any ch sp, 3 ch, 1 dc, 1 ch, 2 dc in first ch sp, *1 ch, 2 dc, 1 ch, 2 dc in next ch sp, rep from * 4 times join with a ss into top of 3 ch. Fasten off B. (6 dc pairs and 12-ch sp)
ROUND 3 Join A into any ch sp, 3 ch, 2 dc into same ch sp, *1 ch, 3 dc into next ch sp, rep from * to end, join with a ss into top of 3 ch. Fasten off A. (12 3-dc and 12-ch sp)
ROUND 4 Join B into any ch sp, work as for round 3. Fasten off B. (12 3-dc and 12-ch sp)
ROUND 5 Join E into any ch sp, 1 ch, * work 1 sc into top of each dc, 1 sc in ch sp, repeat from * to end, join with a ss into top of first ch. Fasten off yarn. Repeat the pattern using shades C, D, and E, plus A, C, and E to make more coasters.

Finishing
Weave in all ends and press according to the ballband instructions to ensure the coaster lies flat.

>> These coasters are made with Rowan Handknit Cotton. 93yds/85m/50g. in A: Bee (364), B: Gooseberry (219), C: Blue John (365), D: Raspberry (356), and E: Ecru (251).

1 To join on a new color, insert the hook into a ch sp, wrap the yarn round the hook and pull it through to the right side of the coaster.

2 Then make a chain to secure the new yarn in place. Work 2 further chains to complete the first 3 ch, then continue with the pattern as usual.

3 For the edging, join the new color in the same way as the other colors. Work 1 sc into each dc and ch sp around. Join with a ss.

Essential information

DIFFICULTY LEVEL Easy

SIZE Striped: 8in (20cm) diameter,
scalloped: 8¾in (22cm) diameter

YARN Any DK weight non-mercerized cotton
will suit this project

A x 1   B x 1   C x 1   D x 1

CROCHET HOOK G/6 US (4mm) hook

NOTIONS Yarn needle

GAUGE Rounds 1–3 measure 3in (8cm)

Both of these pot holders are made up of two layers
of crochet fabric sewn together for extra thickness.
Yarn is a great insulator, so these projects are both
eye-catching and practical. Use washable yarn so you
can put them in the washing machine every so often.

Pot holders

These pot holders will make stylish additions to any kitchen. The shell trim on the scalloped pot holder adds a challenge to an otherwise easy project.

PROJECTS
For more patterns in the round
>> *go to pages 176 and 194*

Striped pot holder (make 2)

With yarn A, work 4 ch, join with a ss to form a ring.

ROUND 1 (RS) Ch 3 (counts as first dc), 11 dc into ring, 1 ss in third of first 3 ch, fasten off A. (12sts)

ROUND 2 (RS) Join B into top of any dc, 3 ch, 1 dc in same place as join, 2 dc in each dc to end of round, 1 ss in top of first 3 ch, fasten off B. (24sts)

Continue working in rounds as follows, always with right side facing:

ROUND 3 Join A into top of any dc, 3 ch, 1 dc in same place as join, *1 dc in next dc, 2 dc in each of next 2 dc, rep from * to last 2 dc, 1 dc in next dc, 2 dc in last dc, 1 ss in 3rd of first 3 ch, fasten off A. (40sts)

ROUND 4 Join B into top of any dc, 3 ch, 1 dc in same place as join, *1 dc in each of next 3 dc, 2 dc in next dc, rep from * to last 3 dc, 1 dc in each of last 3 dc, 1 ss in top of first 3 ch, fasten off B. (50sts)

ROUND 5 Join A into top of any dc, 3 ch, 1 dc in same place as join, *1 dc in each of next 4 dc, 2 dc in next dc, rep from * to last 4 dc, 1 dc

in each of last 4 dc, 1 ss in top of first 3 ch, fasten off A. (60sts)

ROUND 6 Join B into top of any dc, 3 ch, 1 dc in same place as join, *1 dc in each of next 5 dc, 2 dc in next dc, rep from * to last 5 dc, 1 dc in each of last 5 dc, 1 ss in top of first 3 ch, fasten off B. (70sts)

ROUND 7 Join A into top of any dc, 3 ch, 1 dc in same place as join, *1 dc in each of next 6 dc, 2 dc in next dc, rep from * to last 6 dc, 1 dc in each of last dc, 1 ss in top of first 3 ch, fasten off A. (80sts)

Finishing

Weave in all ends and, with wrong sides facing, rejoin B into the top of any double (working through both pieces), 1 sc in each dc to end of round. Do not fasten off. Make hanging loop as follows: ss in last st, 12 ch, skip 6 sc, ss in next sc. Fasten off B. Weave in loose ends.

Scalloped pot holder (make 2)

With yarn C, work 4 ch, join with a ss to form a ring.

ROUND 1 (RS) Ch 3 (counts as first dc), 11 dc into ring, 1 ss in 3rd of first 3 ch, fasten off C. (12sts)

ROUND 2 (RS) Join A into top of any dc, 3 ch, 1 dc in same place as join, 2 dc in each dc to end of round, 1 ss in top of first 3 ch, fasten off A. (24sts)

Continue working in rounds as follows, always with right side facing:

ROUND 3 Join B into top of any dc, 3 ch, 1 dc in same place as join, *1 dc in next dc, 2 dc in each of next 2 dc, rep from * to last 2 dc, 1 dc in next dc, 2 dc in last dc, 1 ss in 3rd of first 3 ch, fasten off B. (40sts)

ROUND 4 Join D into top of any dc, 3 ch, 1 dc in same place as join, *1 dc in each of next 3 dc, 2 dc in next dc, rep from * to last 3 dc, 1 dc in each of last 3 dc, ss in top of first 3 ch, fasten off D. (50sts)

ROUND 5 Join A into top of any dc, 3 ch, 1 dc in same place as join, *1 dc in each of next 4 dc, 2 dc in next dc, rep from * to last 4 dc, 1 dc in each of last 4 dc, 1 ss in top of first 3 ch, fasten off A. (60sts)

ROUND 6 Join B into top of any dc, 3 ch, 1 dc in same place as join, *1 dc in each of next 5 dc, 2 dc in next dc, rep from * to last 5 dc, 1 dc in each of last 5 dc, ss in top of first 3 ch, fasten off B. (70sts)

ROUND 7 Join D into top of any dc, 3 ch, 1 dc in same place as join, *1 dc in each of next 6 dc, 2 dc in next dc, rep from * to last 6 dc, 1 dc in each of last dc, ss in top of first 3 ch, fasten off D. (80sts)

Finishing

Weave in all ends and, with wrong sides facing, rejoin C into top of any double (working through both pieces), 1 sc in each dc to end of round. (80 sc)
Do not turn work, *skip next sc, 5 dc in next sc, skip 1 sc, 1 ss in next sc, rep from * to end, finishing with a ss. Make hanging loop as follows: 12 ch, skip next 5 dc, ss into next st.
Fasten off yarn, weave in ends.

<< The striped pot holder is made with Debbie Bliss Cotton DK, 91yds/84m/50g, in A: Lilac (13067) and B: Aqua (13061). The scalloped pot holder also uses C: Peach (13065) and D: Avocado (13020).

for *Party bunting*
go to page 54

Circular pillow

The perfect project to practice working in the round, this pillow uses the simplest of stitches, a single crochet, and uses basic increasing to work flat circles. The circles are joined with a slip stitch crochet seam.

PROJECTS

For more spiral patterns
>> go to pages 170 and 174

Essential information

DIFFICULTY LEVEL Easy

SIZE Approx 14in (35cm) diameter

YARN You can use any aran weight yarn for this project, or a different weight yarn to create a larger or smaller pillow cover

x 4

CROCHET HOOK H/8 US (5mm) hook

NOTIONS Stitch marker
Yarn needle
14in (35cm) round pillow form

GAUGE Exact gauge is not essential

NOTE This pillow is worked in spirals. Do not join rounds, but place a marker at the first stitch of the round, moving it each round to mark the beginning of the round.

Pattern (make 2)

Work 2 ch and 6 sc into second ch from hook, join round with a ss to first st.

ROUND 1 Ch 1, work 2 sc in each st around, do not join round, place marker. (12sts)

ROUND 2 *2 sc in next st, 1 sc in next st; rep from * to end. (18sts)

ROUND 3 *2 sc in next st, sc in next 2 sts; rep from * to end. (24sts)

ROUND 4 *2 sc in next st, sc in next 3 sts; rep from * to end. (30sts)

ROUND 5 *2 sc in next st, sc in next 4 sts; rep from * to end. (36sts)

ROUND 6 *2 sc in next st, sc in next 5 sts; rep from * to end. (42sts)

Continue in this way, working one extra st between increases for each round until you have worked 23 rounds and have 144 sts.

If you want a larger pillow, you can continue increasing in this way until the desired size is achieved.
Join round with a ss.
Fasten off yarn, weave in ends.

Finishing

Block pieces lightly. Arrange with wrong sides together, attach yarn to both pieces along edge, inserting the hook into a whole stitch of each circular piece. Work a slip stitch seam around edge, trapping pillow form in between when you have worked approximately halfway around the circumference.

>> This pillow is made with Berroco Weekend. 102yds/93m/50g. in Vanilla (5902).

1 To finish the pillow, place the circles with wrong sides together and attach the yarn to the front piece with a ss.

2 Insert the hook through both loops of the next stitch of front piece and through both loops of the corresponding stitch on back. Yo and pull through both stitches and loop on hook to make a ss.

3 When you are about halfway, stuff the pillow form into the middle of the two rounds and continue slip stitching through both sides, joining the last stitch to the first with a slip stitch.

Following a crochet pattern

Followed step-by-step and slowly, crochet patterns are not as difficult to work from as they appear. The guides here for a simple accessory and a garment give many tips for how to approach your first crochet patterns. This section also includes other techniques needed for working from a crochet pattern—finishings such as edgings and button loops, blocking and seams, and darning in yarn.

Simple accessory patterns

A beginner should choose an easy accessory pattern for a first crochet project. A striped pillow cover is given here as an example. Follow the numbered tips of the guide to familiarize yourself with the parts of a simple pattern.

1 The skill level required for the crochet is given at the beginning of most patterns. When starting out, work several easy patterns before progressing to the intermediate level.

2 Check the size of the finished item. If it is a simple square like this pillow, you can easily adjust the size by adding or subtracting stitches and rows.

3 It is best to use the yarn specified. But if you are unable to obtain this yarn, choose a substitute yarn.

8 Make a gauge swatch before starting to crochet and change the hook size if necessary (see opposite).

9 Instructions for working a piece of crocheted fabric always start with how many chains to make for the foundation chain and which yarn or hook size to use. If there is only one hook size and one yarn, these may be absent here.

10 Consult the abbreviations list with your pattern for the meanings of abbreviations (see p. 83).

14 The back of a pillow cover is sometimes exactly the same as the front, or it may have a fabric back. In this example, the stripes are reversed on the back for a more versatile cover.

15 After all the crocheted pieces are completed, follow the Finishing section of the pattern.

Striped pillow cover

Skill level
Easy

Size of finished pillow
16 x 16in (40.5 x 40.5cm)

Materials
7/8oz/7 x 25g (120yds/110m) balls of branded Scottish Tweed 4-Ply in Thatch 00018 (A) 4 x 7/8oz/25g (120yd/110m) balls of branded Scottish Tweed 4-Ply in Skye 00009 (B) Size E/4 US (3.5mm) crochet hook
Pillow form to fit finished cover

Gauge
222 sts and 24 rows to 4in (10cm) over single crochet using size E/4 US (3.5mm) hook or size necessary to achieve correct gauge. To save time, take time to check gauge.

Front
Using size E/4 US (3.5mm) hook and A, ch 89.
Row 1 1 dc in second ch from hook, 1 dc in each of rem ch, turn. (88sts)
Row 2 1 ch (does NOT count as a st), 1 dc in each dc to end, turn.
Rep row 2 throughout to form dc fabric.
Always changing to new color with last yo of last dc of previous row, work in stripes as follows: 26 rows more in A, 8 rows B, (8 rows A, 8 rows B) twice, 28 rows A.
Fasten off.

Back
Work as for Front, but use B for A, and A for B.

Finishing
Darn in loose ends.
Block and press lightly on wrong side, following instructions on yarn label.
With wrong sides facing, sew three sides of back and front together. Turn right-side out, insert pillow form, and sew remaining seam.

4 Always purchase the same total amount in yards (meters) of a substitute yarn; NOT the same amount in weight.

5 If desired, select different colors to suit your décor; the colors specified are just suggestions.

6 Alter the hook size if you cannot achieve the correct gauge with the specified size (see 8 left).

7 Extra items needed for your project are usually listed under Materials, Notions, or Extras.

11 Work in the specified stitch pattern, for the specified number of rows or inches (cm).

12 Colors for stripes are always changed at the end of the previous row before the color change so the first turning chain of the new stripe is in the correct color (see p. 39).

13 Fastening off completes the crochet piece.

16 See page 72 for how to darn in loose ends.

17 Make sure you look at the yarn label instructions before attempting to press any piece of crochet. The label may say that the yarn cannot be pressed or it can be pressed only with a cool iron. (See p. 70 for blocking tips.)

18 See pages 70-71 for seaming options. Take time with seams on crochet, and when working your very first seams, get an experienced crocheter to help you.

Garment patterns

Garment instructions usually start with the Skill Level, followed by the Sizes, Materials, Gauge, and finally the instructions. Most important for successfully making a garment—or other fitted items such as hats, mittens, gloves, and socks—is choosing the right size and making a gauge swatch.

Tips

Choose a skill level that suits your crochet experience. If in doubt or if you haven't crocheted for many years, stick to an Easy or Beginner's level until you are confident you can go to the next level.

White is a good color to use for your first crocheted sweater because the stitches are so easy to see clearly. But if you do choose white yarn, be sure to wash your hands every time you start crocheting; and when you stop, put away the yarn and sweater in a bag to keep it from becoming soiled.

Avoid black or other very dark yarn for a first crocheted sweater, since the stitches are very difficult to distinguish, even for an accomplished crocheter.

Purchase yarn balls that have the same dye-lot number (see p. 15).

Have a set of hook sizes on hand if you are starting to crochet sweaters. When checking gauge (see below), you will need other sizes in order to alter your hook size, if necessary.

Always make the pieces in the order given in the instructions, whether you are crocheting a garment, accessory, or toy. On a garment, the back is usually crocheted first, followed by the front (or fronts, if it is a cardigan or jacket), and finally the sleeves. Pockets that are integrated into the fronts are crocheted before the fronts and those applied as patches are worked last.

Beginners should take care when modifying patterns, since sizing/shaping and stitch patterns are often worked out in detail by the pattern designer and may turn out very differently if altered. However, beginners should not be afraid to try modifying a pattern to suit their preferences, since it can always be ripped out if it does not work as planned.

Choosing a garment size

Sizing advice: Crochet garment sizes are usually listed as specific bust/chest sizes or in generic terms as Small, Medium, Large. (Children's sweater sizes are given in ages and chest sizes.) The best advice is not to stick strictly to choosing your preferred size by these criteria. Decide instead how you want the garment to fit you— how close-fitting or loose-fitting it should be. If you are planning to crochet a sweater, find one in your wardrobe that is comfortable and flattering and has a fabric weight and shape similar to the garment you are going to crochet. Smooth out the sweater and measure the width. Find the same, or closest, width to this on the sweater diagram of your crochet pattern—this is the size for you.

Make a photocopy of your pattern and circle or highlight all the figures that apply to your size throughout the pattern, starting with the number of balls of yarn to purchase, followed by the number of chains in the foundation chain for the sweater back, the length to the armhole, and so on. The figure for the smallest size is given first and all the figures for the larger sizes follow in parentheses. Where there is only one figure given in the instructions—be it a

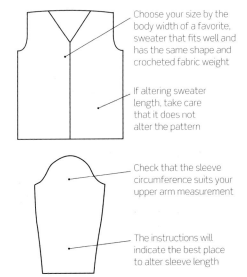

Choose your size by the body width of a favorite, sweater that fits well and has the same shape and crocheted fabric weight

If altering sweater length, take care that it does not alter the pattern

Check that the sleeve circumference suits your upper arm measurement

The instructions will indicate the best place to alter sleeve length

measurement, the number of rows, or the number of stitches—this figure applies to all sizes. Before starting your crochet, always check your gauge (see below).

Measuring gauge

It is essential to check your gauge (stitch size) before beginning a crochet pattern if the final size of the piece matters. Not everyone crochets stitches with exactly the same tightness or looseness, so you may well need to use a different hook size to achieve the stitch size required by your pattern.

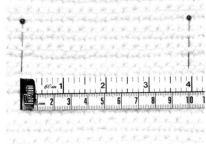

1 Using the specified hook, crochet a swatch about 5in (13cm) square. Mark 4in (10cm) across the center with pins and count the number of stitches between the pins.

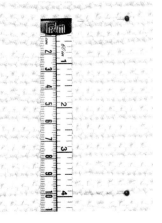

2 Count the number of rows to 4in (10cm) in the same way. If you have fewer stitches and rows than you should, try again with a larger hook size; if you have more, change to a smaller hook size. Use the hook size that best matches the correct gauge. (Matching the stitch width is much more important than matching the row height.)

Basic stitches in symbols and abbreviations

Crochet row instructions can be written out with abbreviations or using symbols for the stitches. There is a more detailed explanation for reading stitch pattern instructions on page 82, but directions for the basic stitches are given in this section in both symbols and abbreviations. This provides an introduction to crochet instructions and a quick reference for how to work crochet fabrics with basic stitches. Please note that left-handed crocheters will need to work the diagram backward. (There are basic instructions for left-handed crocheters on how to hold the hook and yarn on page 22.)

Stitch heights

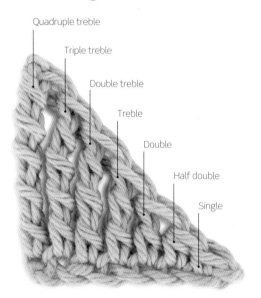

Quadruple treble

Triple treble

Double treble

Treble

Double

Half double

Single

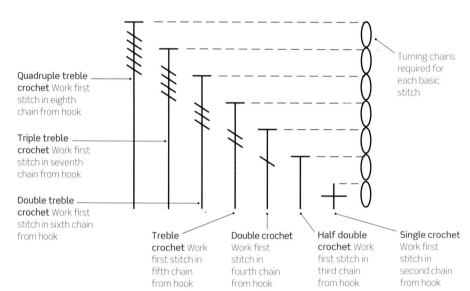

Quadruple treble crochet Work first stitch in eighth chain from hook

Triple treble crochet Work first stitch in seventh chain from hook

Double treble crochet Work first stitch in sixth chain from hook

Treble crochet Work first stitch in fifth chain from hook

Double crochet Work first stitch in fourth chain from hook

Half double crochet Work first stitch in third chain from hook

Single crochet Work first stitch in second chain from hook

Turning chains required for each basic stitch

Stitch symbols: The diagram, above right, shows all the basic stitches in symbols and illustrates approximately how tall the stitches are when standing side by side. A single crochet is roughly one chain tall, a half double crochet two chains tall, a double crochet three chains tall, and so on. (The picture, above left, shows what each stitch actually looks like.) These heights determine the number of turning chains you need to work at the beginning of each row for each of the basic stitches. The diagonal bars are useful, since they indicate how many times you need to wrap the yarn around the hook before working the stitch. Also provided here is a reference for which chain to work into when working the first stitch into the foundation chain.

Single crochet instructions

Single symbol: Crochet symbol instructions, especially for the basic stitches, are very easy to understand. Roughly imitating the size and shape of the stitch, the symbols are read from the bottom of the diagram upward. To get used to very simple crochet instructions, try working single crochet following the written directions and the symbol diagram at the same time (see p. 83 for abbreviations list), then try this with the other basic stitches as well.

Single crochet in abbreviations
Make any number of ch.
Row 1 1 sc in second ch from hook, 1 sc in each of rem ch to end, turn.
Row 2 Ch 1 (does NOT count as a st), 1 sc in each sc to end, turn. Rep row 2 to form sc fabric.

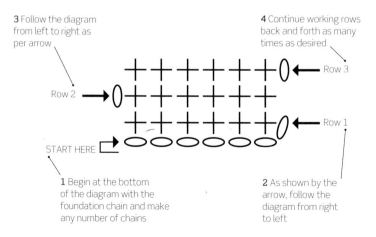

3 Follow the diagram from left to right as per arrow

4 Continue working rows back and forth as many times as desired

Row 3

Row 2

Row 1

START HERE

1 Begin at the bottom of the diagram with the foundation chain and make any number of chains

2 As shown by the arrow, follow the diagram from right to left

Half double crochet instructions

Half double symbol: The symbol for half double is a vertical line with a horizontal bar at the top, and it is about twice as tall as the single crochet symbol, just like the stitch is in reality. Read the written instructions for this basic stitch (below) and look at the chart at the same time. The direction of each arrow indicates whether to read the chart from left to right or right to left.

Half double crochet in abbreviations
Make any number of ch.
Row 1 1 hdc in third ch from hook, 1 hdc in each of rem ch to end, turn.
Row 2 Ch 2 (counts as first st), skip first hdc in row below, *1 hdc in next hdc; rep from * to end, then work 1 hdc in top of 2 ch at end, turn.
Rep row 2 to form hdc fabric.

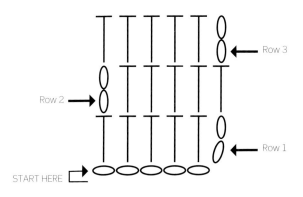

Double crochet instructions

Double symbol: The double symbol has a short diagonal line across its "waist." The diagram shows clearly how the 3-ch turning chain counts as the first stitch of each row.

Double crochet in abbreviations
Make any number of ch.
Row 1 1 dc in fourth ch from hook, 1 dc in each of rem ch to end, turn.
Row 2 Ch 3 (counts as first dc), skip first dc in row below, *1 dc in next dc; rep from * to end, then work 1 dc in top of 3 ch at end, turn.
Rep row 2 to form dc fabric.

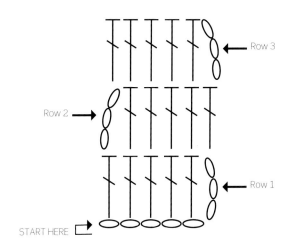

Treble crochet instructions

Treble symbol: Two short diagonal lines cross the "waist" of the treble symbol, echoing the two diagonal yarn strands on the stitch itself.

Treble crochet in abbreviations
Make any number of ch.
Row 1 1 tr in fifth ch from hook, 1 tr in each of rem ch to end, turn.
Row 2 Ch 4 (counts as first tr), skip first tr in row below, *1 tr in next tr; rep from * to end, then work 1 tr in top of 4 ch at end, turn.
Rep row 2 to form tr fabric.

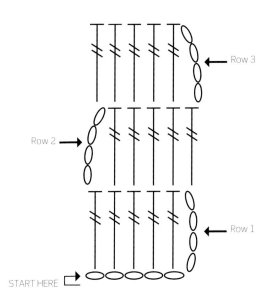

Blocking and seams

Always sew the seams of a garment or accessory using a blunt-ended needle and a matching yarn (a contrasting yarn is used here just to show the seam techniques more clearly); and work them in the order given in the crochet pattern. But before sewing any seams, block your crochet pieces carefully. Press the finished seams very lightly with a cool iron on the wrong side after completion.

Wet blocking

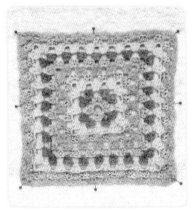

Using water: If your yarn will allow it, wet blocking is the best way to even out crochet. Wet the pieces in a sink full of lukewarm water. Then squeeze out the water and roll the crochet in a towel to remove excess dampness. Smooth the crochet into shape right-side down on layers of dry towels covered with a sheet, pinning at intervals. Add as many pins as is necessary to refine the shape. Do not move the crochet until it is completely dry.

Steam blocking

Using steam: For a speedier process you may prefer steam blocking (if your yarn label allows it). First, pin the crochet right-side down into the correct shape. Then steam the crochet gently using a clean damp cloth, but barely touching the cloth with the iron. Never rest the weight of an iron on your crochet or it will flatten the texture. Leave the steamed piece to dry completely before unpinning it.

Backstitch seam

Backstitch produces durable seams and is frequently recommended in crochet patterns for garments and accessories.

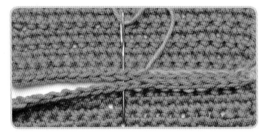

1 Align the crochet pieces, right sides together, and secure the yarn with two or three whipstitches in the same place. Then, inserting the needle near the edge, work the seam, taking one stitch forward and one stitch back.

2 On the backward stitch, be sure to insert the needle through the same place as the end of the last stitch. At the end of the seam, secure the yarn in the same way as at the beginning of the seam.

Whipstitch seam (also called overcast seam)

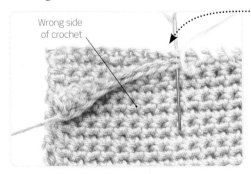

Wrong side of crochet

Simple whipstitch seam: Align the crochet pieces with right sides together and secure the yarn as for backstitch. Then insert the needle close to the edge and make stitches through the two layers as shown.

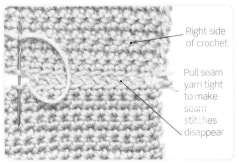

Right side of crochet

Pull seam yarn tight to make seam stitches disappear

Flat whipstitch seam: For a flat seam along the tops of stitches, lay the pieces right-side up and edge-to-edge. Work as for the simple whipstitch seam, but inserting the needle through the back loops of the stitches only.

Mattress stitch (also called edge-to-edge seam)

This method creates a neat flat seam. It can be used, as here, on double crochet as well as on all other types of crochet fabrics.

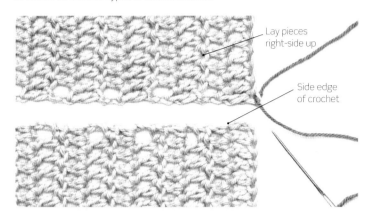

Lay pieces right-side up

Side edge of crochet

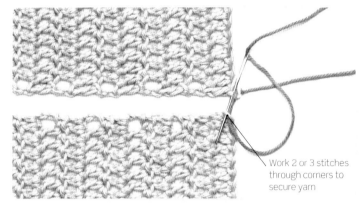

Work 2 or 3 stitches through corners to secure yarn

1 Align the pieces of crochet right-side up and edge-to-edge. Insert the needle through the corner of the top piece, leaving a long loose end.

2 Insert the needle through the corner of the other piece, then through both pieces again in the same place at the corner to secure firmly.

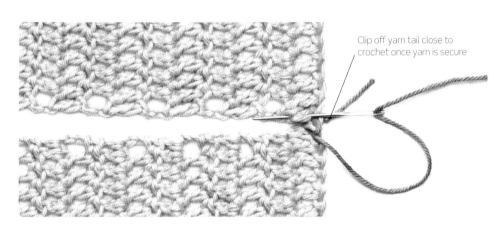

Clip off yarn tail close to crochet once yarn is secure

3 Make the next stitch along the center of the crocheted stitch (a double or a turning chain) at the edge on the top piece of crochet. Make the next crocheted stitch along the center of the stitch or turning chain on the opposite edge.

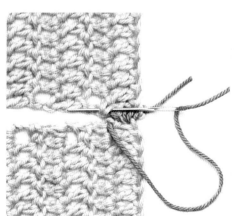

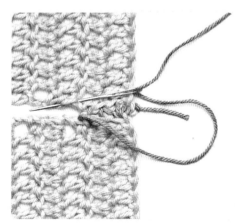

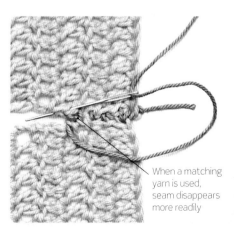

When a matching yarn is used, seam disappears more readily

4 Make the next pair of stitches in the same way, working a stitch along one stitch or turning chain on the top piece, then, on the opposite piece.

5 Continue along the seam, taking a stitch in each side alternately. Take shorter stitches on each piece if the yarn used for the pieces is bulky.

6 After every few stitches, pull the yarn tight so that the seam yarn disappears and is not visible on the right side of the crochet.

Darning in yarn

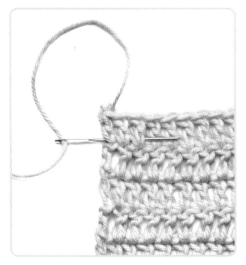

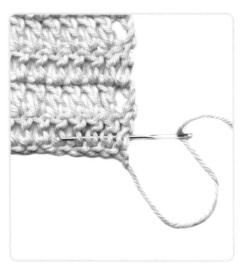

Darning in along top row: Using a blunt-ended yarn needle, darn the yarn tail through the center of the base of 6–8 stitches in the last row. Clip off the remaining end close to the fabric.

Darning in along first row: Using a blunt-ended yarn needle, darn the yarn tail through the center of the base of 6–8 stitches in the first row. Clip off the remaining end close to the fabric.

Darning in along top: You can also weave the yarn in and out of the top of the crochet. This provides a slightly more secure finishing and is good for slippery yarns.

Slip stitch seam

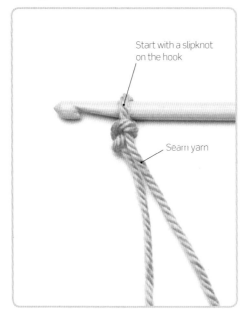

Start with a slipknot on the hook

Seam yarn

1 Instead of using a yarn needle to join your seam, you can use a crochet hook to work a quicker seam. Although seams can be worked with single crochet, slip stitch seams are less bulky. Start by placing a slipknot on the hook.

2 Align the two layers of crochet with the right sides together. Then with the slipknot on the hook, insert the hook through the two layers at the starting end of the seam, wrap the yarn around the hook, and draw a loop through the two layers and the loop on the hook.

3 Continue in this way and fasten off at the end. When working the seam along the tops of stitches (as here), insert the hook through only the back loops of the stitches. Along row-end edges, work through the layers one stitch in from the edge.

This beautiful child's hooded jacket, featured on pages 240-243, contains a number of seams. There are seams on the sleeves and also down the sides of the hoodie.

Handmade yarn embellishments

Yarn embellishments for crochet are easy to make, but be sure to take your time so that they look absolutely perfect. Fringe is often used to edge throws, blankets, rugs, and scarves; tassels are ideal for the corners of a pillow cover or the top of a hat. Instructions for making fringe and tassels are given here, but you can also add pom-poms—handmade or ready-made—to hats, garments, and many different types of accessory.

Making fringe

Wrong side

Right side

1 Cut two lengths of yarn, twice the length of the finished fringe, plus at least 1in (2.5cm) extra for the knots. Align the two strands and fold them in half. With the wrong side of the fabric facing, insert a crochet hook from front to back, ¼in (5mm) from the edge. Draw the loop through.

2 Using the crochet hook, pull the ends of the strands through the loop on the hook. Tighten the loop to secure the fringe. Measure your fringe after making this first fringe knot to be certain that it is long enough, and adjust the length of the strands, if necessary.

3 Add fringe knots along the edge of the fabric, spacing them evenly apart. For a plumper fringe, use more than two strands at a time. If you have trouble pulling the fringe through the fabric, experiment using a smaller or larger hook size. After completing the fringe, trim it slightly to straighten the ends, if necessary.

Making a tassel

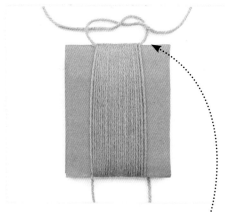

1 Cut a piece of cardboard 3in (8cm) wide and twice as long as the desired length for the finished tassel. Fold the cardboard in half widthwise with the fold at the top. Wrap yarn around and around the cardboard lengthwise to form a plump tassel. Using a blunt-ended needle, pass a length of yarn under the yarn strands at the top and tie tightly.

2 Insert the tip of a pair of scissors between the two layers of cardboard at the lower end of the tassel. Cut through the strands.

3 Wrap one of the long strands at the top several times around the tassel, about ¾in (2cm) from the top. Thread this strand onto a blunt-ended needle and pass it through the center of the tassel and out at the top next to the other strand. Use the long strands to attach the tassel to your crochet.

Care of crochet

Because you have invested so much time and effort in your crochet, take care when cleaning and storing it. Start by referring to the care instructions on the labels supplied with the yarn.

Care of your project

Keep a thorough record of all projects, including the pattern, the gauge swatch, a small amount of the yarn(s), and, most importantly, a yarn label for each of the yarns used. Care instructions for any special ready-made trimming, ribbons, zippers, or snaps should also be included. If you are giving a crochet project as a gift, it is important to attach care information so that the recipient can look after the item properly.

Preparing for washing

Remove any special buttons or trims that can be damaged by water or dry-cleaning. To retain the shape of openings, baste them closed using a fine cotton yarn that can be easily pulled out when dry. Measure the piece in all directions and record these dimensions so you can mold it into the correct shape when it is still damp.

It is often a good idea to sew a care label to your crocheted items for convenience. This works best for larger items such as blankets and garments. Labels can be bought from craft stores, yarn stores, and online. Write the care instructions on the label with a permanent marker before attaching it. The label can then be attached securely with a sewing needle and some matching thread.

Washing

Refer to your yarn label for washing instructions. Yarns labeled "superwash" or "machine washable" can be washed in a washing machine on a gentle cycle and at a cool temperature. Many yarn labels, however, recommend hand-washing.

Wash your animal fiber crochet with great care, avoiding friction (rubbing), agitation (swirling the water), and hot water, which can cause felting in wool yarns and damage other fibers.

Dissolve a mild detergent in a large sink full of lukewarm water. Submerge a single item and gently press up and down on it. Soak for a few minutes, then rinse to remove the soapy water.

Squeeze out the water very gently, pressing the item against the sink. Do not wring. Supporting the damp item, move it onto a large towel. Roll in the towel to remove more moisture.

Drying

Dry washed crochet flat on a fresh towel, turning it over occasionally to speed up the process and prevent damage by mildew.

Large items, such as throws, can be dried on the floor; first, cover the floor with a large plastic sheet, then lay towels on top of this before positioning the throw.

It may be necessary to replace the towels every so often with dry ones if the item is particularly large or thick, in order to help it dry more quickly.

Mold damp crochet into its correct size and shape before leaving to dry, and never leave in direct sunlight or near a heating source. Once completely dry, you can block and steam the piece if necessary (see p. 70).

Never hang up a crocheted item to dry; the weight will cause it to become permanently misshapen, and no amount of blocking will restore it to its original shape and size.

Storage and moth control

Check regularly for telltale holes. If storing all summer, place an antimoth product in the drawer or closet with your wool crochet and renew it as directed.

Before repairing a hole in a moth-infested item, place it in the freezer overnight to kill any eggs. Crochet too large for the freezer, such as throws and afghans, can be placed all day in the sun to achieve the same result.

When a crocheted item is not being used, store it flat. If you hang it up, the stitches will become stretched and any damage will be irreversible. If your crochet is to be stored for any length of time, wrap it in acid-free tissue paper, placing the paper between the folds as well as around the outside.

TOP TIP *Taking good care of your crochet project will prolong its life.*

Stitch techniques

The basic crochet stitches can be combined together in various ways to create endless textures and sculptured effects. Not all the vast range of crochet stitch techniques can be included, but the most commonly used are explained here in detail. When attempting the stitch patterns on pages 84–85, refer back to these step-by-step instructions to see more clearly how to achieve the textures.

Simple textures

The simplest and most subtle crochet textures are created by working into various parts of the stitches or between the stitches in the row below. Before trying out any of these techniques, learn about the parts of the stitches so you can identify them easily.

Parts of stitches

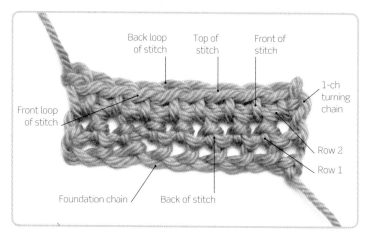

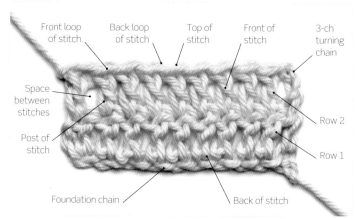

Single crochet stitches: Work two rows of single crochet (see pp. 32-33) and fasten off. Look closely at your sample and make sure you can identify all the parts of the stitch labeled above. If your crochet pattern tells you to work into the stitch below, always insert the hook under BOTH loops (the front loop and the back loop) at the top of the stitch as explained on page 33 for single crochet, unless it tells you to do otherwise.

Double crochet stitches: Work two rows of double crochet (see pp. 42-43) and fasten off. Again, make sure you can identify all the parts of the stitch labeled above. As for single crochet and all other crochet stitches, if your crochet pattern tells you to work into the stitch below, always insert the hook under both loops at the top of the stitch, unless it tells you to do otherwise.

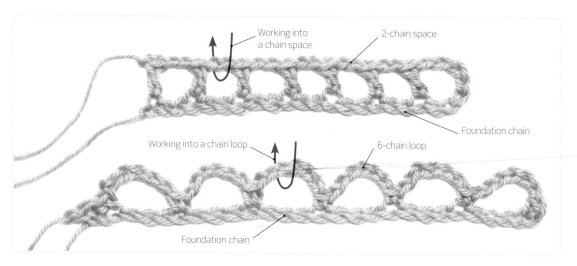

Chain spaces and chain loops: In many stitch patterns chain stitches are introduced between basic stitches to create holes or spaces in the fabric. Spaces formed by short chains are called chain spaces, and those formed by long chains are chain loops. When a crochet pattern instructs you to work into a chain space (or loop), always insert your hook from front to back through the space and not into the actual chain stitches.

Working into the back loop of a single crochet

 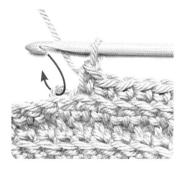

Ridge effect: Working into only the back loops of the stitches in every row of single crochet creates a deep ridged effect. The ridges are formed by the unworked loops.

Working into the front loop of a single crochet

Smooth effect: Working into only the front loop of each single crochet in the row below, on every row, creates a less pronounced texture than working into only the back loop.

Working into the back loop of a double crochet

 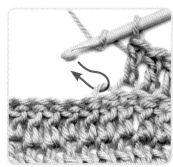

Double ridge: The same techniques shown for working into the back or front of a single crochet can be used on all crochet stitches to create ridges. For this stitch, the fabric will look the same on both sides.

Working into spaces between stitches

 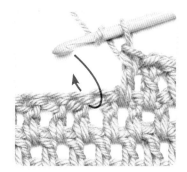

Double space: Another way to achieve a subtly different texture with basic stitches is to work the stitches into the spaces between the stitches in the row below, instead of into the tops of the stitches.

Working into a chain space

Simple texture: Tweed stitch illustrates the simplest of all textures created by working into a chain space. Here, single crochet stitches are worked in the 1-chain spaces between the stitches in the row below, instead of into the tops of the stitches.

Tweed stitch pattern

Because it is such a popular stitch and a perfect alternative to basic single crochet, the pattern for it is given here. (See p. 83 for abbreviations.) Start with an even number of chains.

Row 1 1 sc in second ch from hook, *ch 1, skip next ch, 1 sc in next ch; rep from * to end, turn.

Row 2 Ch 1 (does NOT count as a stitch), 1 sc in first sc, 1 sc in next 1-ch sp, *ch 1, 1 sc in next 1-ch sp; rep from * to last sc, 1 sc in last sc, turn.

Row 3 Ch 1 (does NOT count as a stitch), 1 sc in first sc, *ch 1, 1 sc in next 1-ch sp; rep from * to last 2 sc, ch 1, skip next sc, 1 sc in last sc, turn.

Rep rows 2 and 3 to form patt.

Sculptural textures

These easy raised and grouped crochet stitch techniques produce attractive sculptural textures. Although they can be used to create fairly dense stitch patterns (see pp. 84–85), they are also found in lace stitches (see pp. 113–115).

Front post double crochet

Working around the post is used to make a fabric that imitates knitted ribbing, but it can also be used on its own in rows to create a ridged effect.

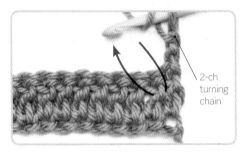

1 Start with a row of doubles. On following rows, work 2 chains, yo and insert the hook from the front around the post of the second double.

2 To complete the double, yo and draw a loop through, then (yo and draw through the first 2 loops on the hook) twice, as shown by the two large arrows.

3 Work a double around each of the following doubles in the row below in the same way. At the end of the row, work a double into the top of the turning chain. Repeat the second row to form a ridged texture.

Back post double crochet

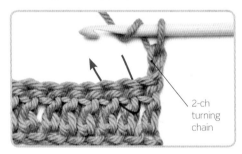

1 Start by working a base row of double crochet. To start the second row, work 2 chains, yo and insert the hook from the back around the post of the second double.

2 To complete the double, yo and draw a loop through, then (yo and draw through the first 2 loops on the hook) twice, as shown by the two large arrows.

3 Work a double around each of the doubles in the row below in the same way. Continue as for step 3 of Front post double (above).

Shells

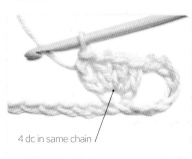

4 dc in same chain

4-dc shell: Shells are the most frequently used of all crochet stitch techniques. Usually made with doubles, they are formed by working several stitches into the same stitch or space. Here 4 doubles have been worked into the same chain to form a 4-dc shell.

5 dc in same chain

5-dc shell: Here 5 doubles have been worked into the same chain to form a 5-dc shell. Any number of doubles can be used to form a shell, but the most commonly used crochet shells have 2, 3, 4, 5, or 6 stitches. Shells can also be made with half doubles and taller basic stitches.

Bobbles

Joining effect: Bobbles are formed using the shell technique and the cluster technique so that the stitches are joined together at the top and the bottom.

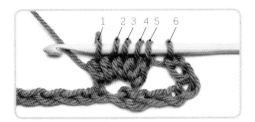  

1 To work a 5-dc bobble, work 5 incomplete doubles (as for a cluster) into the same stitch (as for a shell). There are now 6 loops on the hook.

2 Wrap the yarn around the hook and draw a loop through all 6 loops on the hook.

3 This completes all of the doubles at the same time and joins them at the top. Some bobbles are completed with an extra chain, as shown by the large arrow. Bobbles are usually made with 3, 4, or 5 doubles. Bobbles made with half doubles are called puff stitches.

Clusters

Crocheted clusters look like upside-down shells. They are made by joining the tops of several stitches (each worked into a different stitch below) into a single top.

1 To make a 3-dc cluster, work a double up to the last yo that completes the double. Then work an incomplete double into each of the next 2 stitches in the same way. There are now 4 loops on the hook.

2 Wrap the yarn around the hook and draw a loop through all 4 loops on the hook.

3 This completes all of the doubles at the same time and joins them at the top. Clusters can be made with 2, 3, 4, 5, 6, or more doubles, and with half doubles or taller basic stitches as well.

Popcorns

1 Popcorns are started like shells. To make a 5-dc popcorn, begin by working 5 doubles in the same stitch.

2 Remove the hook from the loop and insert it from back to front through the top of the first double of the group. Draw the working loop through the top of the first double, as shown by the arrow.

3 This pulls the tops of the shells together to form a bobble-type shape. Unlike the top of a bobble, the top of a popcorn protrudes forward because of the method of construction. Popcorns are usually made with 3, 4, or 5 doubles.

Essential information

DIFFICULTY LEVEL Easy

SIZE Small: 1¾in (4.5cm) diameter, Medium: 1¾in (5cm) diameter, Large: 2¼in (5.5cm) diameter

YARN Any 4-ply yarn or crochet thread will work here or use different weight yarns for various sizes of flower

A x 1   **B** x 1   **C** x 1

CROCHET HOOK D/3 US (3mm) hook

NOTIONS Yarn needle

GAUGE Exact gauge is not essential

Flower garland

Flower motifs are quick and easy projects for using all of the stitches you have learned up until now. The use of all the different heights of the stitches together creates curves that are perfect for petals.

PROJECTS
For more multi-stitch patterns
>> *go to pages 186 and 300*

Pattern

NOTE Make three of each color in each sized flower, therefore making nine of each in total.

Big flower (make 9)
Work 5 ch, ss in first ch to form a ring.
ROUND 1 Ch 1, work 16 sc into ring, join round with a ss into first ch.
ROUND 2 Ch 4, (1 tr, 2 ch) into next st, *1 tr into next st, (1 tr, 2 ch) into next st; rep from * to end of round, join round with a ss into top of 4 ch.
ROUND 3 Ch 1, (1 hdc, 2 tr, 1 tr, 2 tr, 1 hdc) all into next 2-ch sp, *1 sc in between next 2 tr, (1 hdc, 2 tr, 1 tr, 2 tr, 1 hdc) all into next 2-ch sp; rep from * to end of round, join round with a ss into first ch.
Fasten off yarn, weave in ends.

Medium flower (make 9)
Work Ch 5, ss in first ch to form a ring.
ROUND 1 Ch 1, work 12 sc into ring, join round with a ss into top of 3 ch.
ROUND 2 Ch 3, (1 tr, 2 ch) into next st, *1 tr into next st, (1 tr, 2 ch) into next st; rep from * to end of round, join round with a ss into top of ch 3.
ROUND 3 Ch 1, (1 hdc, 3 tr, 1 hdc) all into next 2-ch sp, *1 sc in between next 2 tr, (1 hdc, 3 tr, 1 hdc) all into next 2-ch sp; rep from * to end of round, join round with a ss into first ch.
Fasten off yarn, weave in ends.

Small flower (make 9)
Work Ch 4, ss in first ch to form a ring.
ROUND 1 1 ch, work 10 sc into ring, join round with a ss into top of 3 ch.

ROUND 2 Ch 3, (1 tr, 2 ch) into next st, *1 tr into next st, (1 tr, 2 ch) into next tr; rep from * to end of round, join round with a ss into top of ch 3.
ROUND 3 Ch 1, (1 hdc, 3 tr, 1 hdc) all into next 2-ch sp, *1 sc in between next 2 tr, (1 hdc, 3 tr, 1 hdc) all into next 2-ch sp; rep from * to end of round, join round with a ss into first ch.
Fasten off yarn, weave in ends.

Finishing
Work a chain of desired length, threading through the middle of the flowers to create a garland. Alternatively, mount individual flowers onto a safety pin or pin back to create a corsage.

1 Work around the central circle to create five petals. Work a single crochet into the space between the next 2 tr after each petal.

2 Crochet a series of stitches around each flower for petals. You will need single crochet, half double, and double stitch. Work the same number of stitches into each chain space.

Following simple stitch patterns

Working a project from a crochet pattern for the first time can seem difficult for a beginner, especially if an experienced crocheter is not on hand as a guide. The best way to prepare for a crochet pattern is first to practice crocheting rectangles of various stitch patterns using simple stitch techniques. This is a good introduction to following abbreviated written row instructions and symbol diagrams.

Understanding written instructions

As long as you know how to work all the basic stitches and can work them from the simple patterns on pages 68–69 and have reviewed pages 76–79 where special stitch techniques are explained, there is nothing stopping you from trying to work the simple textures stitch patterns on pages 84–85 and page 83. Simply consult the list on pages 68–69 for the meanings of the various abbreviations and follow the written row instructions one step at a time.

Begin by making the required number of chains for the foundation chain, using your chosen yarn and one of the hook sizes recommended for this yarn weight on pages 14–15. Crochet a swatch that repeats the pattern only a few times to test it out. (If you decide to make a blanket or pillow cover with the stitch later, you can adjust the hook size before starting it to obtain the exact flexibility of fabric you desire for your project.)

Work each row of the stitch pattern slowly and mark the right side of the fabric (if there is one) as soon as you start, by tying a contrasting colored yarn to it. Another good tip is to check off the rows as you complete them or put a sticky note under them so you don't lose your place in the pattern. If you do get lost in all the stitches, you can pull out all the rows and start the pattern from the foundation-chain again.

Understanding stitch symbol diagrams

Crochet stitch patterns can also be given in symbols (see p. 83). These diagrams are usually even easier to follow than directions with abbreviations because they create a visual reference of approximately how the finished stitch will look. Each basic stitch on the chart is represented by a symbol that resembles it in some way. The position of the base of each stitch symbol indicates which stitch or chain space it is worked into in the row below. If the symbols are joined at the base, this means that they are worked into the same stitch in the row below.

The beginning of the foundation chain will be marked as your starting point on the diagram. Read each row on the diagram either from right to left or left to right following the direction of the arrow. Although you can consult the written instructions for how many chains to make for a foundation chain and how to repeat the stitch repeat across a row (or a row repeat up the fabric), it is easy to work these out yourself from the diagram once you become proficient in reading diagrams. But to begin with, work from the written instructions and use the diagram as a visual aid. Once you have completed the first few rows of the pattern, you can dispense with the written instructions all together and continue with the diagram as your sole guide. If the stitch is an easy one, you will very quickly be able to work it without looking at any instructions at all.

This symbol diagram for the open shell stitch (see p. 113) is a good introduction to working from a symbol diagram. Start at the bottom of the diagram and follow it row by row with the aid of the numbered tips.

Sample stitch pattern

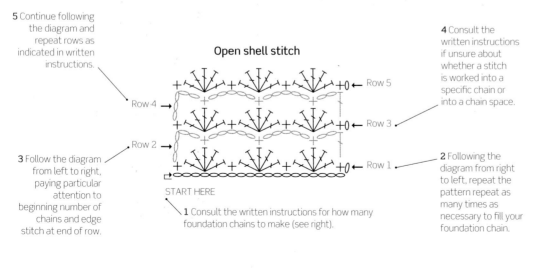

5 Continue following the diagram and repeat rows as indicated in written instructions.

3 Follow the diagram from left to right, paying particular attention to beginning number of chains and edge stitch at end of row.

Open shell stitch

START HERE

1 Consult the written instructions for how many foundation chains to make (see right).

4 Consult the written instructions if unsure about whether a stitch is worked into a specific chain or into a chain space.

2 Following the diagram from right to left, repeat the pattern repeat as many times as necessary to fill your foundation chain.

Crochet instructions

Make a multiple of 6 ch, plus 2 extra.
Row 1 (RS) 1 sc in second ch from hook, *skip next 2 ch, 5 dc in next ch, skip next 2 ch, 1 sc in next ch; rep from * to end, turn.
Row 2 Ch 5 (counts as first dc and a 2-ch sp), 1 sc in center dc of first shell, *ch 5, 1 sc in center dc of next shell; rep from *, ending with ch 2, 1 dc in last sc, turn.
Row 3 Ch 1 (does NOT count as a st), 1 sc in first dc, *5 dc in next sc, 1 sc in next 5-ch loop; rep from * working last sc of last rep in 3rd ch from last sc, turn.
Rep rows 2 and 3 to form patt.

Crochet abbreviations

These are the abbreviations most commonly used in crochet patterns. The abbreviations for the basic stitches are listed first and the other abbreviations found in crochet patterns follow. Any special abbreviations in a crochet pattern will always be explained in the pattern.

Abbreviations for basic stitches
Note: The stitches are listed from shortest to tallest.

ch	chain	foll	follow(s)(ing)	sc3tog	see crochet terminology on p. 311
ss	slip stitch	g	gram(s)	sp	space(s)
sc	single crochet	hdc2tog	see crochet terminology on p. 311	st(s)	stitch(es)
hdc	half double crochet			TBL	through back loop
dc	double crochet	hdc3tog	see crochet terminology p. 311	TFL	through front loop
tr	treble	in	inch(es)	tog	together
dtr	double treble	inc	increas(e)(ing)	WS	wrong side
trtr	triple treble	m	meter(s)	yd	yard(s)
qtr	quadruple treble	mm	millimeter(s)	yo	yarn over
		oz	ounce(s)	*	repeat instructions after asterisk or between asterisks as many times as instructed.
Other abbreviations		patt(s)	pattern(s)		
alt	alternate	rem	remain(s)(ing)		
beg	begin(ning)	rep	repeat(s)(ing)	( )	repeat instructions inside parentheses as many times as instructed.
cm	centimeter(s)	RS	right side		
cont	continu(e)(ing)	sc2tog	see crochet terminology on p. 311	[ ]	used for a repeat within a repeat.
dc2tog	see crochet terminology on p. 311				
dc3tog	see crochet terminology on p. 311				

Crochet stitch symbols

These are the symbols used in this book, but crochet symbols are not universal so always consult the key with your crochet instructions for the symbols used in your pattern.

Basic stitches
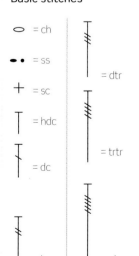

Special stitches and stitch combinations
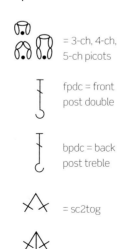
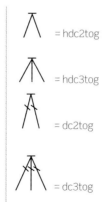
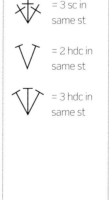

Shells, cluster, bobbles, popcorns
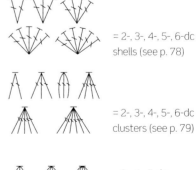

Simple textures stitch patterns

Selected for how easy they are to work, these stitch patterns cover an array of crochet textures, including those made using the techniques shown on pp. 82–83. Although crochet is often identified with lacy openwork fabrics, there are also lots of solid textures like these to choose from. Quick to work and easy to memorize after the first few rows, the following stitches make pretty pillow covers, baby blankets, and throws. They all look good on both sides of the fabrics and two are reversible.

Crochet rib stitch

Crochet diagram

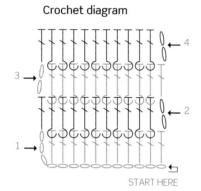

START HERE

Crochet instructions
Make a multiple of 2 ch.
Row 1 1 dc in fourth ch from hook, 1 dc in each of rem ch, turn.
Row 2 Ch 2 (counts as first st), skip first dc, *1 dc around post of next dc from front, 1 dc around post of next dc from back; rep from * to end, 1 dc in top of turning ch at end, turn.
Rep row 2 to form patt.

Simple crossed stitch

Crochet diagram

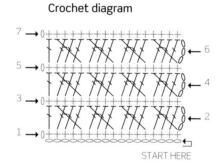

START HERE

Crochet instructions
Make a multiple of 4 ch, plus 2 extra.
Row 1 1 sc in second ch from hook, 1 sc in each of rem ch, turn.
Row 2 (RS) Ch 3 (counts as first dc), skip first sc, 1 dc in each of next 3 sc, yo and insert hook from front to back in first sc (the skipped sc), yo and draw a long loop through (extending the loop that so it reaches back to position of work and does not squash 3-dc group just made), (yo and draw through first 2 loops on hook) twice (called long dc), *skip next sc, 1 dc in each of next 3 sc, 1 long dc in last skipped sc; rep from * to last sc, 1 dc in last sc, turn.
Row 3 Ch 1 (does NOT count as a st), 1 sc in each dc to end (do NOT work a sc in 3-ch turning chain), turn.
Rep rows 2 and 3 to form patt.

Close shells stitch

Crochet diagram

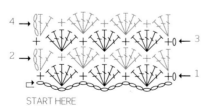

START HERE

Crochet instructions
Make a multiple of 6 ch, plus 2 extra.
Row 1 1 sc in second ch from hook, *skip next 2 ch, 5 dc in next ch, skip next 2 ch, 1 sc in next ch; rep from * to end, turn.
Row 2 Ch 3 (counts as first dc), 2 dc in first sc, *skip next 2 dc, 1 sc in next dc, 5 dc in next sc (between shells); rep from *, ending last rep with 3 dc in last sc (instead of 5 dc), turn.
Row 3 Ch 1 (does NOT count as a st), 1 sc in first dc, *5 dc in next sc (between shells), skip next 2 dc, 1 sc in next dc; rep from *, working last sc in top of 3 ch at end, turn.
Rep rows 2 and 3 to form patt.

Cluster and shell stitch

Crochet diagram

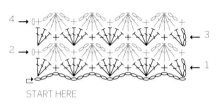

START HERE

Crochet instructions

Note: cluster (also called sc5tog) = over next 5 sts (which include 2 dc, 1 sc, 2 dc) work (yo and insert hook in next st, yo and draw a loop through, yo and draw through first 2 loops on hook) 5 times (6 loops now on hook), yo and draw through all 6 loops on hook (see p. 79).
Make a multiple of 6 ch, plus 4 extra.

Row 1 (RS) 2 dc in fourth ch from hook, skip next 2 ch, 1 sc in next ch, *skip next 2 ch, 5 dc in next ch, skip next 2 ch, 1 sc in next ch: rep from * to last 3 ch, skip next 2 ch, 3 dc in last ch, turn.

Row 2 Ch 1 (does NOT count as a st), 1 sc in first dc, *2 ch, 1 cluster over next 5 sts, 2 ch, 1 sc in next dc (center dc of 5-dc group); rep from *, working last sc of last rep in top of 3 ch at end, turn.

Row 3 Ch 3 (counts as first dc), 2 dc in first sc, skip next 2 ch, 1 sc in next st (top of first cluster), *5 dc in next sc, skip next 2 ch, 1 sc in next st (top of next cluster); rep from *, ending with 3 dc in last sc, turn.
Rep rows 2 and 3 to form patt.

Simple bobble stitch

Crochet diagram

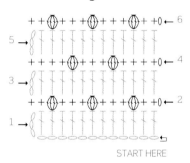

START HERE

Crochet instructions

Note: bobble = (yo and insert hook in specified st, yo and draw a loop through, yo and draw through first 2 loops on hook) 4 times all in same st (5 loops now on hook), yo and draw through all 5 loops on hook (see p. 79).

Row 1 (WS) 1 dc in fourth ch from hook, 1 dc in each of rem ch, turn.

Row 2 (RS) Ch 1 (does NOT count as a st), 1 sc in each of first 2 dc, *1 bobble in next dc, 1 sc in each of next 3 dc; rep from * to last 2 dc, 1 bobble in next dc, 1 sc in next dc, 1 sc in top of 3-ch at end, turn.

Row 3 Ch 3 (counts as first dc), skip first sc and work 1 dc in each st to end, turn.

Row 4 Ch 1 (does NOT count as a st), 1 sc in each of first 4 dc, *1 bobble in next dc, 1 sc in each of next 3 dc; rep from *, ending with 1 sc in top of 3 ch at end, turn.

Row 5 Rep row 3.
Rep rows 2–5 to form patt, ending with a patt row 5.

Shells and chains

Crochet diagram

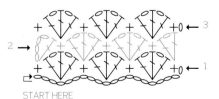

START HERE

Crochet instructions

Make a multiple of 6 ch, plus 2 extra.

Row 1 (RS) 1 sc in second ch from hook, *skip next 2 ch, work (1 dc, ch 1, 1 dc, ch 1, 1 dc) in next ch, skip next 2 ch, 1 sc in next ch; rep from * to end, turn.

Row 2 Ch 4 (counts as 1 dc and a 1-ch sp), 1 dc in first sc, skip next dc, 1 sc in next dc (center dc of shell), *work (1 dc, ch 1, 1 dc, ch 1, 1 dc) all in next sc (between shells), skip next dc, 1 sc in next dc (center dc of shell); rep from *, ending with (1 dc, ch 1, 1 dc) in last sc, turn.

Row 3 Ch 1 (does NOT count as a st), 1 sc in first dc, *work (1 dc, ch 1, 1 dc, ch 1, 1 dc) all in next sc, skip next dc, 1 sc in next dc (center dc of shell); rep from *, working last sc of last rep in third of 4 ch made at beg of previous row, turn.
Rep rows 2 and 3 to form patt.

Embellishments for crochet

There are many ways to add subtle or bold embellishments to your crochet. Although it may seem unimportant, choosing the right buttons when they are required comes at the top of the list, so always select buttons carefully and take your finished crochet along to try them out before purchasing any. Other adornments that will dress up your crochet include beads, ribbons, pom-poms, fringe, edgings, and embroidery.

Beaded crochet

Beads can be sewn onto your finished crochet if you are only adding a few. But for an allover effect, work the beads into the fabric as you crochet. The most common beaded crochet technique uses single crochet as the background to the beads.

Working beaded single crochet

Beaded crochet is suitable for a range of simple spaced-out allover geometric patterns. But beware of using too many beads on the crochet or beads that are too big, since they can add so much extra weight to the fabric that they stretch it out.

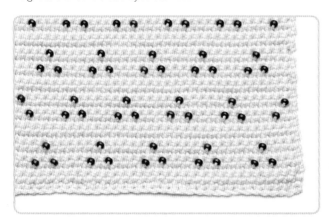

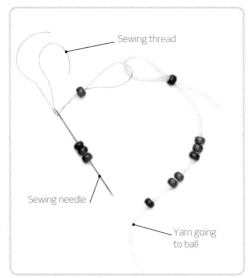

Sewing thread

Sewing needle

Yarn going to ball

1 Beaded single crochet is usually worked from a chart that shows the positions of the beads on the fabric. The chart is read as for a chart for colorwork (see p. 91) and the key provided with the chart indicates which stitches are worked as plain single crochet and which have beads. Loop the end of the yarn into a loop of sewing thread as shown, then thread the beads onto the needle and down onto the yarn.

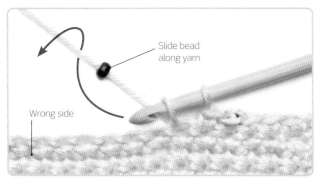

Slide bead along yarn

Wrong side

2 Follow the chart for the bead pattern, sliding the beads along the yarn until they are needed. The beads are always positioned on wrong-side rows. When a bead position is reached, work the next single crochet up to the last yo—there are now 2 loops on the hook. Slide a bead up close to the crochet and wrap the yarn around the hook.

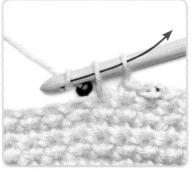

3 Draw a loop through both loops on the hook to complete the single crochet.

4 Complete the single crochet tightly so that the bead sits snugly against the fabric on the right side of the crochet.

Embroidery on crochet

Because single crochet creates such a firm fabric, it is easy to work embroidery onto it. Many embroidery stitches are suitable for crochet and a few of the most popular are given here. Use the same yarn for the embroidery as the yarn used for the crochet, or choose a slightly thicker yarn, so that the stitches will show up clearly. Always work the stitches with the same type of blunt-ended yarn needle that is used for seams.

Blanket stitch

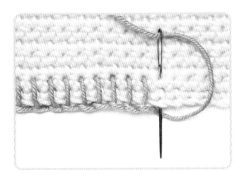

Edging: Blanket stitch creates an excellent crisp, decorative finish. Secure the yarn with 2 or 3 whipstitches worked at the edge of the crochet. Then make stitches that are spaced evenly apart from left to right, as shown here.

Chain stitch

Motif: Chain stitch is perfect for curved motifs. Hold the yarn on the wrong side of the fabric and draw loops through with the hook. To fasten off, pull the yarn end through the last loop and then back to the wrong side over the loop. Darn in the ends on the wrong side.

Cross-stitch

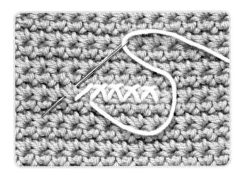

1 Work each individual cross-stitch on single crochet over one single crochet stitch. Complete each cross-stitch before moving on to the next. Keep the stitches fairly loose so they don't distort the crochet.

2 Adding lines of cross-stitches is an effective way to create an interesting plaid pattern on a base of plain single crochet. This is the perfect technique for dressing up a simple piece of single crochet.

Edgings on crochet

Several edging patterns are provided on pages 90–95 because they are an excellent simple adornment for your crochet. Some edgings can be worked directly onto your crochet (see pp. 90–91), and others made separately and then sewn on, as shown below.

Adding edgings

Attach an edging: To sew an edging in place, use a yarn that matches the base crochet and a blunt-ended yarn needle. Secure the yarn at the right-hand end of the seam with 2 or 3 whipstitches. Then work evenly spaced whipstitches through both the base crochet and the edging, as shown.

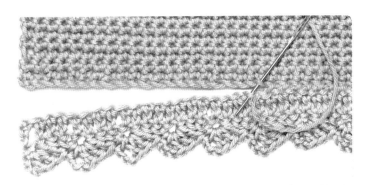

Finishing details

Finishings require slightly different crochet techniques. Some of the techniques most frequently used are shown here. Take your time with all finishings and practice the methods on small swatches before adding them to your completed pieces.

Single crochet edging

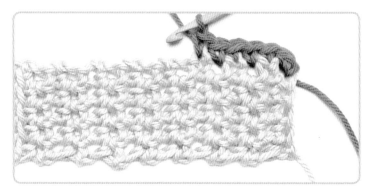

Along top or bottom of a piece of crochet: Adding a simple single crochet edging is a good way to neaten up the edges of a crochet project. To work a single crochet edging along the top or bottom of a piece of crochet, join the yarn to the first stitch with a slip stitch, work 1 ch, 1 sc in the same place as the slip stitch, then work 1 sc in each stitch below all along the edge.

Along row-ends of a piece of crochet: A single crochet edging is worked the same way along the row-ends of a piece of crochet, but it is not as easy to achieve an even edging. To create a perfect result, experiment with how many stitches to work per row-end. If the finished edging looks flared, try working fewer stitches per row-end; and if it looks puckered, try working more stitches per row-end.

Crocheting edging directly onto edge

Any of the edgings starting with a row of single crochet on pages 90–95 can easily be worked directly onto the crochet.

1 Using a contrasting color for the edging, start by working the row of single crochet onto the base, then turn and work the next row of the edging (the second row of the simple shell edging on p. 92 is being worked here).

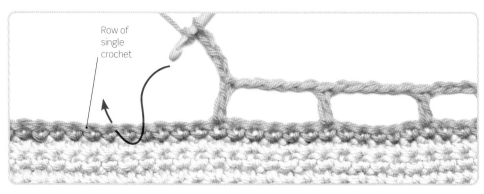

Row of single crochet

2 At the end of the second row, turn the crochet and work the remaining rows of the edging (the third and final row of the simple shell edging is being worked here).

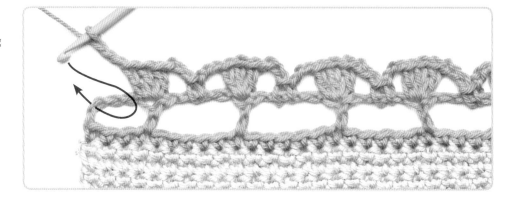

Round buttons

Making matching crochet buttons is a great finishing detail. Experiment with different yarn and hook sizes to make round buttons of the desired size. The buttons here are made using a superfine cotton yarn and a size 5 steel or B/1 US (2mm) hook for a button approximately ½in (1.5cm) in diameter.

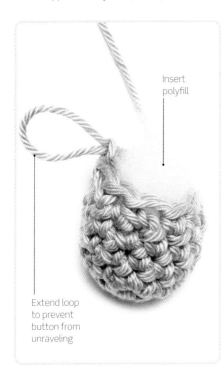

Insert polyfill

Extend loop to prevent button from unraveling

1 Make each button as follows: Ch 4 and join with a sl st to first ch to form a ring.
Round 1 (RS) Ch 1, 8 sc in ring (working over yarn tail while working sc into ring), join with a sl st to first sc. (Do not turn at end of rounds, but work with RS always facing.)
Round 2 Ch 1, 1 sc in same sc as last sl st, 2 sc in next sc, (1 sc in next sc, 2 sc in next sc) 3 times, join with a ss to first sc. (12 sc)
Round 3 Ch 1, 1 sc in each sc to end, join with a sl st to first sc.
Round 4 Ch 1, 1 sc in same sc as last ss, (sc2tog over next 1 sc, 1 sc in next sc) 3 times, sc2tog over last 2 sc, join with a sl st to first sc. (8 sc)
Take the loop off the hook and extend it to prevent the button from unraveling. Push the yarn tail from round 1 into the inside of the button and stuff the button firmly.

2 Slip the loop back on the hook and tighten it. Then continue the button as follows: **Round 5** Ch 1, sc2tog over first 2 sc (same sc as last ss and next sc), (2 sc over next 2 sc) 3 times, join with a ss to first sc. (4 sc)
Fasten off, leaving a long loose end at least 8in (20cm) long. Push more stuffing inside, if necessary. Then using a blunt-ended yarn needle and the long yarn tail, sew the opening at the back of the button closed.

Retain long yarn tail for sewing on button

3 Do not cut off the yarn tail, but keep it for sewing on the button.

Button loops

Button loops are very easy to make along the edge of a pillow cover, the front of a cardigan, or for closings on baby garments.

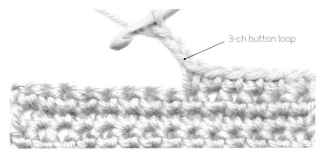

3-ch button loop

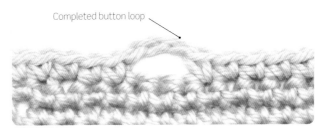

Completed button loop

1 Work in single crochet to the position of the button loop. Make 2, 3, or more chains, depending on the size of the button.

2 Skip the same number of stitches on the edge and work the next single crochet in the next stitch. Test the size of the first completed button loop with the button and adjust the number of chains, if necessary.

3 Continue along the edge, working single crochet and button loops until the edging is complete. To make stronger loops, work a second row of single crochet along the first row, working the same number of single crochet stitches as chains into each loop.

Simple edging patterns

Adding a decorative crochet edging to an otherwise mundane-looking piece of crochet can transform it, giving it a touch of elegance. All the simple crochet edgings that follow are worked widthwise, so you start with a length of chain roughly equivalent to the length of edging you need. Suitable even for beginners, these edgings are perfect for dressing up towels, throws, baby blankets, necklines, and cuffs. When making an edging that will encircle a blanket, be sure to add extra for turning the corners; the edging can then be gathered at each corner to allow for the turning. Use a short test swatch to calculate how much extra you will need at each corner. See page 83 for abbreviations and symbols.

Chain fringe

Crochet instructions

Note: This fringe is worked onto a row of sc. The length of the fringe can be altered by changing the number of chains in each fringe loop. To start the edging, make 1 ch more than the required number of sc.
Row 1 (WS) 1 sc in second ch from hook, 1 sc in each of rem ch, turn.
Row 2 (RS) Ch 1, 1 sc in first sc, ch 29, 1 sc in same place as last sc, *1 sc in next sc, ch 29, 1 sc in same place as last sc; rep from * to end. Fasten off.

Crochet diagram

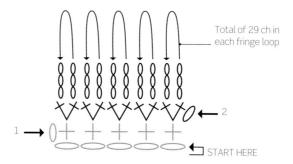

Total of 29 ch in each fringe loop

START HERE

Step edging

Crochet instructions

Make a multiple of 4 ch, plus 3 extra.
Row 1 (WS) 1 dc in fourth ch from hook, 1 dc in each of rem ch, turn.
Row 2 (RS) Ch 3, 3 dc in first dc, *skip next 3 dc, work (1 sc, ch 3, 3 dc) all in next dc; rep from * to last 3 dc, skip last 3 dc, 1 sc in top of 3-ch at end.
Fasten off.

Crochet diagram

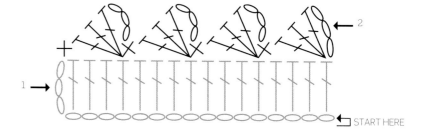

START HERE

Picot scallop edging

Crochet instructions

Make a multiple of 4 ch, plus 2 extra.
Row 1 (WS) 1 sc in second ch from hook, *ch 5, skip next 3 ch, 1 sc in next ch; rep from * to end, turn.
Row 2 (RS) Ch 1, *work (4 sc, ch 3, 4 sc) all in next 5-ch loop; rep from * to end.
Fasten off.

Crochet diagram

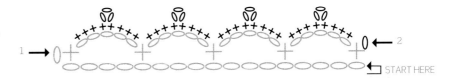

Double loop edging

Crochet instructions

To start edging, make a multiple of 5 ch, plus 2 extra.
Row 1 (WS) 1 sc in second ch from hook, 1 sc in next ch, *ch 5, skip next 2 ch, 1 sc in each of next 3 ch; rep from * to last 4 ch, ch 5, skip next 2 ch, 1 sc in each of last 2 ch, turn.
Row 2 (RS) Ch 1, 1 sc in first sc, *ch 8, 1 sc in center sc of next group of 3-sc (at other side of 5-ch loop); rep from * working last sc in last sc of row 1.
Fasten off.

Crochet diagram

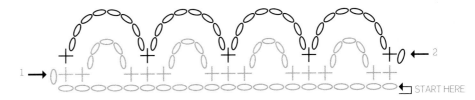

Grand eyelet edging

Crochet instructions

Make a multiple of 7 ch, plus 2 extra.
Row 1 (WS) 1 sc in second ch from hook, 1 sc in each of rem ch, turn.
Row 2 (RS) Ch 1, 1 sc in first sc, 1 hdc in next sc, 1 dc in next sc, 1 tr in next sc, *ch 5, skip next 3 sc, 1 sc in next sc, 1 hdc in next sc, 1 dc in next sc, 1 tr in next sc; rep from * to last 4 sc, ch 5, skip next 3 sc, 1 sc in last sc.
Fasten off.

Crochet diagram

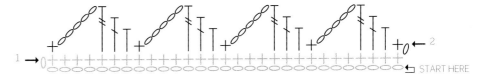

Pillar edging

Crochet instructions

Make a multiple of 10 ch, plus 2 extra.

Row 1 (WS) 1 sc in second ch from hook, 1 sc in each of rem ch, turn.

Row 2 (RS) Ch 1, 1 sc in first sc, *2 ch, skip next sc, 1 dc in next sc, (ch 2, skip next sc, 1 tr in next sc) twice, ch 2, skip next sc, 1 dc in next sc, ch 2, skip next sc, 1 sc in next sc; rep from * to end.

Fasten off.

Crochet diagram

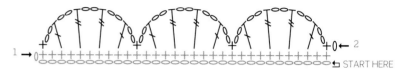

Simple shell edging

Crochet instructions

Make a multiple of 6 ch, plus 2 extra.

Row 1 (RS) 1 sc in second ch from hook, 1 sc in each of rem ch, turn.

Row 2 Ch 5, skip first 3 sc, 1 dc in next sc, *5 ch, skip next 5 sc, 1 dc in next sc; rep from * to last 3 sc, ch 2, skip next 2 sc, 1 dc in last sc, turn.

Row 3 Ch 1, 1 sc in first dc, ch 3, 3 dc in next dc, *ch 3, 1 sc in next 5-ch space, ch 3, 3 dc in next dc; rep from *, ending with ch 3, skip first 2 ch of last 5 ch, 1 sc in next ch.

Fasten off.

Crochet diagram

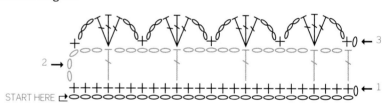

Twirl fringe

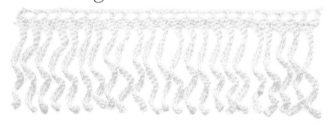

Crochet instructions

Note: The fringe will twirl naturally; do not press out the twirls.

To start edging, make a multiple of 2 ch.

Row 1 (WS) 1 tr in fourth ch from hook, *ch 1, skip next ch, 1 tr in next ch; rep from * to end, turn.

Row 2 (RS) Ch 1, 1 sc in first tr, *ch 24, 1 sc in second ch from hook, 1 sc in each of rem 22 ch, 1 sc in next tr; rep from * to end.

Fasten off.

Crochet diagram

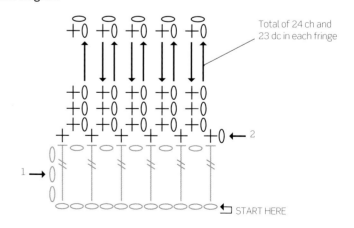

Total of 24 ch and 23 dc in each fringe

Triple picot edging

Crochet instructions

Make a multiple of 6 ch, plus 2 extra.
Row 1 (WS) 1 sc in second ch from hook, 1 sc in each of rem ch, turn.
Row 2 (RS) Ch 5, work (1 sc, [ch 5, 1 sc] twice) all in first sc, *ch 4, skip next 5 sc, (1 sc, [ch 5, 1 sc] 3 times) all in next sc; rep from * to end.
Fasten off.

Crochet diagram

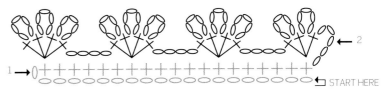

Cluster and shell edging

Crochet instructions

Make a multiple of 8 ch, plus 4 extra.
Row 1 (WS) 1 dc in fourth ch from hook, *skip next 3 ch, 6 dc in next ch (to make a shell), skip next 3 ch, work (1 dc, ch 1, 1 dc) all in next ch; rep from * to last 8 ch, skip next 3 ch, 6 dc in next ch, skip next 3 ch, 2 dc in last ch, turn.
Row 2 (RS) Ch 1, skip first dc, 1 sc in next dc, *ch 4, (yo, insert hook in next dc, yo and draw a loop through, yo and draw through first 2 loops on hook) 6 times (once into each of 6 dc of shell), yo and draw through all 7 loops on hook to complete cluster, ch 6, 1 ss in top of cluster just made, ch 4, 1 sc in next 1-ch sp (between 2 dc); rep from * to end, working last sc of last rep in top of 3 ch at end.
Fasten off.

Crochet diagram

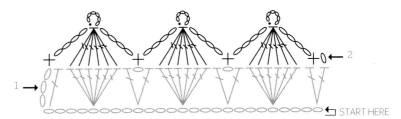

Bold scallop edging

Crochet instructions

Make a multiple of 10 ch, plus 2 extra.
Row 1 (RS) 1 sc in second ch from hook, 1 sc in each of rem ch, turn.
Row 2 Ch 1, 1 sc in first sc, ch 2, skip next 2 sc, 1 sc in next sc, ch 7, skip next 3 sc, 1 sc in next sc, *ch 6, skip next 5 ch, 1 sc in next sc, ch 7, skip next 3 sc, 1 sc in next sc; rep from * to last 3 sc, ch 2, skip next 2 sc, 1 sc in last sc, turn.
Row 3 Ch 1, 1 sc in first sc, 13 dc in 7-ch loop, *1 sc in next 6-ch sp, 13 dc in next 7-ch loop; rep from *, ending with 1 sc in last sc.
Fasten off.

Crochet diagram

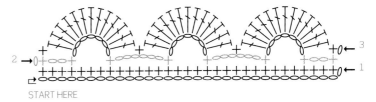

Long loop edging

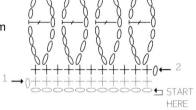

Crochet instructions

Make a multiple of 3 ch.

Row 1 (WS) 1 sc in second ch from hook, 1 sc in each of rem ch, turn.

Row 2 (RS) Ch 1, 1 sc in first sc, ch 9, 1 dc in sixth ch from hook, ch 4, *1 sc in each of next 3 sc, ch 9, 1 dc in sixth ch from hook, ch 4; rep from * to last sc, 1 sc in last sc. Fasten off.

Crochet diagram

Diamond edging

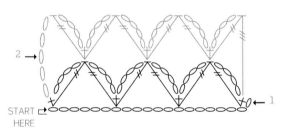

Crochet instructions

Make a multiple of 6 ch, plus 2 extra.

Row 1 (RS) 1 sc in second ch from hook, *ch 4, yo twice and insert hook in same place as last sc, (yo and draw first 2 loops on hook) twice, yo twice, skip next 5 ch and insert hook in next ch, (yo and draw first 2 loops on hook) twice, yo and draw through all 3 loops on hook (called tr2tog), ch 4, 1 sc in same place as last tr; rep from * to end, turn.

Row 2 Ch 5, 1 tr in first tr2tog, ch 4, 1 sc in same place as last tr, *4 ch, tr2tog over last tr worked into and next tr, ch 4, 1 sc in same place as last tr; rep from *, ch 4, yo twice and insert hook in same place as last sc, (yo and draw first 2 loops on hook) twice, yo 3 times and insert hook in last sc in previous row, (yo and draw first 2 loops on hook) 3 times, yo and draw through all 3 loops on hook. Fasten off.

Crochet diagram

Double scallop edging

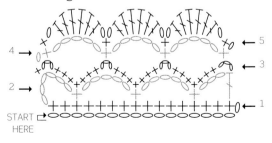

Crochet instructions

Make a multiple of 5 ch, plus 2 extra.

Row 1 (RS) 1 sc in second ch from hook, 1 sc in each of rem ch, turn.

Row 2 Ch 6, skip first 2 sc, 1 sc in next sc, *ch 5, skip next 4 sc, 1 sc in next sc; rep from * to last 3 sc, 3 ch, skip next 2 sc, 1 dc in last sc, turn.

Row 3 Ch 3, 3 sc in first 3-ch sp, 1 sc in next sc (between loops), *work (3 sc, ch 3, 3 sc) all in next 5-ch loop, 1 sc in next sc; rep from *, ending with (3 sc, ch 3, 1 sc) in last 6-ch loop, turn.

Row 4 Ch 1, 1 sc in first 3-ch picot, *ch 5, 1 sc in next 3-ch picot; rep from * to end, turn.

Row 5 Ch 1, 1 sc in first sc, *ch 1, 6 dc in next 5-ch loop, ch 1, 1 sc in next sc; rep from * to end. Fasten off.

Crochet diagram

Simple multiple-stitch edging

Crochet instructions

Make a multiple of 8 ch, plus 2 extra.

Row 1 (WS) 1 sc in second ch from hook, 1 sc in each of rem ch, turn.

Row 2 (RS) 1 ch, 1 ss in first sc, *1 sc in next sc, 1 hdc in next sc, 1 dc in next sc, 3 tr in next sc, 1 dc in next sc, 1 hdc in next sc, 1 sc in next sc, 1 ss in next sc; rep from * to end. Fasten off.

Crochet diagram

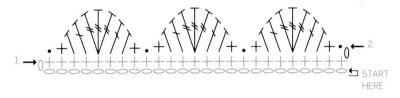

Petal edging

Crochet instructions

Make a multiple of 14 ch, plus 2 extra.

Row 1 (RS) 1 sc in second ch from hook, 1 sc in each of rem ch, turn.

Row 2 Ch 1, 1 sc in first sc, *ch 6, skip next 6 sc, work (2 dc, ch 2, 2 dc) all in next sc, ch 6, skip next 6 sc, 1 sc in next sc; rep from * to end, turn.

Row 3 Ch 1, 1 sc in first sc, *ch 6, work (2 dc, ch 2, 2 dc) all in next 2-ch sp, ch 6, 1 sc in next sc; rep from * to end. Fasten off.

Note: When blocking this edging, pin out each point at each 2-ch sp to achieve correct shape.

Crochet diagram

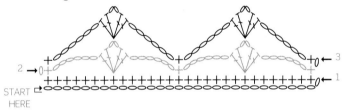

Circles edging

Crochet instructions

Make a multiple of 6 ch.

Row 1 (RS) 1 sc in ninth ch from hook, *ch 7, skip next 5 ch, 1 sc in next ch; rep from * to last 3 ch, ch 3, skip next 2 ch, 1 sc in last ch, turn.

Row 2 Ch 1, 1 sc in first dc, ch 2, 1 dc in next sc, *ch 5, 1 dc in next sc; rep from *, ending with ch 2, 1 sc in 4th ch from last sc in previous row, turn.

Row 3 Ch 1, 1 sc in first sc, *ch 3, 1 dc in next dc, ch 3, 1 sc in 7-ch loop of row 1 (catching 5-ch loop in previous row inside sc); rep from * to end working last sc of last rep in last sc of row 2.
Fasten off.

Crochet diagram

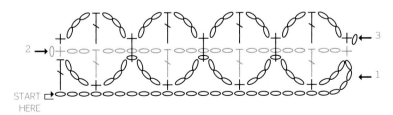

Working crocheted edges

Crocheted edgings are extremely versatile, since you can work them separately or as an integral part of your fabric. If you work the edge separately, in a strip or ribbon, you must then attach the edge to your piece by simply sewing it to the fabric with a whipstitch (see p. 87). Working an edging directly onto the main fabric is usually preferable, since it creates a seamless, unified fabric with less finishing.

Edgings worked into woven fabrics

Non-knitted/crocheted fabrics can also be edged in crochet. Towels, pillows, pillowcases, napkins, and dish towels with a fancy crocheted edge elevate the everyday household items into desirable decorative interior pieces. Woven fabric may need a bit more preparation before an edge is worked, especially with a tight weave or an edge likely to fray. To prevent fraying under the crochet when using

a fabric ground, you may need to hem the material first before attempting to edge it. If the fabric is not too dense, you may be able to insert the hook straight through it on the first row. However, a neater, more even finish can be achieved when you prepare the edge first. You can do this in various ways with differing results to the finished edge.

Attaching a crocheted edging using the punched hole method

1 First, mark where you want the hook to be inserted, at regular intervals along the seam or selvage.

2 Make a series of holes in the edge of the fabric by using the tip of the hook, a large darning needle, or a fabric eyelet hole punch if you are using bulky yarn and a large hook. Make sure that you make the appropriate multiple of holes required for the edge.

3 Join the yarn to the first space with a slip stitch (see p. 26), and then work 1 chain stitch.

4 Work 1 single crochet (see p. 32) into the first hole. Do not pull the yarn tightly or the fabric will pucker.

5 Then work 1 single crochet into each hole evenly along the edge, making sure to keep the stitches loose.

Attaching a crocheted edging using the blanket stitch method

1 Choose a sewing or embroidery thread, or the crochet thread you intend to use for the edge. This could be the same color as the edging or a complementary shade. A contrasting color to both the edge and the fabric can also look effective.

2 Sew an even, traditional blanket stitch (see p. 87) along the edge of the fabric. Make sure that the number of stitches used is a multiple that works with the stitches in the edge to create a neat finish.

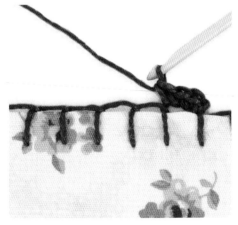

3 Attach the edging yarn to the horizontal top edge of the first blanket stitch.

4 Work the first single crochet row into the blanket stitches.

5 Make sure that you work the same multiple of edge stitches into each blanket stitch, around the top horizontal line of each. Fasten off the yarn and weave in all ends.

Crochet-edged pillows

Adding an attractive crocheted embellishment to a pillow or bolster is a quick and easy way to personalize store-bought home furnishing. Turn to pages 96–97 for detailed information about working a crocheted edge.

PROJECTS

For more pillow patterns
>> *go to pages 122 and 152*

Essential information

DIFFICULTY LEVEL Intermediate

SIZE To fit the length of your pillow

YARN Any cotton yarn will suit a fine print or silky fabric. Use a DK yarn for a heavier weight edging

x 1

CROCHET HOOK B/1 US (2.5mm) hook

NOTIONS Yarn needle
Pillow cover ready to embellish

GAUGE Exact gauge is not essential

SPECIAL ABBREVIATIONS

3-DC CLUSTER: 3-double cluster. (Yo, insert hook into ch sp, yo and draw a loop through, yo and draw through first 2 loops on hook) 3 times in next 6-ch sp, 4 loops now on hook, yo and draw through all 4 loops on hook to close 3-dc group.

>> These edgings are made with DMC Size 8 Pearl Cotton, 95yds/90m/10g, in Red (321).

Either make your own pillows or use bought ones with a matching or contrasting thread for the edging.

Cluster scallop pillow

Prepare the edge to be embellished by making holes at regular intervals along the edge, approx $1/4$in (5mm) from the edge. You will need a multiple of eight, plus one hole for this edging to work.

With RS facing, attach yarn to the edge to be embellished, work 1 ch.

ROW 1 Work 1 sc into each hole along the edge.

ROW 2 Ch 1, 3 sc, *6 ch, skip next 3 sc, 5 sc; rep from * to last 6 sc, 6 ch, skip next 3 sc, 1 sc in each of last 3 sc, turn.

ROW 3 Ch 3, 1 3-dc cluster in next 6 ch sp, *4 ch, 1 3-dc cluster in same ch sp, 4 ch, 1 3-dc cluster in same ch sp, but do not close the cluster (leave last 4 loops on hook), 1 3-dc cluster in next 6-ch sp and close this cluster

and last cluster at the same time by drawing the loop through all 7 loops on hook; rep from * to last 6-ch sp, (4 ch, 1 3-dc cluster in same ch sp) twice, 1 dc in last sc.
Fasten off.

Triple picot variation pillow

Prepare the edge to be embellished by working a blanket stitch along the RS of the edge, using the yarn you will be edging with. Make a multiple of 4 blanket stitches.

Attach yarn to the first blanket stitch, with WS facing.

ROW 1 Work 4 sc into the first blanket stitch, then work 3 sc into each of next blanket stitches along edge, turn.

ROW 2 Ch 5, work (1 sc, [5 ch, 1 sc] twice) all in first sc, *4 ch, skip next 5 sc, sc into next sc, 4 ch, skip next 5 sc, (1 sc, [5 ch, 1 sc] 3 times) all in next sc; rep from * to end.
Fasten off.

Cluster scallop diagram

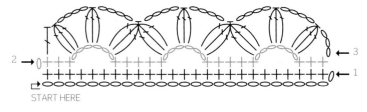

START HERE

Triple picot variation diagram

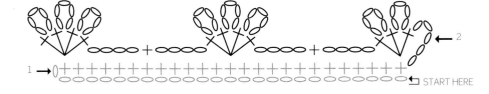

START HERE

It is very easy to adapt the stitch patterns on pages 90–95 to suit your own project. The edging above has changed the triple picot edging on page 93 by taking out every other picot and adding in a single crochet instead for a simple variation.

The cluster scallop edging is a reversible design that looks pretty from all angles. This edging is attached to the pillow using the punched hole method. Pages 96–97 give detailed instructions, plus information about the blanket stitch method.

Circular crochet

Crochet can be worked not only back and forth in rows, but also around and around in circles to form tubes or flat shapes started from the center (called medallions). The basic techniques for crocheting in the round are very easy to learn, even for a beginner, so it is not surprising that many popular crochet accessories are made with circular crochet, including flowers and afghan motifs, as well as seamless toys, hats, mittens, containers, and bags.

Crocheting tubes

Tubular crochet is started on a long chain of foundation stitches that are joined at the ends to form a ring. The subsequent rounds of stitches are then worked around this foundation ring. The easiest of all crochet cylinders is a single crochet tube, shown below, which is worked in a spiral without turning chains.

Starting a tube

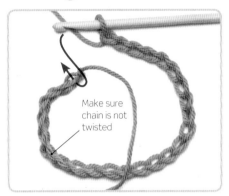

Make sure chain is not twisted

1 Start the crochet cylinder, or tube, with the length of chain specified in your crochet pattern. Then, insert the hook through the first chain.

Completed slip stitch joint

2 Draw a loop through the chain and at the same time through the loop on the hook to complete the slip stitch. This joins the chain into a ring. Work the first and following rounds as directed in your pattern.

Single crochet spiral tube

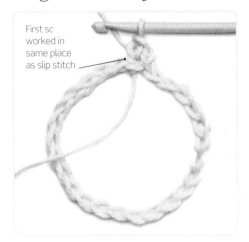

First sc worked in same place as slip stitch

1 Make the foundation ring and work one chain. Work the first single crochet into the same place as the slip stitch. Then work 1 sc into each of the remaining chains of the ring.

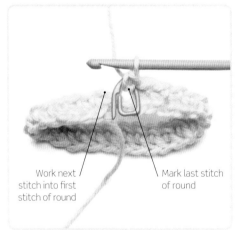

Work next stitch into first stitch of round

Mark last stitch of round

2 Place a stitch marker on the last stitch of the first round to keep track of where the rounds begin and end. To begin the second round, work the next stitch into the first stitch of the previous round.

Move marker up at end of each round

Work with right side always facing

3 On the second round, work 1 sc in each sc in the round below. At the end of the round, move the marker up onto the last stitch of this round. (As the spiral grows, the beginning of the round moves gradually to the right.) Continue around and around in the same way until the crochet tube is the required length.

Double crochet tube without turns

When basic stitches taller than single crochet are used to make crochet tubes, each round is started with a turning chain.

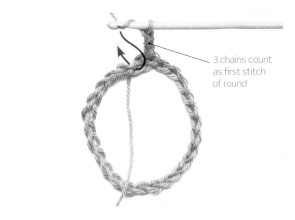

3 chains count as first stitch of round

1 To work a double crochet tube with the right side of the work always facing (without turns), begin with 3 chains. Then work 1 dc into the next chain and each of the remaining chains around the ring.

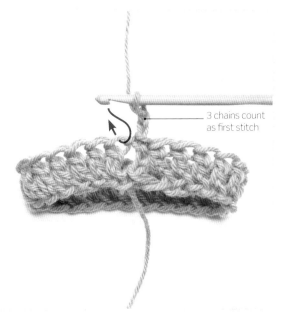

3 chains count as first stitch

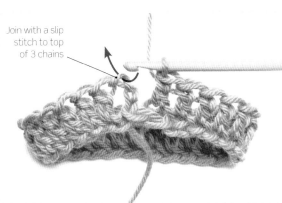

Join with a slip stitch to top of 3 chains

2 At the end of the round, join the last stitch to the top of the turning chain at the beginning of the round by working a slip stitch into the third of the 3 chains.

3 Start the second round with 3 chains. There is no need to mark the end of the round with a stitch marker since the turning chain shows where each round begins. Continue around the tube again, working 1 dc into each dc in the previous round. At the end of the second round, join the last stitch to the top of the turning chain with a slip stitch. Continue in the same way, beginning all following rounds with 3 chains.

Double crochet tube with turns

If a double crochet tube needs to match crochet worked in rows in other parts of an item, then the work can be turned at the end of each round.

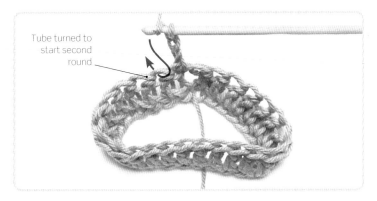

Tube turned to start second round

Second round shows backs of doubles

First round shows fronts of doubles

1 Work the first round in double crochet as for a tube without turns. Then turn the work, make 3 chains as shown, and complete the round.

2 To begin the third round, turn the work and start with 3 chains. Continue in this way, joining the last stitch with a slip stitch to the top of the turning chain at the end of each round, then turning the work to start the next round. The fabric looks just like double crochet that has been worked in ordinary rows.

A basic granny square

If you are new to crochet, the granny square, medallion, or motif (also called an afghan square), is an excellent practice project, and a great way to perfect your double crochet. If you are a seasoned crocheter, there are many variations on the basic granny square that you can try.

Practice square: Use a different color for each round until you are confident making granny squares.

1 Work 6 chains and join with a slip stitch to form a ring. For round 1, work 3 chains, then 2 doubles in the ring, then 3 more chains; *then 3 doubles in the ring and 3 chains.

2 Rep from * 2 more times. Join the round with a slip stitch to the top of the first chain. Break off yarn at the end of this and every round for a striped medallion, adding different colors randomly for each round.

Turn the square as you work.

3 For round 2, join new yarn in any 3-ch sp, chain 3, work 2 doubles, chain 3 and work 3 doubles in the same space; *chain 1, work 3 doubles, chain 3 and work 3 doubles all in the next 3-ch sp. Repeat from * 2 more times, then chain 1. Join round with a slip stitch to the top of the first chain.

4 For round 3, join the yarn in any 3-ch sp, chain 3, work 2 doubles, chain 3 and work 3 doubles in the same space. Chain 1, work 3 doubles in the next 1-ch sp; *chain 1, work 3 doubles, chain 3 and work 3 doubles all in the next 3-ch sp for the corner. Chain 1, work 3 doubles in the next 1-ch sp. Repeat from * around, then chain 1. Join round with a slip stitch to the top of the first chain.

Joining medallions

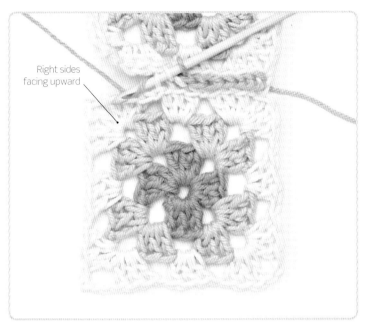

Right sides facing upward

Right sides together

Flat slip-stitch seam: Working seams with crochet stitches is the quickest way to join medallions. For a slip-stitch seam, lay the two medallions side by side. Work each slip stitch through only 1 loop (the back loop) of the top of a stitch on each medallion. (Use a hook one size smaller than the hook used for the medallions, but work the stitches very loosely.)

Single-crochet seam: A single-crochet seam is also quick to work, but it forms a ridge, so is best worked on the wrong side. Place the two medallions with the right sides together. Then work each single crochet through only 1 loop of the top of a stitch on each medallion (the loop closest to you on the top medallion and the loop farthest from you on the bottom medallion).

The join-as-you-go method

When making medallions, you can create a neat and practically invisible seam by joining each medallion to the others as you work. To demonstrate the technique, a traditional granny square method is described, but you can apply the same technique to other types of medallion. First, crochet one complete medallion, then work the second medallion up to the penultimate round, but don't fasten off. Work along the edge of the second medallion, right up until you are about to make the corner chain. Work 1 chain and attach with a slip stitch into one of the corner chains on the first medallion, and finish off the corner space with 1 chain and a group of three doubles into the corner space.

Instead of working 1 chain before the next group of doubles, join with a slip stitch into the next 1-chain space on the first medallion. Work the next group of doubles along the edge of your second medallion, before joining it to the first medallion with a slip stitch as before.

Continue in this way until you get to the next corner, then join the corner chain of the second medallion to the corner chain of the first in the same way as before. Now, continue around the edges to complete the second medallion. Once you have completed the second medallion, fasten off. Repeat for all following medallions, noting that some will need to be joined along two edges.

Simple medallion patterns

Making crochet medallions is a great way to use up yarn scraps, and this was probably the reason they became so popular. You can sew medallions together to form small items like bags or pillow covers, or to form larger items like throws and baby blankets. Joined medallions also make great scarves and shawls, especially when made in gossamer mohair. But if you are a beginner, stick to less hairy yarns when making your first medallions since it is easier to learn the technique with a smooth, standard lightweight or medium-weight wool yarn. When following diagrams, use colors as explained in the written instructions. The tones used in the diagram are used to distinguish the rows and do not indicate color changes. (See p. 83 for a list of crochet abbreviations and basic stitch symbols.) Join on new colors (see p. 57). Do not turn the medallions at the end of the rounds, but work with the right side always facing.

Traditional afghan square

Crochet diagram

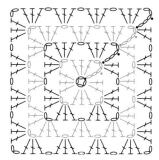

Crochet instructions

This square is worked in 4 colors (A, B, C, D), a different color for each round.
With A, ch 4 and join with a ss to first ch to form a ring.

Round 1 (RS) With A, ch 5 (counts as 1 dc and a 2-ch sp), (3 dc in ring, 2 ch (these 2-ch form a corner sp)) 3 times, 2 dc in ring, join with a ss to third of 5 ch. Fasten off A.

Round 2 With B, join with a ss to a 2-ch corner sp, ch 5, 3 dc in same corner sp, *ch 1, (3 dc, ch 2, 3 dc) in next 2-ch corner sp; rep from * twice more, ch 1, 2 dc in same corner sp as 5 ch at beg of round, join with a ss to third of 5 ch. Fasten off B.

Round 3 With C, join to a 2-ch corner sp, ch 5, 3 dc in same corner sp, *ch 1, 3 dc in next 1-ch sp, ch 1, (3 dc, ch 2, 3 dc) in next 2-ch corner sp; rep from * twice more, ch 1, 3 dc in next 1-ch sp, ch 1, 2 dc in same sp as 5-ch at beg of round, join with a ss to third of 5 ch. Fasten off C.

Round 4 With D, join to a 2-ch corner sp, ch 5, 3 dc in same corner sp, *(ch 1, 3 dc in next 1-ch sp) twice, 1 ch, (3 dc, ch 2, 3 dc) in next 2-ch corner sp; rep from * twice more, (ch 1, 3 dc in next 1-ch sp) twice, ch 1, 2 dc in same sp as 5 ch at beg of round, join with a ss to third of 5 ch.
Fasten off.

Plain square

Crochet diagram

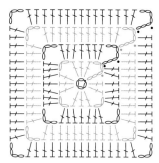

Crochet instructions

This square is worked in 4 colors (A, B, C, D).
Using A, ch 4 and join with a ss to first ch to form a ring.

Round 1 (RS) Ch 5 (counts as 1 dc and a 2-ch sp), (3 dc in ring, ch 2) 3 times, 2 dc in ring, join with a ss to third of 5 ch.

Round 2 1 ss in next ch, ch 7 (counts as 1 dc and a 4-ch sp), 2 dc in same 2-ch corner sp, *1 dc in each of next 3 dc, (2 dc, ch 4, 2 dc) in next 2-ch corner sp; rep from * twice more, 1 dc in each of next 3 sts (working last of these dc in top of turning ch at beg of previous round), 1 dc in same sp as 7 ch at beg of round, join with a s to third of 7 ch. Fasten off A.

Round 3 With B, join to a 4-ch corner sp, ch 7, 2 dc in same corner sp, *1 dc in each of dc along this side of square, (2 dc, ch 4, 2 dc) in next 4-ch corner sp; rep from * twice more, 1 dc in each of dc along this side of square (working last of these dc in top of turning ch at beg of previous round), 1 dc in same sp as 7 ch at beg of round, join with a ss to third of 7 ch. Fasten off B.

Round 4 With D, rep round 3.
Fasten off.

Flower hexagon

Crochet diagram

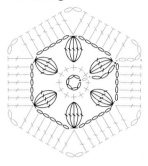

Crochet instructions
Note: bobble = (yo and insert hook in sc, yo and draw a loop through, yo and draw through first 2 loops on hook) 5 times all in same sc (6 loops now on hook), yo and draw through all 6 loops on hook.

This hexagon is worked in 2 colors (A, B).

With A, ch 6 and join with a ss to first ch to form a ring.

Round 1 (RS) Ch 1, 12 sc in ring, join with a ss to first sc.

Round 2 Ch 3, (yo and insert hook in same sc as last ss, yo and draw a loop through, yo and draw through first 2 loops on hook) 4 times all in same sc (5 loops now on hook), yo and draw through all 5 loops on hook (counts as first bobble), *ch 5, skip next sc, 1 bobble in next sc; rep from * 4 times more, ch 5, join with a ss to top of first bobble. Fasten off A.

Round 3 With B, join with a ss to top of a bobble, ch 5 (counts as 1 dc and a 2-ch sp), 1 dc in same place as ss, *5 dc in next 5-ch sp, (1 dc, ch 2, 1 dc) in top of next bobble; rep from * 4 times more, 5 dc in next 5-ch sp, join with a ss to third of 5 ch at beg of round. Fasten off.

Simple hexagon

Crochet diagram

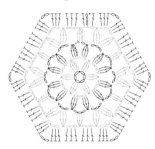

This hexagon is worked in 3 colors (A, B, C).

Using A, ch 6 and join with a ss to first ch to form a ring.

Round 1(RS) Ch 3, dc2tog (counts as first cluster), (ch 3, 1 cluster in ring) 5 times, ch 1, join with 1 hdc in top of first cluster.

Round 2 Ch 3, dc2tog in sp formed by 1-hdc, *ch 3, (1 cluster, 3 ch, 1 cluster) in next 3-ch sp; rep from *4 times more, ch 3, 1 cluster in next 1-ch sp, 1 ch, join with 1 hdc in top of first cluster changing to B with last yo of hdc. Cut off A.

Round 3 With B, ch 3, dc2tog in sp formed by 1-hdc, *ch 3, (1 cluster, ch 3, 1 cluster) in next 3-ch sp, ch 3, 1 cluster in next 3-ch sp; rep from * 4 times more, ch 3, (1 cluster, ch 3, 1 cluster) in next 3-ch sp, ch 1, join with 1 hdc in top of first cluster changing to C with last yo of hdc. Cut off B.

Round 4 With C, ch 3, 1 dc in sp formed by 1-hdc, *3 dc in next 3-ch sp, (3 dc, ch 2, 3 dc) in next 3-ch sp, 3 dc in next 3-ch sp; rep from * 4 times more, 3 dc in next 3-ch sp, (3 dc, ch 2, 3 dc) in next 3-ch sp, 1 dc in next 1-ch sp, join with a ss to third of 3 ch at beg of round.
Fasten off.

Crochet instructions
Note: cluster = (yo and insert hook in sp, yo and draw a loop through, yo and draw through first 2 loops on hook) 3 times all in same sp (4 loops now on hook), yo and draw through all 4 loops on hook.

Circle

Crochet diagram

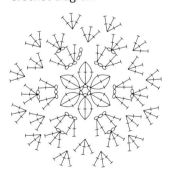

Crochet instructions
Cluster (cl): Work 3 half finished doubles into the next stitch, then finish them off together. Yo, insert into st, pull loop through, yo, pull through 2 loops, (yo, insert into same st, pull loop through, yo, pull through 2 loops) twice, 4 loops on hook, yo and pull through all loops.

With yarn A, 5 ch, join into round with ss.

Round 1 Ch 3, (1 cluster, 2 ch) 6 times in ring.
Change to yarn B, attaching to any 2-ch sp.

Round 2 Ch 3, (1 dc, 2 ch, 2 dc), (2 dc, 2 ch, 2 dc) in each 2-ch sp around, join round with ss. Change to yarn C, attaching to any 2-ch sp.

Round 3 Ch 3, 2 dc in same sp, 2 ch, (3 dc, 2 ch) into each sp around, join round with ss. Change to yarn D, attaching to any 2-ch sp.

Round 4 As round 3. Fasten off.

Triangle

Crochet diagram

Crochet instructions

With yarn A, work 5 ch, ss in first ch to join round.
Round 1 Ch 3, (2 dc, 3 ch) into ring, (3 dc, 2 ch) twice in ring, join round with ss. Change to yarn B, attaching to any 3-ch sp.
Round 2 Ch 3, (2 dc, 3 ch, 3 dc) into same ch sp, *2 ch, (3 dc, 3 ch, 3 dc) into next ch sp; rep from * twice, join round with ss.

Round 3 Ch 3, (2 dc, 3 ch, 3 dc) in same ch sp, 2 ch, 3 dc in next 2-ch sp, *(3 dc, 3 ch, 3 dc) into next ch sp, 2 ch, 3 dc in next 2-ch sp, 2 ch; rep from * to end, join round with ss. Change to yarn D, attaching to any 3-ch sp.
Round 4 Ch 3, (2 dc, 3 ch, 3 dc) in same ch sp, 2 ch, (3 dc in next 2-ch sp, 2 ch) twice, *(3 dc, 3 ch, 3 dc) into next ch sp, 2 ch, (3 dc in next 2-ch sp, 2 ch) twice; rep from * to end, join round with ss.

Simple flower patterns

Crochet flowers are very seductive—even simple ones like these, which are all easy and very quick to make. You may want to try them out right away but wonder what to do with them. First, they make great pins, which, in turn, are perfect gifts. Just sew a safety pin to the back and maybe a button or an artificial pearl to the flower center. Flowers and leaves can also be used to decorate crocheted (or knitted) hats, the ends of scarves, glove cuffs, or bags.

Sprinkled over a pillow cover, they will make a bold statement in a room as well. When following diagrams, use colors as explained in written instructions. The symbol tones are used to distinguish the rows and do not indicate color changes. (See p. 83 for a list of crochet abbreviations and basic stitch symbols.) Join on new yarn colors as explained on page 57. Do not turn at the end of the rounds, but work with the right side of the flowers always facing.

Heptagon flower

Crochet diagram

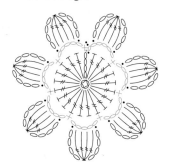

Crochet instructions

Note: cluster = (yo twice and insert hook in sp, yo and draw a loop through, [yo and draw through first 2 loops on hook] twice) 4 times all in same sp (5 loops now on hook), yo and draw through all 5 loops on hook.
This flower is worked in 2 colors (A, B).
With A, make ch 4 and join with a ss to first ch to form a ring.
Round 1 (RS) Ch 4 (counts as first tr), 20 tr in ring, join with a ss to fourth of 4 ch. Fasten off A.
Round 2 With B, join with a ss to same place as last ss, ch 1 (does NOT count as a st), 1 sc in same place as last ss, (5 ch, skip next 2 tr, 1 sc in next tr) 6 times, ch 5, join with a ss to first sc of round.
Round 3 *Work (1 ss, ch 4, 1 cluster, ch 4, 1 ss) all in next 5-ch loop; rep from * 6 times more, join with a ss to last sc in round 2.
Fasten off.

Short loop flower

Crochet diagram

Crochet instructions

This flower is worked in 2 colors (A, B).
With A, Ch 4 and join with a ss to first ch to form a ring.
Round 1 (RS) Ch 1 (does NOT count as a st), 8 sc in ring, join with a ss to first sc of round.
Round 2 Ch 1 (does NOT count as a st), 2 sc in same place as ss, *2 sc in next sc; rep from * to end, join with a ss to first sc of round. (16 sc) Fasten off A.
Round 3 With B, join with a ss to a sc, ch 1, work (1 sc, ch 9, 1 sc) all in same place as last ss, 1 sc in next sc, *work (1 sc, ch 9, 1 sc) all in next sc, 1 sc in next sc; rep from * 6 times more, join with a ss to first sc of round. Fasten off.

Long loop flower

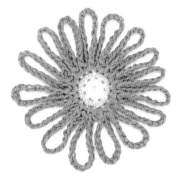

Crochet diagram

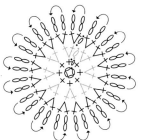

Crochet instructions

This flower is worked in 3 colors (A, B, C).

With A, Ch 4 and join with a ss to first ch to form a ring.

Round 1 (RS) Ch 2 (does NOT count as a st), 8 sc in ring, join with a ss to first sc of round. Fasten off A.

Round 2 With B, join with a ss to a sc, ch 1 (does NOT count as a st), 2 sc in same place as last ss, *2 sc in next sc; rep from * to end, join with a ss to first sc of round. 16 sc. Fasten off B.

Round 3 With C, join with a ss to a sc, ch 1, work (1 sc, ch 17, 1 sc) all in same place as last ss, *work (1 sc, ch 17, 1 sc) all in next sc; rep from * 14 times more, join with a ss to first sc of round.

Fasten off.

Pentagon flower

Crochet diagram

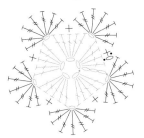

Crochet instructions

This flower is worked in 2 colors (A, B).

With A, ch 5 and join with a ss to first ch to form a ring.

Round 1 (RS) Ch 3 (counts as first dc), 4 dc in ring, (ch 1, 5 dc in ring) 4 times, ch 1, join with a ss to top of 3-ch at beg of round. Fasten off A.

Round 2 With B, join with a ss to a center dc of a 5-dc group, ch 1, 1 sc in same place as last ss, (7 tr in next 1-ch sp, 1 sc in center dc of next 5-dc group) 4 times, 7 tr in next 1-ch sp, join with a ss to first sc of round.

Fasten off.

Square petal flower

Crochet diagram

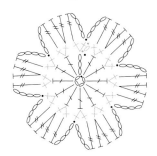

Crochet instructions

This flower is worked in 3 colors (A, B, C).

With A, make 4 ch and join with a ss to first ch to form a ring.

Round 1 (RS) Ch 3 (counts as first dc), 11 dc in ring, join with a ss to top of 3 ch at beg of round. Fasten off A.

Round 2 With B, join with a ss same place as last ss, ch 1 (does NOT count as a st), 2 sc in same place as last ss, 2 sc in each dc to end, join with a ss to first sc of round. (24 sc) Fasten off B.

Round 3 With C, join with a ss to a sc, *ch 4, 1 tr in next sc, 2 tr in next sc, 1 tr in next sc, ch 4, 1 ss in next sc; rep from * 5 times more working last ss in same place as first ss of round.

Fasten off.

Simple leaf

Crochet diagram

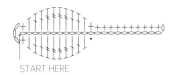

START HERE

Crochet instructions

Note: The leaf is worked in one row, around both sides of the foundation chain. To begin leaf and stem, ch 23.

Row 1 (RS) Working into only one loop of each foundation chain, work 1 sc in second ch from hook, 1 sc in each of next 10 ch (this completes the stem), 1 hdc in next ch, 1 dc in each of next 2 ch, 1 tr in each of next 4 ch, 1 dc in each of next 2 ch, 1 hdc in next ch, 1 sc in next ch (this is the last ch), ch 3, then continue working around other side of foundation ch (working into other loop of each ch) as follows—1 sc in first ch, 1 hdc in next ch, 1 dc in each of next 2 ch, 1 tr in each of next 4 ch, 1 dc in each of next 2 ch, 1 hdc in next ch, 1 ss in next ch. Fasten off. Press stem flat.

Openwork

Whether worked with fine threads for lace collars, pillow edgings, and tablecloths or with soft yarns for shawls, throws, and scarves, openwork crochet has an enduring appeal. As illustrated by the easy techniques on this page and the next, these airy lace textures are produced by working chain spaces and chain loops between the basic stitches.

Simple lace techniques

A few of the openwork stitch patterns on pages 113–115 are explained here to provide an introduction to some popular openwork crochet techniques—chain loops, shells, and picots. Refer to the instructions for the stitches when following the steps.

Chain loop mesh

1 After working the first row of chain loops into the foundation chain as explained (see p. 113), work the 5-chain loops of the following rows into the loops below, joining them on with a sc as shown here.

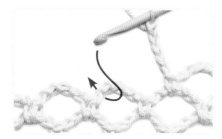

2 Remember to work the last sc of each row into the space inside the turning chain made at the beginning of the previous row. If you don't, your lace will become narrower.

Shell mesh stitch

1 On the shell row of this stitch (see p. 114) start each shell with a sc in a chain loop. Then work all the dc of the shell into a single sc as shown.

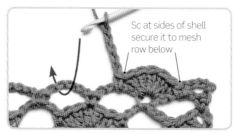

Sc at sides of shell secure it to mesh row below

2 Complete the shell with a sc worked into the following chain loop. Then work a chain loop and join it to the next chain loop with a sc as shown.

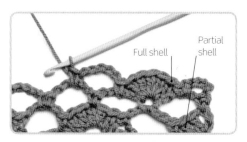

Full shell   Partial shell

3 Continue alternating shells and chain loops to complete the shell row. Work mesh and shell rows alternately, working partial shells at ends on alternate shell rows.

Picot net stitch

1 In this stitch pattern (see p. 113), work 4 chains for each picot. Close the picot-ring by working a slip stitch in the fourth chain from the hook as shown.

2 Work 3 sc between each of the picots in each picot row as shown.

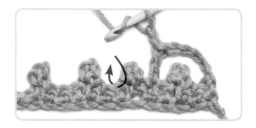

3 After each picot row, work a 2-chain space above each picot and a dc between the picots, as shown.

Filet crochet

Filet crochet is the easiest of all the openwork techniques to make. Once you learn how to work the simple structure of the open filet mesh and the solid filet blocks, all you need to do is follow is a simple chart to form the motifs and create the repeating patterns.

Making basic filet mesh

When working the foundation chain for the basic filet mesh, there is no need to start with an exact number of chains—just make an extra-long chain and unravel the unused excess later when finishing your crochet.

Filet mesh in symbols and words: The diagram provides the best explanation of how filet mesh is worked. If in doubt, work a mesh from the written pattern as follows: Make a multiple of 3 ch (3 ch for each mesh square needed), plus 5 extra (to form the right side edge and top of the first mesh square of the first row).
Row 1 1 dc in eighth ch from hook, *Ch 2, skip next 2 ch, 1 dc in next ch; rep from * to end.
Row 2 Ch 5, skip first dc, 1 dc in next dc, *ch 2, 1 dc in next dc; rep from * working last dc in 3rd ch from last dc in row below.

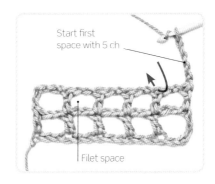

Start first space with 5 ch

Filet space

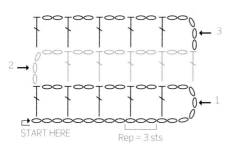

START HERE   Rep = 3 sts

Making filet blocks

The pattern motifs on filet crochet are created by filling in some of the mesh squares and leaving others empty. In other words, the designs are built up with solid squares and square holes. Having learned how to work the filet mesh, understanding how to fill them in to form blocks is easy.

Filet blocks in symbols: The diagram illustrates how the blocks are made—instead of working 2 chains to form an empty square, work 2 doubles to fill in the square. An individual block consists of a double on each side and 2 doubles in the center. To work a block above a filet space, work the 2 center doubles into the 2-chain space. To work a block above another block, work a double into each of the doubles below.

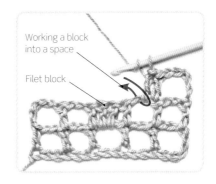

Working a block into a space

Filet block

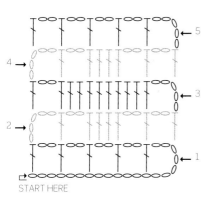

START HERE

Reading filet charts

This chart on the right shows the simple motif in the block symbol diagram above. Although actual filet charts are bigger and have elaborate patterns (see pp. 110–112), the principle is the same as for this tiny chart. Each square on the chart represents either a filet space or a filet block. Please note that left-handed crocheters will need to work the diagram and instructions in a mirror image.

To start working from a chart, make 3 chains for each of the squares along the bottom row of the chart, plus 5 chains extra. (You can work the chart stitch-repeat as many times as desired.) Working the chart from the bottom upward, make the blocks and spaces on the chart, while reading the first row and all following odd-numbered rows from right to left, and the even-numbered rows from left to right.

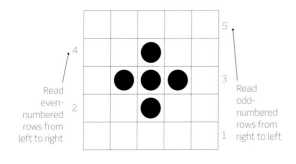

Read even-numbered rows from left to right

Read odd-numbered rows from right to left

Key   ☐ = filet space   ▣ = filet block

Filet stitch patterns

Follow the instructions on page 109 to work filet crochet from these charts. The best yarn to use for filet lace is a superfine cotton yarn and a suitably small-sized crochet hook (see recommended hook sizes on p. 14). This technique forms patterns by filling in parts of a chain stitch mesh with treble crochet stitches. Because filet crochet is reversible, it makes great curtains. It can also be used for edgings along the ends of pillowcases and hand towels, or even wall hangings.

Special note and symbol key

Repeat the charted motifs as many times as desired widthwise and work across the stitches in rows until the chart is complete. To continue the pattern upward, start at row 1 again.

Key
☐ = filet space
▣ = filet block

Diamonds border

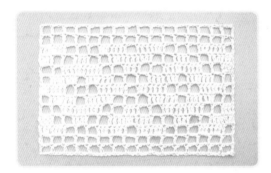

Crochet chart

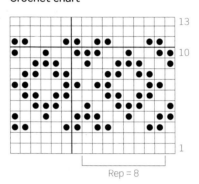

Flowers and circles

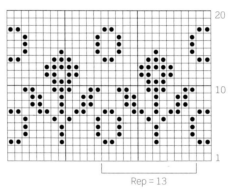

Zigzag border

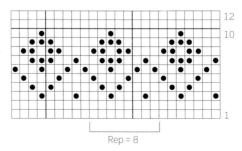

Apple

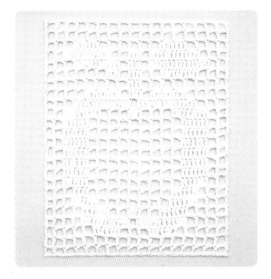

Crochet chart

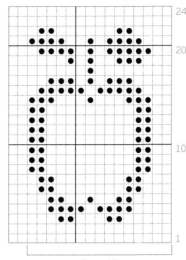

Rep = 15

Bloom

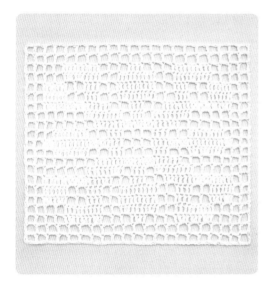

Crochet chart

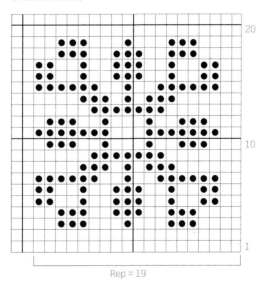

Rep = 19

Crosses border

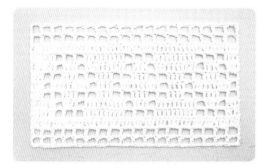

Crochet chart

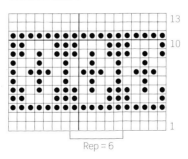

Rep = 6

Heart

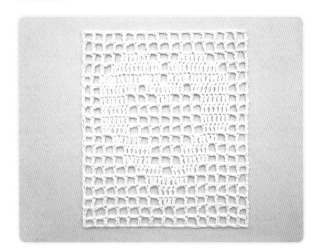

Crochet chart

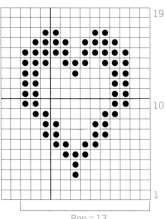

Rep = 13

Dog

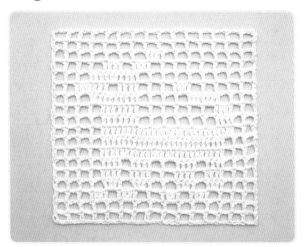

Crochet chart

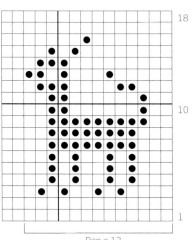

Rep = 13

Bird

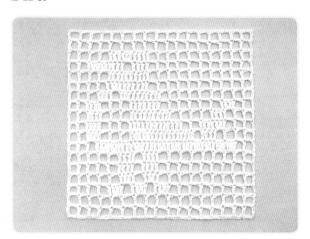

Crochet chart

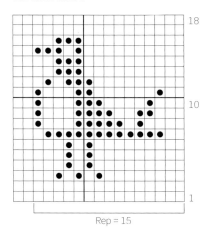

Rep = 15

Simple openwork stitch patterns

Openwork crochet stitches are always popular because of their lacy appearance (see scarf on pp. 116–117) and because they are quicker to work than solid crochet textures. The written instructions below explain how many chains to start with. So if working from the diagram, consult the written instructions to make the foundation chain. When working a wide piece, such as a blanket, it is difficult to count and keep track of the number of foundation chains being made. In these cases, make a chain about an inch longer than the correct length and unravel the excess later.

Chain loop mesh

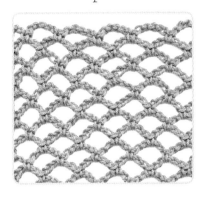

Crochet diagram

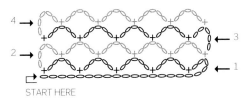

START HERE

Crochet instructions

Make a multiple of 4 ch, plus 2 extra.
Row 1 1 sc in sixth ch from hook, *ch 5, skip next 3 ch, 1 sc in next ch; rep from * to end, turn.
Row 2 *Ch 5, 1 sc in next 5-ch loop; rep from * to end, turn.
Rep row 2 to form patt.

Picot net stitch

Crochet diagram

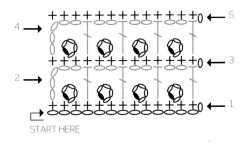

START HERE

Crochet instructions

Make a multiple of 3 ch, plus 2 extra.
Row 1 (RS) 1 sc in second ch from hook, 1 sc in next ch, *ch 4, 1 ss in fourth ch from hook (called 1 picot), 1 sc in each of next 3 ch; rep from * omitting 1 sc at end of last rep, turn.
Row 2 Ch 5 (counts as 1 dc and a 2-ch sp), skip first 3 sc (which includes 2 sc before picot and 1 sc after picot), 1 dc in next sc, *ch 2, skip next 2 sc (which includes 1 sc on each side of picot), 1 dc in next sc; rep from * to end, turn.
Row 3 Ch 1 (does NOT count as a st), 1 sc in first dc, *work (1 sc, 1 picot, 1 sc) all in next 2-ch sp, 1 sc in next dc; rep from * working last sc of last rep in third ch from last dc, turn.
Rep rows 2 and 3 to form patt.

Open shell stitch

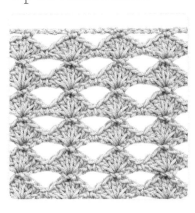

Crochet diagram

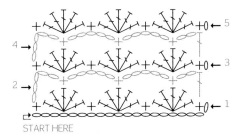

START HERE

Crochet instructions

Make a multiple of 6 ch, plus 2 extra.
Row 1 (RS) 1 sc in second ch from hook, *skip next 2 ch, 5 dc in next ch, skip next 2 ch, 1 sc in next ch; rep from * to end, turn.
Row 2 Ch 5 (counts as first dc and a 2-ch sp), 1 sc in center dc of first shell, *ch 5, 1 sc in center dc of next shell; rep from *, ending with ch 2, 1 dc in last sc, turn.
Row 3 Ch 1 (does NOT count as a st), 1 sc in first dc, *5 dc in next sc, 1 sc in next 5-ch loop; rep from * working last sc of last rep in third ch from last sc, turn.
Rep rows 2 and 3 to form patt.

Arched mesh stitch

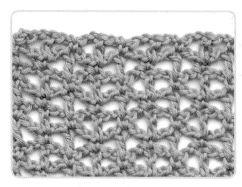

Crochet diagram

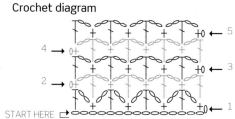

START HERE

Crochet instructions

Make a multiple of 4 ch.

Row 1 1 sc in second ch from hook, ch 2, skip next ch, 1 dc in next ch, *ch 2, skip next ch, 1 sc in next ch, ch 2, skip next ch, 1 dc in next ch; rep from * to end, turn.

Row 2 Ch 1 (does NOT count as a st), 1 sc in first dc, ch 2, 1 dc in next sc, *ch 2, 1 sc in next dc, ch 2, 1 dc in next sc; rep from * to end, turn.

Rep row 2 to form patt.

Banded net stitch

Crochet diagram

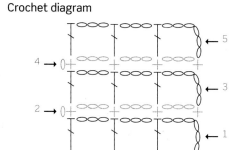

START HERE

Crochet instructions

Make a multiple of 4 ch, plus 2 extra.

Row 1 (RS) 1 dc in tenth ch from hook, *ch 3, skip next 3 ch, 1 dc in next ch; rep from * to end, turn.

Row 2 Ch 1 (does NOT count as a st), 1 sc in first dc, *ch 3, 1 sc in next dc; rep from *, ending with ch 3, skip next 3 ch, 1 sc in next ch, turn.

Row 3 Ch 6 (counts as 1 dc and a 3-ch sp), skip first sc and first 3-ch sp, 1 dc in next sc, *ch 3, 1 dc in next sc; rep from * to end, turn.

Rep rows 2 and 3 to form patt.

Shell mesh stitch

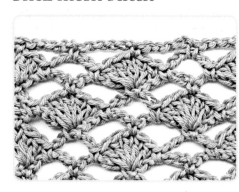

Crochet diagram

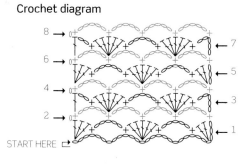

START HERE

Crochet instructions

Make a multiple of 12 ch, plus 4 extra.

Row 1 (RS) 2 dc in fourth ch from hook, *skip next 2 ch, 1 sc in next ch, ch 5, skip next 5 ch, 1 sc in next ch, skip next 2 ch, 5 dc in next ch; rep from *, ending last rep with 3 dc (instead of 5 dc) in last ch, turn.

Row 2 Ch 1 (does NOT count as a st), 1 sc in first dc, *ch 5, 1 sc in next 5-ch loop, ch 5, 1 sc in 3rd dc of next 5-dc shell; rep from * working last sc of last rep in top of 3 ch at end, turn.

Row 3 *Ch 5, 1 sc in next 5-ch loop, 5 dc in next sc, 1 sc in next 5-ch loop; rep from *, ending with ch 2, 1 dc in last sc, turn.

Row 4 Ch 1 (does NOT count as a st), 1 sc in first dc, *ch 5, 1 sc in third dc of next 5-dc shell, ch 5, 1 sc in next 5-ch loop; rep from * to end, turn.

Row 5 Ch 3 (counts as first dc), 2 dc in first sc, *1 sc in next 5-ch loop, ch 5, 1 sc in next 5-ch loop, 5 dc in next sc; rep from * ending last rep with 3 dc (instead of 5 dc) in last sc, turn.

Rep rows 2–5 to form patt.

Blocks lace

Crochet diagram

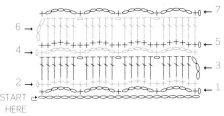

Note: When working from diagram, rep rows 2–7 to form patt.

Crochet instructions

Make a multiple of 5 ch, plus 2 extra.

Row 1 (RS) 1 sc in second ch from hook, *ch 5, skip next 4 ch, 1 sc in next ch; rep from * to end, turn.

Row 2 Ch 1 (does NOT count as a st), 1 sc in first sc, *5 sc in next 5-ch loop, 1 sc in next sc; rep from * to end, turn.

Row 3 Ch 3 (counts as first dc), skip first sc, 1 dc in each of next 5 sc, *ch 1, skip next sc, 1 dc in each of next 5 sc; rep from * to last sc, 1 dc in last sc, turn.

Row 4 Ch 1 (does NOT count as a st), 1 sc in first dc, *Ch 5, 1 sc in next 1-ch sp; rep from * working last sc of last rep in top of 3-ch at end, turn.

Rep rows 2–4 to form patt.

Tiara lace

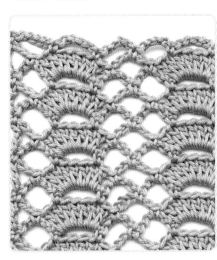

Crochet diagram

Crochet instructions

Make a multiple of 12 ch.

Row 1 (WS) 1 sc in second ch from hook, *ch 5, skip next ch 3, 1 sc in next ch; rep from *to last 2 ch, ch 2, skip next ch, 1 dc in last ch, turn.

Row 2 (RS) Ch 1 (does NOT count as a st), 1 sc in first st, skip next 2-ch sp, 7 dc in next 5-ch loop, 1 sc in next 5-ch loop, *ch 5, 1 sc in next 5-ch loop, 7 dc in next 5-ch loop, 1 sc in next 5-ch loop; rep from *, ending with ch 2, 1 tr in last sc, turn.

Row 3 Ch 1 (does NOT count as a st), 1 sc in first tr, ch 5, 1 sc in second of next 7-dc shell, ch 5, 1 sc in sixth dc of same shell, *ch 5, 1 sc in next 5-ch loop, ch 5, 1 sc in second of next 7-dc shell, ch 5, 1 sc in sixth dc of same shell; rep from *, ending with ch 2, 1 tr in last sc, turn.

Rep rows 2 and 3 to form patt.

Fans stitch

Crochet diagram

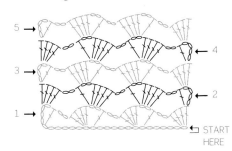

Crochet instructions

Make a multiple of 7 ch, plus 4 extra.

Row 1 1 dc in fifth ch from hook, ch 2, skip next 5 ch, 4 dc in next ch, *ch 2, 1 dc in next ch, ch 2, skip next 5 ch, 4 dc in next ch; rep from * to end, turn.

Row 2 Ch 4, 1 dc in first dc, *ch 2, skip next 2-ch sp and work (4 dc, ch 2, 1 dc) all in following 2-ch sp; rep from * to last 2-ch sp, skip last 2-ch sp and work 4 dc in 4-ch loop at end, turn.

Rep row 2 to form patt.

Shell mesh scarf

This openwork scarf, using lace crochet techniques and fine yarn, is warm but delicate enough to carry you from fall through to spring. Turn to pages 113–115 for a collection of alternative openwork stitch patterns.

PROJECTS
For more openwork patterns
>> go to pages 200 and 250

Essential information

DIFFICULTY LEVEL Intermediate

SIZE Approx 50 x 5½in (125 x 14cm), with 4in (10cm) tassels

YARN Use any fine merino for the same effect

x 1

CROCHET HOOK E/4 US (3.5mm) hook

NOTIONS Yarn needle

GAUGE Exact gauge is not essential

Pattern
Work 64 ch (any multiple of 12 sts plus 4 extra will work).

ROW 1 2 dc in fourth ch from hook. *skip 2 sts, 1 sc in next st, 5 ch, skip 5 sts, 1 sc in next st, skip 2 sts, 5 dc in next st. Repeat from * and ending last repeat with 3 dc (instead of 5) in last st. Turn.

ROW 2 Ch 1, 1 sc in first dc, *5 ch, 1 sc in next ch loop, ch 5, 1 sc in third dc of next 5 dc shell, repeat from * and work last sc of last repeat in top of ch at end. Turn.

ROW 3 *Ch 5, 1 sc in next ch loop, 5 dc in next sc, 1 sc in next ch loop. Repeat from * and ending with 2 ch, 1 dc in last sc. Turn.

ROW 4 Ch 1, 1 sc in first dc, *5 ch, 1 sc in third dc of next 5 dc shell, 5 ch, 1 sc in next ch loop. Repeat from * to end. Turn.

ROW 5 Ch 3 (counts as first dc), 2 dc in first sc, *1 sc in next ch loop, 5 ch, 1 sc in next ch loop, 5 dc in next sc. Repeat from * ending last repeat with 3 dc (instead of 5) in last sc. Turn. Repeat rows 2–5 to form pattern until the scarf is the required length.
Fasten off, weave in ends.

Making the tassels
Cut the yarn into 10in (25cm) lengths. Tie bundles of 15 lengths together in an overhand knot through each chain loop space at the ends of the scarf—this scarf has 10 tassels at either end.

>> This scarf is made with Rowan Fine Lace. 437yds/400m/50g, in Aged (933).

1 To crochet the shell pattern used for this scarf, insert your hook into the single crochet stitch from the row below.

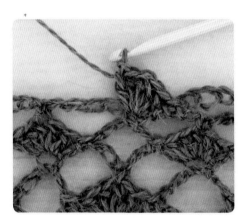

2 Work the double stitches for the shell, see pattern above, into the sc. Complete the shell by working 5 doubles into the same sc stitch.

3 Encourage the shell to "fan out" within the scarf by working a sc into the next chain space before working the next shell sequence.

Colorwork

One-color crochet has its charms, but using your creative imagination to combine colors is both more challenging and more rewarding. All of the crochet colorwork techniques are easy to master and worth experimenting with. They include colorwork stitch patterns (see pp. 119–121), stripes, jacquard, and intarsia (see p. 39 and below).

Jacquard and intarsia colorwork

Jacquard and intarsia crochet are both worked in single crochet stitches. Jacquard is usually worked with only two colors in a row; the color not in use is carried across the top of the row below and stitches are worked over it to enclose it. When a color is used only in an area of the crochet rather than across the entire row, the intarsia technique is required; a different length of yarn is used for each section of color.

Colorwork charts

The charted crochet design will reveal which technique to use—jacquard or intarsia. If the pattern on the chart shows two colors repeated across each horizontal row of squares, then the jacquard technique is required. Motifs worked in isolation require the intarsia technique. Each square on the charts represent one single crochet.

Jacquard chart

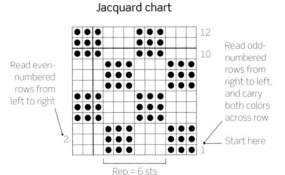

Read even-numbered rows from left to right

Read odd-numbered rows from right to left, and carry both colors across row

Start here

Rep = 6 sts

Intarsia chart

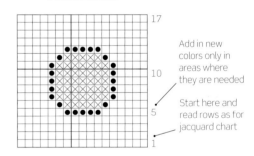

Add in new colors only in areas where they are needed

Start here and read rows as for jacquard chart

Jacquard technique

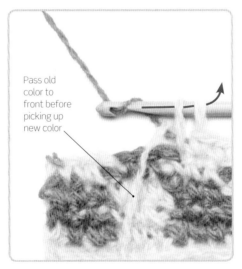

1 To change to a new color in jacquard, work up to the last yo of the single crochet stitch before the color change, then pass the old color to the front of the work over the top of the new color and use the new color to complete the stitch.

Pass old color to front before picking up new color

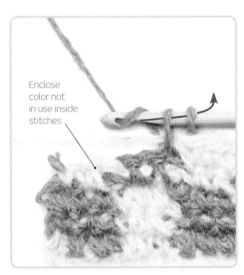

2 Work the next stitch in the new color in the usual way, but keep the old yarn positioned along the top of the row below so that the single crochet stitches in the new color enclose it.

Enclose color not in use inside stitches

Intarsia technique

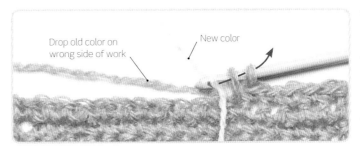

Drop old color on wrong side of work

New color

1 To change to a new color in intarsia, work to the position on the chart where the motif begins, but stop before working the last yo of the previous stitch. Then use the new color to complete the single crochet.

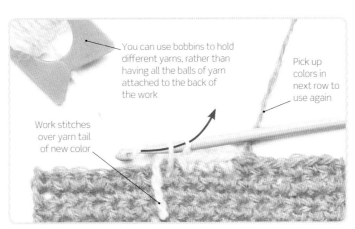

You can use bobbins to hold different yarns, rather than having all the balls of yarn attached to the back of the work

Pick up colors in next row to use again

Work stitches over yarn tail of new color

2 Work all the required stitches in the new color as shown. Then join in another ball (or length of yarn) for the next area of background color. Use a separate yarn for each area of color.

Simple colorwork stitch patterns

Crochet colorwork stitch patterns are lots of fun to work. This selection of stitches, all easy-to-work, includes an array of textures, so you are sure to find one that catches your eye. Although some of the stitches have a right and wrong side, the back and front of these fabrics still look very similar. The reversibility of crochet is one of its best features. If you want to make a scarf, shawl, baby blanket, throw, or pillow cover with one of these stitches, take your time to choose the right color combination. See page 83 for abbreviations and basic stitch symbols. Any special symbols are given with the individual diagram.

Simple zigzag stitch

Crochet diagram

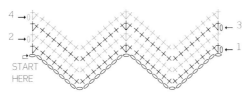

Note: When working from diagram, rep rows 2 and 3 for stitch pattern.

Crochet instructions

This pattern is worked in 3 colors (A, B, C).
With C, make a multiple of 16 ch, plus 2 extra.
Row 1 (RS) With A, 2 sc in second ch from hook, *1 sc in each of next 7 ch, skip next ch, 1 sc in each of next 7 ch, 3 sc in next ch; rep from * to end, working 2 sc (instead of 3 sc) in last ch, turn.
Row 2 With A, ch 1 (does NOT count as a st), 2 sc in first sc, *1 sc in each of next 7 sc, skip next 2 sc, 1 sc in each of next 7 sc, 3 sc in next sc; rep from * to end, working 2 sc (instead of 3 sc) in last sc, turn.
Rows 3 and 4 With B, rep row 2.
Rows 5 and 6 With C, (rep row 2) twice.
Rows 7 and 8 With A, (rep row 2) twice.
Rep rows 3–8 to form patt.

Colored tweed stitch

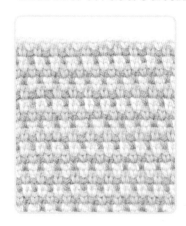

Crochet diagram

START HERE

Crochet instructions

This pattern is worked in 3 colors (A, B, C).
With A, make a multiple of 2 ch.

Row 1 With A, 1 sc in second ch from hook, *ch 1, skip next ch, 1 sc in next ch; rep from * to end, turn.

Row 2 With B, ch 1 (does NOT count as a st), 1 sc in first sc, 1 sc in next 1-ch sp, *ch 1, 1 sc in next 1-ch sp; rep from * to last sc, 1 sc in last sc, turn.

Row 3 With C, ch 1 (does NOT count as a st), 1 sc in first sc, *ch 1, 1 sc in next 1-ch sp; rep from * to last 2 sc, ch 1, skip next sc, 1 sc in last sc, turn.

Row 4 With A, rep row 2.

Row 5 With B, rep row 3.

Row 6 With C, rep row 2.

Row 7 With A, rep row 3.

Rep rows 2–7 to form patt.

Spike stitch stripes

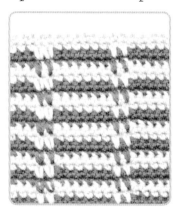

Crochet diagram

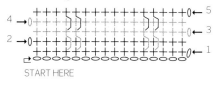

START HERE

KEY   spike st in st one row below next st

Crochet instructions

NOTE: spike st = do not work into next st, but instead insert hook front to back through top of st one row below this st, yo and draw a loop through, lengthening the loop to the height of the row being worked (and enclosing the skipped st), yo and a draw through both loops on hook to complete an elongated sc.

This pattern is worked in 2 colors (A, B).
Using A, make a multiple of 8 ch, plus 1 extra.

Row 1 (RS) With A, 1 sc in 2nd ch from hook, 1 sc in each of rem ch, turn.

Row 2 With A, ch 1 (does NOT count as a st), 1 sc in each sc to end, turn.

Row 3 With B, ch 1 (does NOT count as a st), *1 sc in each of next 3 sc, (1 spike st in top of st one row below next st) twice, 1 sc in each of next 3 sc; rep from * to end, turn.

Row 4 With B, rep row 2.

Row 5 With A, rep row 3.

Rep rows 2–5 to form patt.

Colored cluster and shell stitch

Crochet instructions

This pattern is worked in 2 colors (A, B).
Work as for cluster and shell stitch on page 85 as follows:
With A, make the foundation ch. Then work in stripe patt, repeating the following stripe sequence—2 rows A, 2 rows B.

Bobble stripe

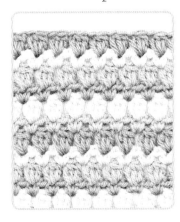

Crochet diagram

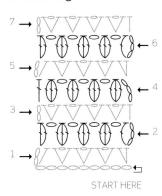

START HERE

Crochet instructions

NOTE: bobble = (yo and insert hook in specified st, yo and draw a loop through, yo and draw through first 2 loops on hook) 3 times all in same st (4 loops now on hook), yo and draw through all 4 loops on hook to complete 3-dc bobble (see p. 79).

This pattern is worked in 3 colors (A, B, C).

With A, make a multiple of 2 ch, plus 1 extra.

Work the following rows in stripes, repeating this stripe sequence—1 row A, 1 row B, 1 row C.

Row 1 (WS) 1 hdc in third ch from hook, *skip next ch, work (1 hdc, ch 1, 1 hdc) all in next ch; rep from * to last ch 2, skip next ch, 2 hdc in last ch, turn.**Row 2 (RS)** Ch 3 (counts as first dc), 1 dc in first hdc, *ch 1, 1 bobble in next 1-ch sp; rep from *, ending with ch 1, work (yo and insert hook in top of 2-ch at end of row, yo and draw a loop through, yo and draw through first 2 loops on hook) twice all in same place (3 loops now on hook), yo and draw through all 3 loops on hook, turn.

Row 3 Ch 2 (counts as first hdc), *work (1 hdc, ch 1, 1 hdc) all in next 1-ch sp; rep from *, ending with 1 hdc in top of 3-ch, turn.

Row 4 Ch 3 (counts as first dc), 1 bobble in next 1-ch sp, *ch 1, 1 bobble in next 1-ch sp; rep from *, ending with 1 dc in top of 2-ch at end, turn.

Row 5 Ch 2 (counts as first hdc), 1 hdc in first dc, *work (1 hdc, ch 1, 1 hdc) all in next 1-ch sp; rep from *, ending with 2 hdc in top of 3-ch at end, turn.

Rep rows 2–5 to form patt, while continuing stripe sequence.

Triangles spike stitch

Crochet diagram

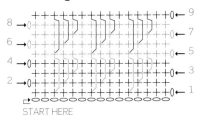

START HERE

KEY

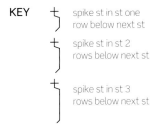

spike st in st one row below next st

spike st in st 2 rows below next st

spike st in st 3 rows below next st

Crochet instructions

NOTE: spike st = do not work into next st, but instead insert hook front to back through top of st 1, 2 or 3 rows below this st, yo and draw a loop through, lengthening the loop to the height of the row being worked (and enclosing the skipped st), yo and a draw through both loops on hook to complete an elongated sc.

This pattern is worked in 2 colors (A, B).

With A, make a multiple of 4 ch.

Row 1 (RS) With A, 1 sc in second ch from hook, 1 sc in each of rem ch, turn.

Row 2 With A, ch 1 (does NOT count as a st), 1 sc in each sc to end, turn.

Rows 3 and 4 With A, (rep row 2) twice.

Row 5 (RS) With B, ch 1 (does NOT count as a st), 1 sc in first sc, *1 sc in next sc, 1 spike st in top of sc one row below next sc, 1 spike st in top of sc 2 rows below next sc, 1 spike st in top of sc 3 rows below next sc; rep from * to last 2 sc, 1 sc in each of last 2 sc, turn.

Rows 6, 7, and 8 With B, (rep row 2) 3 times.

Row 9 (RS) With A, rep row 5.

Rep rows 2–9 to form patt, ending with a patt row 5 or 9.

Colored close shells stitch

Crochet instructions

This pattern is worked in 3 colors (A, B, C).

Work as for close shells stitch on page 84 as follows:

With A, make the foundation ch. Then work in stripe patt, repeating the following stripe sequence—1 row A, 1 row B, 1 row C.

Essential information

DIFFICULTY LEVEL Intermediate

SIZE 12 x 20in (30 x 50cm)

YARN Any DK weight yarn will work for this project

A x 4 **B** x 2

CROCHET HOOK F/5 US (4mm) hook

NOTIONS Yarn needle

GAUGE 15 sts x 20 rows per 4in (10cm) square

Intarsia pillow

This simple bolster pillow is worked in two pieces and has an attractive diamond and stripe intarsia pattern. The pattern includes the option for a double-sided pillow or for crocheting one side in plain crochet.

PROJECTS

For more pillow patterns
>> go to pages 152, 154, and 156

NOTE When changing yarn color: with yarn A insert hook into next st, pull through a loop, change to yarn B, yo and crochet both loops on hook. Work the next stitch in yarn B. Changing the yarn is completed in the final step of the previous stitch.

Pillow front

With yarn A, work 76 ch.

ROW 1 sc into second ch from hook, sc to end. (75sts)

ROW 2 Ch 1, sc to end of row.

ROWS 3–9 Repeat row 2.

ROW 10 With yarn B, 1 ch, sc to end of row.

ROW 11 Repeat row 10.

ROW 12 With yarn A, 1 ch, sc to end of row.

ROW 13 Repeat row 12.

ROW 14–17 With yarn B, 1 ch, sc to end of row.

ROW 18-21 With yarn A, 1 ch, sc to end of row.

ROW 22 See chart, below right, for the colorwork intarsia design.

Working in intarsia and changing yarn color before the final stage in the last stitch, with yarn A (referred to as A) 1 ch, 10 sc, yarn B (referred to as B) 1 sc, *A17 sc, B1 sc; repeat from * 2 more times, A10 sc.

ROW 23 Repeat row 22.

ROW 24 With A, 1 ch, 9 sc, B3 sc, *A15 sc, B3 sc; repeat from * two more times, A9 sc.

ROW 25 Repeat row 24.

ROW 26 With A, 1 ch, 8 sc, B2 sc, A1 sc, B2 sc, *A13 sc, B2 sc, A1 sc, B2 sc; repeat from * 2 more times, A8 sc.

ROW 27 Repeat row 26.

ROW 28 With A, 1 ch, 7 sc, B2 sc, A3 sc, B2 sc, *A5 sc, B1 sc, A5 sc, B2 sc, A3 sc, B2 sc; repeat from * 2 more times, A7 sc.

ROW 29 Repeat row 28.

ROW 30 With A, 1 ch, 6 sc, B2 sc, A2 sc, B1 sc, A2 sc, B2 sc, *A3 sc, B3 sc, A3 sc, B2 sc, A2 sc, B1 sc, A2 sc, B2 sc; repeat from * 2 more times, A6 sc.

ROW 31 Repeat row 30.

ROW 32 Repeat row 28.

ROW 33 Repeat row 32.

ROW 34 Repeat row 26.

ROW 35 Repeat row 34.

ROW 36 Repeat row 24.

ROW 37 Repeat row 36.

ROW 38 Repeat row 22.

ROW 39 Repeat row 38.

ROW 40 With A, 1 ch, sc to end of row.

ROWS 41–43 Repeat row 40.

ROWS 44–47 With B, 1 ch, sc to end of row.

ROWS 48–49 With A, 1 ch, sc to end of row.

ROWS 50–51 With B, 1 ch, sc to end of row.

ROWS 52–60 With A, 1 ch sc to end of row. Fasten off.

Pillow back

Repeat instructions for pillow front.
For the plain version, work as follows:
With yarn A, work 76 ch.

ROW 1 Sc into second ch from hook, sc to end of row. (75sts)

ROW 2 Ch 1, sc to end of row.

ROWS 3–60 Repeat row 2.
Fasten off.

Finishing

With right sides together, sew the pillow, leaving one shorter side open. Turn inside out and insert pillow form. Either sew edges together or insert a zipper.

<< This intarsia pillow is made with Rowan Pure Wool DK, 142yds/130m/50g, in A: Cream (00013) and B: Blue (00008).

Unusual stitches

If you want to try some stitches that are a little more unusual, you could try either Tunisian Simple stitch or Broomstick stitch. While they are not difficult stitches to work, it is best to make sure you have mastered the basics of crochet before you try them out.

Tunisian crochet

Tunisian crochet combines elements of both knitting and crochet. It produces a fabric that looks very similar to either a woven fabric or knitted stockinette stitch, depending on the stitch variation. A row is completed by working two "passes" (a "forward" and a "return" pass) as opposed to one regular row in crochet, and these are worked with a special hook (see p. 19). This is because you need room for the many loops on the hook during one of the passes of each row.

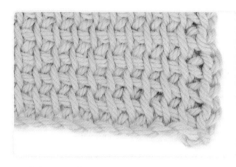

Tunisian crochet: Tunisian Simple stitch is the easiest Tunisian stitch and produces a dense fabric. Always work with the RS facing you.

1 Tunisian crochet begins with a regular chain, after which each row is composed of two passes. The first row is the foundation row. Insert the hook into the first chain, yo and draw a loop through, leaving this loop on the hook.

2 Repeat the last step for each chain to the end. You will have the same number of loops on the hook as the number of chains you began with. The foundation forward pass is now complete.

3 Now begin the return pass of the foundation row. When you get to the end of the first forward pass, do not turn, but simply work one chain.

4 Then, yo and pull through the first two loops on the hook.

5 Repeat this, working off the loops in pairs until one loop is left on the hook. The foundation, or first row (a forward and a return pass), is complete.

6 For the forward pass of row 2, (the first regular row), do not work a turning chain—the loop on the hook counts as the first stitch. Skip the vertical stitch directly under the hook and insert the hook into the next vertical stitch from right to left.

7 Yo and pull through the stitch, then repeat, pulling a loop through each vertical stitch to the end of the row, leaving each loop on the hook. Work each following forward pass of every row in this way. Now work the return pass for this (and every following) row in the same way as for steps 3 and 4. Continue working Tunisian Simple stitch in this way until the project is the desired length.

Broomstick lace

Broomstick lace was originally made using a broom handle to create the lacy effect. Basic broomstick stitch is normally worked using a regular hook and a 35 to 50 US (20mm–25mm/³⁄₄in–1in) diameter knitting needle to create the large, lacy loops typical of this stitch.

Broomstick combination: Also known as peacock eye crochet, this stitch can be combined with regular crochet stitches to create pattern variations.

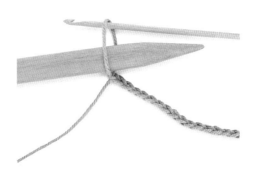

1 Make a chain as usual, making the last chain larger by pulling up with the hook, and placing it onto the knitting needle.

2 Insert the hook into the next chain, yo, and pull a loop through.

3 Place the loop onto the knitting needle.

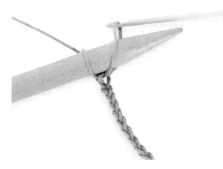

4 Continue to work steps 2 and 3 until all the loops are on the knitting needle.

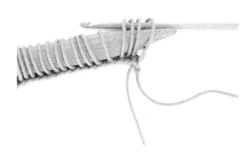

5 Slide the hook through the first groups of loops (the pattern will tell you how many), and pull them off the needle.

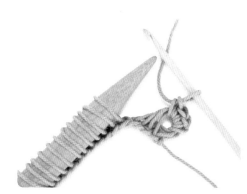

6 Yo and pull through all the loops on the hook, then work a multiple of dc stitches into the group of loops (again, the pattern will indicate how many).

7 Continue in this way until all the loops have been crocheted into, and this completes a row of broomstick lace. You can continue in the same way, drawing up loops through each stitch, or continue in regular crochet, or a mixture of both to create beautiful broomstick lace patterns.

Unusual yarns

If you want to break the monotony of working with wool yarns, why not try out some unusual materials? String, wire, rag strips, and plastic strips are lots of fun to crochet with, and the materials used can be recycled ones. To take you through the techniques involved, a quick-to-make item is shown with each of these "yarns." It isn't advisable to try to learn to crochet with unusual yarns, so make sure you are deft at forming single crochet stitches before attempting to work with them.

String crochet

Tightly crocheted string forms a sturdy fabric suitable for containers. Because it is usually neither too thick nor too thin, garden twine is a good choice for a first string crochet project. It is also easy to obtain and forms a fabric that holds its shape well.

Crocheting a round string container

Use a safety pin as the stitch marker

1 Select a hook size for your chosen string that will form a firm, tight single crochet fabric. As an example, a size 7 US (4.5mm) crochet hook was used here with a natural garden twine. To try out string crochet, make a small round container. Start with round 1 of the flat circle instructions on page 56.

Move marker up at end of each round

2 Continue to follow the circle pattern, and work rounds 2 and 3. Work the stitches as tightly as you can. If the crochet doesn't seem tight enough, start again with a smaller hook size.

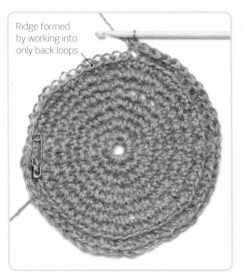

Ridge formed by working into only back loops

3 Keep working rounds of the circle pattern until the circle is the desired size for the base of the container. Then to start the sides of the container, work 1 sc into the back loop only of the top of each stitch in the next round as shown. This forms a ridge.

4 On all the remaining rounds of the container, work 1 sc in each stitch of the previous round, working through both loops of the top of the stitch below in the usual way. This will form a tube (see p. 100 for tips on working spiral crochet). Continue until the container is the desired height.

Wire crochet

As long as it is fine enough, wire is easy to crochet with, even though it takes a little practice to produce even stitches. As with string crochet, it is best to stick to simple single crochet for wire—more exotic stitches are difficult to distinguish among the bending, airy wire loops. Adding beads to wire crochet is the best way to jazz it up and turn it into simple jewelry like the easy-to-make, flexible bangle shown here.

Crocheting a beaded wire bangle

The easiest wire thickness to crochet with is a 28 gauge (0.3mm) copper wire, which can be obtained online from craft stores or stores that sell jewelry supplies. For this wire size, you will need a size D-3 US (3mm) crochet hook.

1 Thread all the beads onto the wire before you begin crocheting with it. The bangle worked here uses about 27 glass beads (6-7mm in diameter), but it is always best to string on about 10 more than you think you'll need, in case you have miscalculated.

2 Make your own chart for your bead jewelry, showing where the beads are to be placed. This is the chart used for the simple bangle. (See p. 86 for how to work bead crochet.)

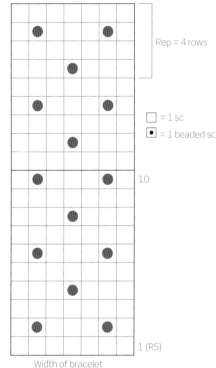

Rep = 4 rows

□ = 1 sc
■ = 1 beaded sc

10

1 (RS)

Width of bracelet

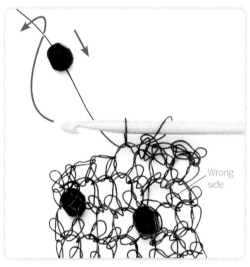

Wrong side

3 Using the wire with the beads on it, make 8 chains to start the featured bangle. Then follow the chart to work the beaded crochet, working the stitches loosely. Whenever the position of a bead is reached (always on a wrong-side row), work up to the last yo of the stitch, then slide the bead up close to the crochet and complete the stitch.

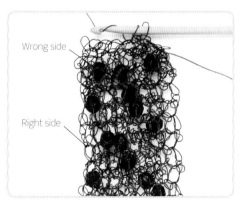

Wrong side

Right side

4 Work the bangle until it is the desired length. End with a right-side (non-bead) row so that the wrong side will be facing for the next row. Place the other end of the bangle behind the next row and work the last row through both layers of the bangle by inserting the hook through the foundation chain of the second layer as shown.

5 After completing the single crochet seam, cut the wire and fasten off. Darn in the wire tails along the single crochet seam, using a blunt-ended yarn needle and wrapping the wire tightly a few times around the edge of the crochet. Then cut off the remaining wire close to the bangle. Turn the bangle right side out.

Alternative bangle

You can also make plain wire crochet bangles and decorate them once they have been completed. This bangle has been worked plain without any beads. Buttons have been sewn along the center of the bangle with a bright, contrasting, silk-button thread.

Rag-strip crochet

The biggest advantage of rag-strip crochet is its limitless color palette—the "yarn" can be made from any cotton shirt-weight or patchwork-weight fabric. To try out the technique, work circles with rag strips, and make them into a bag.

Preparing fabric strips

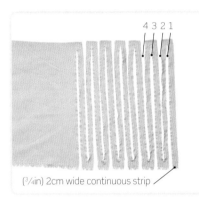

4 3 2 1

(¾in) 2cm wide continuous strip

1 To make a continuous fabric strip ¾in (2cm) wide, cut or tear the fabric from selvage to selvage, stopping each tear/cut about ½in (1.5cm) from the edge.

2 As you tear the strips, wind them into balls. Rag crochet uses up a lot of fabric. To start your project, you can prepare some rag yarn in each of the colors you need and make more later as required.

Crocheting two circles for a bag

A large paper clip is the best stitch marker for rag-strip crochet

1 For a firm crochet fabric, use a size N-15 US (10mm) crochet hook and ¾in (2cm) wide patchwork-fabric-weight cotton strips. Simple single crochet is the best stitch to use for rag crochet. To begin a circle for a bag, work round 1 of the flat circle pattern on p. 56 (but leave the yarn tail at the back of the work and do not attempt to work the stitches of this round over it).

Change to a new color with last yo of a round

2 Continuing to follow the circle pattern, introduce new colors for stripes as desired. Work the circle until it is the size you want for a bag front. Then work a second circle the same size. Using the hook, pull any yarn tails through a few stitches on the wrong side to secure them and trim off the ends.

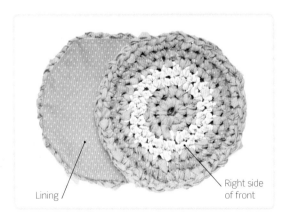

Lining

Right side of front

3 Line the two circles with a harmonizing fabric print. (The edge of the lining should reach the base of the tops of the single crochet stitches of the last row.)

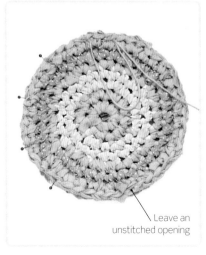

Leave an unstitched opening

4 With the wrong sides facing, pin the bag front and back together. Then using a sewing needle and matching thread or thin cotton yarn, stitch the seam just under the tops of the single crochet stitches of the last round, leaving an opening at the top. For a bag strap, make a long braid with some of the fabric strip yarn or use a long ready-made cord.

Plastic-strip crochet

Recycling your colorful plastic bags is a great way to help the environment. You can create plastic yarn (or plarn) very quickly using the quick cutting technique shown here. Then use it to experiment with plastic-strip crochet by making a simple bag.

Preparing plarn strips

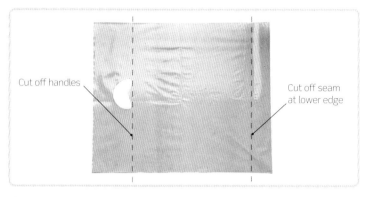

Cut off handles

Cut off seam at lower edge

1 Use lightweight plastic bags for plarn. To cut a continuous strip from a bag, begin by laying it flat and smoothing it out. Trim off the seam at the lower edge of the bag and the handles at the top.

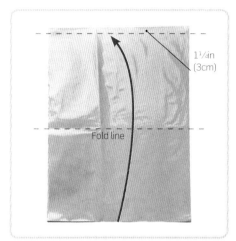

1¼in (3cm)

Fold line

2 Fold the plastic tube in half, bringing the fold at the lower edge up to 1¼in (3cm) from the top fold.

3 Fold the bag twice more, bringing the lower edge up to within 1¼in (3cm) of the top with each fold.

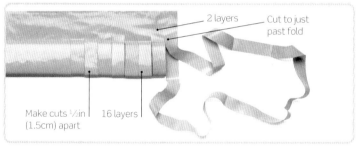

2 layers

Cut to just past fold

Make cuts ½in (1.5cm) apart

16 layers

4 Make vertical cuts through the 16 layers at ½in (1.5cm) intervals, stopping each cut about ½in (1.5cm) from the two-layer top fold. Make cuts in this way all along the folded bag.

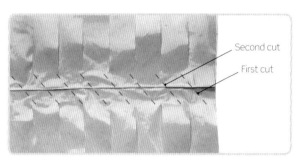

Second cut

First cut

5 Open out the bag so that you can see the area where the strips are still joined together. To create the continuous strip, make diagonal cuts as shown and wind the strip into a ball.

Crocheting a plarn makeup bag

If strip breaks just knot ends together

1 Use a size H-8 US (5mm) hook to crochet plarn prepared as shown above. To make a small makeup bag, work a spiral tube of single crochet (see p. 100).

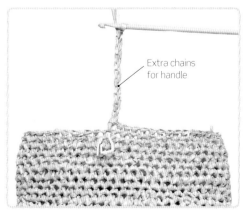

Extra chains for handle

2 To add a loop handle, make extra chains before starting the next round. Work single crochet stitches along the extra chains. Work more rounds until the handle is the desired width, then fasten off. Join the seam along the lower edge by working a row of single crochet through both layers. Sew the two layers of the handle together level with the side edge of the bag to form an open loop. Line the bag and add a zipper.

Crocheted toys

Although crocheted toys look difficult, they are relatively easy to make, and quick as well. This step-by-step guide to crocheting a toy provides tips for making the pieces, stuffing, sewing the parts together, and for adding facial features (see pp. 132–135 for the pattern).

Toy techniques

This cute teddy bear has been designed for intermediate crocheters, and its pattern on pages 132-135 has an easy-to-follow style. Because the toy has a step-by-step guide, it is an ideal first toy project. Being able to see what the pieces look like before they are stuffed will give you confidence that your crocheted toy is turning out the shape that it should.

The tips in the steps apply to crocheted toys in general. Start your toy project by selecting the yarns and hook required. For the sample teddy bear, you only need two colors of yarn. Select a crochet hook that will produce a tight single-crochet fabric, one to two sizes smaller than the size recommended for the yarn weight category (see p. 14).

You will need two balls of a lightweight or medium-weight yarn, one in A (main color) and one in B

Polyfill

Velvet ribbon for neck

Blunt-ended yarn needle

Toy safety eyes

Stitch marker

Six-stranded cotton embroidery thread (for nose and mouth)

Plastic safety-eye backs

Choose a crochet hook one or two sizes smaller than the size recommended for the yarn weight

The extras needed for the teddy bear are the same as those for most toys—embroidery thread for the facial features, safety eyes or buttons for the eyes, and polyfill. Be VERY careful if you are making any toy for a small child; for these toys, it is best to embroider the eyes or select toy safety eyes that meet safety regulations.

1 Place a stitch marker or scrap of different-colored yarn as you crochet at the position for each eye, so that when you have finished making the head, you will be able to attach the safety eyes symmetrically.

2 Begin stuffing the head just after you have begun decreasing, when the opening is still large enough to do so easily. Make sure you insert enough polyfill to fill the head completely.

3 When you have finished the head, there will be a small hole left. To sew this up, make sure you leave a long tail of yarn for sewing. Thread the yarn tail all around the opening with a yarn needle.

4 Now pull tightly on the thread to close the hole. Secure the closure with a few stitches to make sure that it does not open. You can also use this long tail to sew the body onto the head; if you wish to do so, do not fasten it off.

5 Attach the safety eyes and then sew the muzzle onto the face by sewing with a whipstitch (see p. 70) in the same color as the muzzle.

Start with the nose

6 Using the embroidery thread, embroider a mouth and nose onto the muzzle as shown, or to your own design, creating an individual personality for the teddy bear.

7 Attach the head to the body using neat stitches (mattress stitch works well—see p. 71), taking a stitch from the body then the head alternately as you go around. You can use any neat stitch technique you are comfortable with; just make sure the head is fastened securely and does not flop over.

Push stuffing down with crochet hook

8 To stuff the limbs, use the blunt end of the crochet hook or any long object, such as a knitting needle, to push down the polyfill. Make sure that the polyfill is pushed all the way to the bottom. Use this technique to insert more stuffing and be sure that the limbs are stuffed tightly.

9 Attach the limbs to the body in the position shown, in a similar way to the head. While making sure that you attach the limbs securely so they do not fall off, also be sure that they are not sewn so tightly that they do not move. Sew from one spot at the side of the arm or leg (rather than at the tip) onto the body so that they are moveable.

Essential information

DIFFICULTY LEVEL Intermediate

SIZE Approx 11 x 6¼in (28 x 16cm)

YARN You can use any DK weight yarn

A x 1   **B** x 1

CROCHET HOOK F US (3.75mm) hook

NOTIONS 2 stitch markers
Yarn needle
½in (12mm) black safety toy eyes
Brown embroidery thread and needle
Brown felt for inner ears
Polyfill
⅜in- (1cm-) wide velvet ribbon

GAUGE Exact gauge is not essential

SPECIAL ABBREVIATIONS
ADJUSTABLE RING: Wind the yarn twice around
your finger. Insert the hook and wrap the yarn
around it. Pull the hook back through and work a
chain. Work the first round of sts into the "ring",
then pull the tail of yarn gently to close it, before
joining the sts into a round using a ss.

Teddy bear

You never forget your first bear and this one is sure to become a true keepsake. Worked in the round using adjustable rings for neatly curved paws and feet, this project is quick and satisfying to make.

PROJECTS
For more toy patterns
>> go to pages 266 and 274

NOTE The teddy bear is worked in spirals. Do not join rounds, but place a marker at first stitch of the round, moving it each round to mark the beginning of the next round.

Pattern
Follow this pattern and then refer to pages 130–131 when assembling your toy.

Head
With yarn A, make an adjustable ring and work 6 sc into the ring. (6sts)
ROUND 1 2 sc into each st to the end. (12sts)
ROUND 2 *1 sc, 2 sc in the next st; rep from * to end. (18sts)
ROUND 3 *2 sc, 2 sc in the next st; rep from * to end. (24sts)
ROUND 4 *3 sc, 2 sc in the next st; rep from * to end. (30sts)
ROUND 5 *9 sc, 2 sc in the next st; rep from * to end. (33sts)
ROUND 6 *10 sc, 2 sc in the next st; rep from * to end. (36sts)
ROUND 7 *11 sc, 2 sc in the next st; rep from * to end. (39sts)

ROUND 8 *12 sc, 2 sc in the next st; rep from * to end. (42sts)
ROUND 9 *13 sc, 2 sc in the next st; rep from * to end. (45sts)
Place 2 stitch markers on the next row 10 sts apart to mark where you will put the toy eyes.
ROUND 10 *14 sc, 2 sc in next st; rep from * to end. (48sts)
ROUND 11 *15 sc, 2 sc in next st; rep from * to end. (51sts)
ROUND 12 *16 sc, 2 sc in next st; rep from * to end. (54sts)
ROUNDS 13–14 Sc in each st to end.
ROUND 15 *sc2tog, 7 sc; rep from * to end. (48sts)
ROUND 16 *sc2tog, 6 sc; rep from * to end. (42sts)
ROUND 17 *sc2tog, 5 sc; rep from * to end. (36sts)
ROUND 18 *sc2tog, 4 sc; rep from * to end. (30sts)
ROUND 19 *sc2tog, 3 sc; rep from * to end. (24sts)
ROUND 20 *sc2tog, 2 sc; rep from * to end. (18sts)
ROUND 21 *sc2tog, 1 sc; rep from * to end. (12sts)
Add some stuffing to the head now.
ROUND 22 *sc2tog; rep from* to end. (6sts)
Put the working loop on a stitch holder and attach the toy eyes to the head in the places you marked on round 10.
Finish stuffing the head. Weave the cut yarn through the last 6 sts, pull to close the hole at the base of the head. Weave in yarn to secure and cut off any loose ends.

Muzzle
With yarn B, make an adjustable ring and work 6 sc into the ring. (6sts)
ROUND 1 2 sc into each st to end. (12sts)
ROUND 2 *3 sc, 2 sc in the next st; rep from * to end. (15sts)
ROUND 3 Sc in each st to end.
ROUND 4 *4 sc, 2 sc in next st; rep from * to end. (18sts)
ROUNDS 5–6 Sc in each st to end.
ROUND 7 *5 sc, 2 sc in next st; rep from * to end. (21sts)
ROUND 8 Sc in each st to end.
Cut the yarn leaving a long tail and pull through loop to secure. Position the muzzle and sew it onto the face. Use embroidery thread to sew the nose and mouth detail on the muzzle. Weave in and cut off loose ends.

Body
Stuff the body as you go along.
With yarn A, make an adjustable ring and work 6 sc into the ring. (6sts)
ROUND 1 2 sc into each st to end. (12sts)
ROUND 2 *3 sc, 2 sc in next st; rep from * to end. (15sts)
ROUND 3 *4 sc, 2 sc in next st; rep from * to end. (18sts)
ROUND 4 Sc in each st to end.
ROUND 5 *5 sc, 2 sc in next st; rep from * to end. (21sts)
ROUND 6 Sc in each st to end.
ROUND 7 *6 sc, 2 sc in next st; rep from * to end. (24sts)
ROUND 8 Sc in each st to end.
ROUND 9 *7 sc, 2 sc in next st; rep from * to end. (27sts)

The legs are worked from the feet upward. Start with an adjustable ring (see p. 57) and maintain even gauge as you increase the number of stitches on each round. Stuff the legs as they evolve.

ROUND 10 Sc in each st to end.
Add some stuffing to the body now.
ROUND 11 *8 sc, 2 sc in next st; rep from * to end. (30sts)
ROUND 12 Sc in each st to end.
ROUND 13 *9 sc, 2 sc in next st; rep from * to end. (33sts)
ROUND 14 Sc in each st to end.
ROUND 15 *10 sc, 2 sc in next st; rep from * to end. (36sts)
ROUND 16 Sc in each st to end.
ROUND 17 *sc2tog, 10 sc; rep from * to end. (33sts)
ROUND 18 *sc2tog, 9 sc; rep from * to end. (30sts)
ROUND 19 *sc2tog, 3 sc; rep from * to end. (24sts)
ROUND 20 *sc2tog, 2 sc; rep from * to end. (18sts)
ROUND 21 *sc2tog, 1 sc; rep from * to end. (12sts)
ROUND 22 *sc2tog; rep from * to end. (6sts)
Cut the yarn leaving a long tail and pull through loop to secure.
Finish stuffing the arm. Thread the cut yarn onto a yarn needle and weave through the last

6 stitches, pull the yarn to close the hole at the top of the body. Sew the body firmly to the head. Weave in and cut off any loose ends.

Arms (make 2)
Stuff the arms as you go along.
With yarn A, make an adjustable ring and work 6 sc into the ring. (6sts)
ROUND 1 2 sc into each st to end. (12sts)
ROUND 2 *1 sc, 2 sc in the next st; rep from * to end. (18sts)
ROUND 3 *2 sc, 2 sc in the next st; rep from * to end. (24sts)
ROUNDS 4-6 Sc in each st to the end.
ROUND 7 *sc2tog, 2 sc; rep from * to end. (18sts)
ROUND 8 *sc2tog, 4 sc; rep from * to end. (15sts)
ROUND 9 *sc2tog, 3 sc; rep from * to end. (12sts)
ROUNDS 10-19 Sc in each st to end.
ROUND 20 Sc2tog, sc in each st to end. (11sts)
ROUNDS 21-25 Sc in each st to end.
ROUND 26 sc2tog, sc in each st to end. (10sts)
ROUNDS 27-28 Sc in each st to end.
Cut the yarn leaving a long tail and pull through loop to secure.
Finish stuffing the arm firmly.
Thread the cut yarn onto a wool needle and weave through the last 10 stitches, pull the yarn to close the hole at the top of the arm, weave in yarn to secure.
Position the arms carefully in place and sew them onto the body.

Legs (make 2)
Stuff the legs as you go along.
With yarn A, make an adjustable ring and work 6 sc into the ring. (6sts)
ROUND 1 2 sc into each st to end. (12sts)
ROUND 2 2 sc, 2 sc in the next st, 2 sc, 3 hdc in the next st, 2 hdc, 3 hdc in the next st, 2 sc, 2 sc in the last st. (18sts)
ROUND 3 3 sc, 2 sc in the next st, 2 sc, 1 hdc, 2 hdc in the next st, 4 hdc, 2 hdc in the next st, 1 hdc, 1 sc, 2 sc in the next st, 2 sc. (22sts)
ROUND 4 2 sc in the first st, 8 sc, 3 hdc in the next st, 5 hdc, 3 hdc in the next st, 6 sc. (27sts)

ROUND 5 Sc in each st to end.
ROUND 6 1 sc, sc2tog, 8 sc, sc2tog, 6 sc, sc2tog, 6 sc. (24sts)
ROUND 7 11 sc, hdc3tog, 3 hdc, hdc3tog, 4 sc. (20sts)
ROUND 8 3 sc, sc2tog, 4 sc, sc2tog, 1 sc, sc2tog, 1 sc, sc2tog, 3 sc. (16sts)
ROUND 9 8 sc, sc2tog, 1 sc, sc2tog, 3 sc. (14sts)
ROUND 10 Sc in each st to end.
ROUND 11 Sc2tog, sc in each st to end. (13sts)
ROUNDS 12-16 Sc in each st to end.
ROUND 17 Sc2tog, sc in each st to end. (12sts)
ROUNDS 18-22 Sc in each st to end.
ROUND 23 Sc2tog, sc in each st to end. (11sts)
ROUNDS 24-28 Sc in each st to end.
ROUND 29 Sc2tog, sc in each st to end. (10sts)
Cut the yarn leaving a long tail and pull through loop to secure.
Finish stuffing the legs firmly.
Thread the cut yarn onto a wool needle and weave through the last 10 stitches, pull the yarn to close the hole at the top of the leg, weave in yarn to secure. Position the legs carefully and sew onto the body.

Ears (make 2)
With yarn A, make an adjustable ring and work 6 sc into the ring. (6sts)
ROUND 1 2 sc into each st to end. (12sts)
ROUND 2 *1 sc, 2 sc in next st; rep from * to end. (18sts)
ROUND 3 Sc in each st to end.
ROUND 4 *2 sc, 2 sc in next st; rep from * to end. (24sts)
ROUND 5 sc in each st to end.
ROUND 6 *3 sc, 2 sc in next st; rep from * to end. (30sts)
ROUNDS 7-8 Sc in each st to end.
ROUND 9 Sc2tog, sc in each st to end. (29sts)
ROUND 10 Sc2tog, sc in each st to end. (28sts)
Cut the yarn, leaving a long tail, and secure.
Cut two pieces of felt and stitch them inside the ears using running stitch. Try not to allow the stitches to go through to the outer ear.
Sew the ears onto the head. Weave in and cut off any loose ends. Tie a velvet ribbon around the bear's neck.

Felted crochet

When felted, crochet shrinks, and it is not possible to control the exact amount of shrinkage. Luckily, there are many things you can make from felted crochet that do not require precise sizes, from pillow covers to simple bags. Motifs cut from felt also make great brooches or decoration on other crochet.

Felting basics

If you are a beginner, avoid attempting a felted garment pattern until you have gained some experience with felting smaller items. Before taking the plunge into a specific project, read all about the felting basics below and discover some helpful tips. The best yarns for felted crochet are 100 percent wool yarns and other animal fiber yarns that have not been spun too tightly, such as roving yarns. As a rule, the longer the fibers of a yarn, the more easily they felt. A mixed fiber yarn with at least 50 percent wool or feltable animal fiber will felt to varying degrees, and it is best to try a test swatch first to see if a yarn felts, since some wools have been treated to prevent felting. Always avoid wool yarns marked "machine washable," since these will not felt.

Preparing a swatch for test-felting

By testing a swatch of your yarn, you can determine how much it will shrink when felted. But keep in mind that felting is not an exact science because of all these variables—washing machine agitation, water temperature, detergent type, and yarn fiber content, spin, and color.

Work a swatch in single crochet that is approximately 8in (20cm) square; accurate shrinkage measurements cannot be obtained with smaller swatches because they shrink more than is usual.

To measure the gauge before and after felting, tie yarn markers around stitches in the crochet using a different-colored yarn, which preferably does not felt. Place them about 20 stitches apart on one row horizontally and about 20 rows apart vertically, making a note of how many stitches are in between. You then have obvious markers once the piece has been felted, so that you can take a measurement of distance between stitches and rows. Since you know the number of rows and stitches within those markers, you can calculate the gauge per in/cm and therefore the amount that your swatch has shrunk.

Prepare a swatch as explained above, then put it in your washing machine and add in a large hand towel. (The towel increases the agitation in the water to enable the felting process and should always be put in with your felting.) Add half the amount of laundry detergent normally used for a full load. Use a water temperature of warm for yarn that contains any mohair, and hot for 100 percent wool yarns.

Wash the sample using the full washing cycle and the full spin for that cycle. Tug the washed swatch gently in both directions, then lay it right-side up on your ironing board and pat it into a rectangular shape.

Leave it to dry completely—the shrinkage is only complete when the felt is totally dry. If necessary, do more tests with new swatches, altering the temperature or the length of the wash cycle. Keep detailed records of your testing, listing gauge, hook size, sizes of pre-felted and felted swatch, machine setting, and the type and amount of detergent.

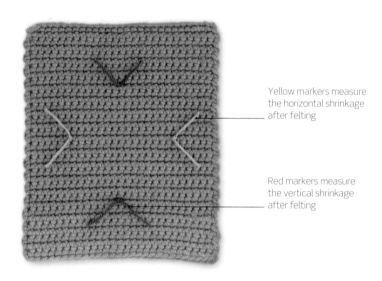

Yellow markers measure the horizontal shrinkage after felting

Red markers measure the vertical shrinkage after felting

Tips for felting

- If you are trying out felting for the first time, make several test swatches in different weights of yarn and felt them together in the same washing-machine load, so you can get a feel for the different thicknesses of crocheted felt.
- Do not tightly crochet your projects before felting because they will felt better with more room to move within the stitches, since agitation is the most important part of creating a felted item.
- When using highly contrasting colors in the same piece of crochet or putting them in the same felting load, put a color catcher in the washing machine. This absorbs loose dye and will prevent colors from running.
- Wool will fade slightly when felted, due to the high temperatures and the detergent, but this adds an attractive quality to the felt.
- Clean your washing machine after a felting load by wiping it out with a damp cloth to remove any stray fibers.

Before and after felting

Crochet changes character when it is felted, softening and shrinking—sometimes more widthwise than lengthwise, but it depends on the yarn. Integrated decorative effects can be achieved with crocheted stripes or embroidery worked onto the crochet prior to felting.

Single crochet swatches

You can see that the felted swatch is considerably smaller than the unfelted, but when compared to the half double swatch below, it is not as completely felted. You can still see the stitches quite clearly. This happens for two reasons: first, a single crochet is a small, tight stitch, so the yarn within the fabric has very little room to move and create the desired amount of friction to aid felting. Second, the sample is striped, and different colors have a bearing on felting. Two yarns of different colors may felt slightly differently, due to the diverse chemical makeup in the dyes, and because the yarn might have already felted slightly during the dye process.

Single crochet swatch before felting
Width = 8in (20cm);
Length = 8in (20cm)

Single crochet swatch after felting
Width = 6½in (16.5cm);
Length = 7¼in (18.5cm)

Half double swatches

The half double stitch is a looser, taller stitch, with more gaps in the fabric than a single crochet stitch. This has resulted in a much more tightly felted fabric than the single crochet test swatch (above), since the yarn has more room to create the desired amount of friction. You can work out the amount that your final project will felt from this test, by working out the ratio of shrinkage in the measurements.

Remember that if your project is made of different pieces sewn together, you must do this first since each piece will felt slightly differently and unevenly—this can be seen in the irregular edges at the bottom of the single crochet felted swatch. Also, the sewing up of the pieces might affect the felting. Felting is always an unknown quantity, and the test swatching is purely for a guide to gauge.

Half double crochet swatch before felting
Width = 8in (20cm);
Length = 8in (20cm)

Half double crochet swatch after felting
Width = 6¼in (16cm);
Length = 6¾in (17cm)

Project patterns

Blankets and pillows

Essential information

DIFFICULTY LEVEL Intermediate

SIZE Approx 31½ x 47¼ (35½ x 67:39½ x 74¾)in/ 80 x 120 (90 x 170:100 x190)cm

YARN Use any DK yarn, wool or acrylic, or a mix will work well, or use scraps of DK

A x 4 B x 1 C x 1 D x 1 E x 1

F x 1 G x 1 H x 1 I x 1 J x 1

K x 1 L x 1

CROCHET HOOK G/6 US (4mm) hook

NOTIONS Yarn needle

GAUGE Exact gauge is not essential

SPECIAL ABBREVIATIONS

PUFF: (Yo, insert hook into st, yo and pull through loop, drawing it up to height of hdc) 4 times, 9 loops on hook, yo and pull through all loops on hook.

POPCORN: See p. 79

Flower blanket

This vibrant update of the vintage-inspired flower blanket is crocheted together, not sewn, so it looks great from both sides without any ugly seams. This blanket is an ideal project for using up scraps of yarn.

PROJECTS
For more flower patterns
>> *go to pages 80 and 148*

Flower motifs

ROUND 1 With any contrast shade, work 3 ch to count as first dc, work 1 dc into third ch from hook, then work 10 further dc into same chain. Join round with a ss.
Change color.
ROUND 2 Ch 2, work 1 puff into first dc, 1 ch, *1 puff, 1 ch; rep from * to end of round, join round with a ss. Change color.
ROUND 3 Ch 3, work popcorn into bottom of chain, 3 ch, *work popcorn into next 1-ch sp, 3 ch; rep from * to end of round, join round with a ss.
Make enough flower motifs in the same way for the desired size of blanket. For a small blanket, work 96 flowers; for a medium blanket, work 153 flowers; for a large blanket work 190 flowers.

Joining the motifs

With the border shade, work a final row around one flower motif as follows:
Join yarn to any 3-ch sp. 3 ch, (1 dc, 3 ch, 2

dc) all into same sp, *(2 dc, 1 ch, 2 dc) into next 3-ch sp twice, (2 dc, 3 ch, 2 dc) into next 3-ch sp; rep from * twice more, (2 dc, 1 ch, 2 dc) into next 3-ch sp twice, join round with a ss.
To join the next flower to the first finished motif, work border around the next flower as follows:
With the border shade, join yarn to any 3-ch sp. 3 ch, (1 dc, 3 ch, 2 dc) all into same sp, (2 dc, 1 ch, 2 dc) into next 3-ch sp twice, (2 dc, 1 ch) into next 3-ch sp, work a ss into the central ch of any 3-ch corner sp of first motif to join the corners, 1 ch, 2 dc back into original 3-ch sp of second motif. *2 dc into next 3-ch sp, ss into next 1-ch sp of first motif, 2 dc back into original 3-ch sp of second motif; rep from * once more, (2 dc, 1 ch) into next 3-ch sp, ss into central ch of next corner ch of first motif, 1 ch, 2 dc back into original 3-ch sp of second motif, (2 dc, 1 ch, 2 dc) into next 3-ch sp twice, (2 dc, 3 ch, 2 dc) into next 3-ch sp, (2 dc, 1 ch, 2 dc) into next 3-ch sp twice, join round with a ss.
Work all following motifs from first row in the same way as this, joining each subsequent flower to the previous motif along one side. On the second row of motifs, join first flower of the row to the motif below in the same way as previously stated. For all following motifs, join along two sides to the motifs immediately adjacent and below it in the same way as before. For a small blanket arrange 8 motifs wide by 12 motifs long. For a medium blanket, arrange 9 motifs wide by 17 motifs long. For a large blanket, arrange 10 motifs wide by 19 motifs long.

Finishing

With the border shade, attach yarn to any corner of blanket.
Ch 3, 4 dc into same corner sp, continue around the whole blanket working (2 dc, 1 ch, 2 dc) into every 1-ch sp, (2 dc, 1 ch, 2 dc) into each joining sp of two motifs and 5 dc into each corner sp. Join round with a ss.
Weave in all ends and block very lightly to shape, being careful not to flatten the 3-D nature of the flower motifs.

Each flower motif measures approx 3in (8cm) in diameter and makes a quick project to work up when time is short. If you have any left over, sew pin backs onto them and turn them into pins.

Lap blanket

This warm and cozy blanket works up surprisingly quickly thanks to the super bulky yarn and large hook. The tweed stitch is simply composed of single crochet and chain stitch, creating a luxurious texture with minimal effort.

PROJECTS
For more single crochet patterns
>> *go to pages 34 and 292*

Essential information

DIFFICULTY LEVEL Easy

SIZE Approx 38½ x 47¼in (98 x 120cm)

YARN Any super bulky weight wool or acrylic yarn will substitute. Try alpaca for a heavyweight blanket

A x 8   **B** x 2

CROCHET HOOK N/15 US (10mm) hook

NOTIONS Yarn needle

GAUGE Exact gauge is not essential

SPECIAL ABBREVIATIONS
CRAB STITCH: Means simply working sc in reverse, working round the row, or round in this case, from left to right, instead of right to left. After completing a row of sc, do not turn the work around; work 1 ch, *insert the hook into the next stitch to the right, not in the stitch you just completed, but the next one. Draw a loop through. Yo as normal and pull through both loops on the hook; rep from * across row.

Adding a trim around the blanket will give your project a professional finish, with an even edge around all sides. See pp. 174 and 240 for more projects with crab stitch edging.

Pattern
With yarn A, work 81 ch.
ROW 1 1 sc into second ch from hook, (1 ch, skip 1 ch, sc in next ch) to end.
ROW 2 Ch 1, sc in first sc, sc in ch sp, (1 ch, 1 sc into ch sp) to end, sc into last sc.
ROW 3 Ch 1, sc in first sc, (1 ch, sc into ch sp) to last ch sp, skip next sc, sc in last sc. Rep last two rows until work measures approximately 47¼in (120cm) long, or desired length. Fasten off yarn.

Finishing
Block blanket lightly.
Attach yarn B to any point around edge and work evenly in sc around entire edge, working 3 sc into each corner. Join round with a ss, but do not turn; instead, work 1 row in crab stitch.
Fasten off yarn, weave in ends, and block edge lightly.

>> This blanket is made with Lion Brand Wool Ease Thick & Quick, 49yds/45m/50g, in A: Fisherman (099) and B: Cranberry (138).

Colorful granny blanket

Reminiscent of a rainbow, this blanket uses the bright tones of the yarn to great effect. The join-as-you-go technique, using the white yarn, creates a pretty border and saves time, which is great when creating a large item such as this.

PROJECTS

For more blanket patterns
>> go to pages 142, 144, and 148

Essential information

DIFFICULTY LEVEL Intermediate

SIZE Approx 71 x 43½in (180 x 110cm)

YARN Any weight or fiber content will work here. Try wool for a warmer blanket. Change the hook to suit the yarn and remember that the blanket may come out a different size or texture

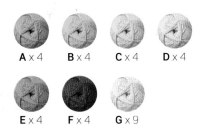

A x 4   B x 4   C x 4   D x 4

E x 4   F x 4   G x 9

CROCHET HOOK G/6 US (4mm) hook

NOTIONS Yarn needle

GAUGE Exact gauge is not essential

Pattern

Work 4 ch, join with a ss to form a ring.
ROUND 1 Ch 3 (counts as first dc), 2 dc in ring, 3 ch, *3 dc in ring, 3 ch; rep from * twice. Join round with ss to top of first ch.
ROUND 2 Ss to next corner sp, 3 ch, (1 dc, 3 ch, 2 dc) into corner sp, 3 dc, *(2 dc, 3 ch, 2 dc) into next corner sp, 3 dc; rep from * to end of round. Join round with ss to top of first ch.
ROUND 3 Ss to next corner sp, 3 ch, (1 dc, 3 ch, 2 dc) into corner sp, 1 dc into each dc to next corner sp, *(2 dc, 3 ch, 2 dc) into next corner sp, 1 dc into each dc to next corner sp; rep from * to end of round. Join round with ss to top of first ch.
Rep last round twice.
Fasten off yarn.
Make 14 squares of each color; 84 squares in total. Block all pieces lightly.

Joining

Arrange each set of colors in order as in the photograph. Attach yarn G to corner sp of first square and complete next round as round 3. Take next square and work round 2 sides as per round 3, when you get to the corner sp, work 2 dc, 1 ch into corner, then attach square 2 to square 1 with a ss to the corresponding corner, 1 ch, 2 dc into corner, ss to the corresponding st of square 1, then *work 3 sts along the next side as usual, ss to the corresponding st of square 1; rep from * to next corner, 2 dc, 1 ch into corner, join to the corresponding corner ch, then work along the remaining side as normal without a join. Two squares are joined.

Continue joining the first row of 7 squares in the same way, then join each square of the next row to the top of the first in the same way; you will need to join along two sides of some squares from this row.

Edging

Join yarn G to any corner space.
Work 1 row of doubles all around, working (2 dc, 3 ch, 2 dc) into the corner spaces as before.

Turn to pages 102–106 for more information about the classic granny square, plus additional patterns for different squares, triangles, and other motifs.

>> This blanket is made with Classic Elite Wool Bamboo DK, 118ds/108m/50g, in A: True blue (1692), B: Treasure (1660), C: Artichoke green (1672), D: Solid gold (1680), E: Watermelon (1689), F: Mulberry (1634), and G: White (1616).

Baby blanket

This charming throw is made using the "join-as-you-go" method, so that you don't have all the squares to join at the end.

PROJECTS
For more granny square patterns
>> *go to pages 146 and 154*

Essential information

DIFFICULTY LEVEL Easy/Intermediate

SIZE Approx 36¼ x 42in (92 x 107cm)

YARN You can use any DK wool or wool-mix yarn to achieve a similar effect

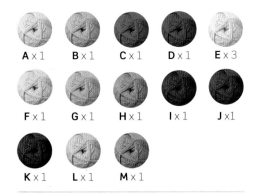

A x 1   B x 1   C x 1   D x 1   E x 3

F x 1   G x 1   H x 1   I x 1   J x 1

K x 1   L x 1   M x 1

CROCHET HOOK G/6 US (4mm) hook

GAUGE Exact gauge is not essential

NOTIONS Yarn needle

SPECIAL ABBREVIATIONS

WORKING BETWEEN POSTS/STITCHES: Rather than inserting your hook under the top "V" of the stitch of the previous round (in this case, a double) you will insert your hook underneath the actual stitch and therefore between the posts of the stitches of the previous round. This is done so that the "petals" will open up and separate once the square is complete.

SLIP STITCH JOIN FOR JOIN-AS-YOU-GO:
Holding one square, which has been completed up to and including round 2, to a complete square (up to and including round 3) to join as you go, you replace the 3-ch corner sp with 1 ch, 1 ss join, 1 ch, after making the first cluster for that corner. Replace the 1-ch sp between clusters along the side with 1 ss join.

TO COMPLETE THE STITCH: Insert the hook into the sp (either 3-ch corner sp or 1-ch edge sp), yo, bring yarn from back of ch sp to the front, and also through the loop on the hook.

SLIP STITCH JOIN: Put hook into stitch, yo, bring yarn through stitch, and loop on hook.

Pattern

Make 168 squares in total for a blanket of the same size as the one shown here.

For all squares

FOUNDATION With your choice of color, 4 ch, ss into first st to form a ring.

ROUND 1 Ch 3 (counts as a dc), 11 dc into ring. Join with a ss to third ch of 3 ch. Fasten off. (12sts)

ROUND 2 With a second color, join new color working between the posts/stitch of the stitches of round 1 throughout. Ch 3 (counts as a double) and 1 dc into same sp between posts, 2 dc in each sp to end. Join with a ss to third ch of 3 ch. Fasten off. (24sts)

For first square only

ROUND 3 With a third color, join new color working between the posts/stitch of the stitches of round 2 throughout. Ch 3 (counts as a double), 2 dc into same place. Ch 3 (corner sp), 3 dc into same place (forms a corner). *Ch 1, skip 3 sts from round 2, 3 dc in next sp. Ch 1, skip 3 sts from round 2, 3 dc, 3 ch, 3 dc into next sp. Repeat from *2 times, ch 1, skip 3 sts from round 2, 3 dc in next sp, 1 ch, join with a ss into third ch of 3 ch. Fasten off, weave in ends.

For all other squares

Hold unfinished square against a finished (to round 3) square, RS facing.

When joining to 1 completed square

ROUND 3 When joining to 1 completed square, with your third color choice join new color, work between the posts/stitch of the stitches of round 2 throughout. Ch 3 (counts as a double), 2 dc into same place. Ch 1, 1 ss join into 3-ch corner sp of completed square, 1 ch, 3 dc into same place (forms a corner). 1 ss join into next 1-ch sp of completed square, skip 3 sts from round 2, 3 dc in next sp. 1 ss join into next 1-ch sp of completed square, skip 3 sts from round 2, 3 dc in next sp, 1 ch, 1 ss join into 3-ch corner sp of completed square, 1 ch, 3 dc into same sp. *Ch 1, skip 3 sts from round 2, 3 dc in next sp,

>> This blanket is made with Rowan Pure Wool DK, 137yds/125m/50g, in A: Pier (006), B: Cypress (007), C: Marine (008), D: Indigo (010), E: Enamel (013), F: Avocado (019), G: Tea rose (025), H: Hyacinth (026), I: Kiss (036), J: Port (037), K: Dahlia (042), L: Gold (051), and M: Orchid (052).

Plan the color scheme for your blanket before buying any yarn. This project contains a vast array of colors and you need to make sure that the shades work together before buying expensive balls of yarn. Make a color sketch to suit your palette and then crochet a few squares as samples.

1 ch, skip 3 dc from round 2, 3 dc, 3 ch, 3 dc into next sp. Repeat from * once. Ch 1, skip 3 sts from round 2, 3 dc into next sp, 1 ch, join with a ss into third ch of 3 ch. Fasten off, weave in ends.

When joining to 2 squares

Hold the unfinished square against the finished squares, RS facing (one square above, one square to the left of that square).

ROUND 3 Join new color and work between the posts/stitch of the stitches of round 2 throughout. Ch 3 (counts as a double), 2 dc into same place. Ch 1, 1 ss join into 3-ch corner sp of completed square above, 1 ch, 3 dc into same place (forms a corner). 1 ss join into next 1-ch sp of completed square above, skip 3 sts from round 2, 3 dc in next sp, 1 ss join into next 1-ch sp of completed square above, skip 3 sts from round 2, 3 dc in next sp, 1 ss join into 3-ch corner sp of completed square above, 1 ss join into 3-ch corner sp of completed square to top left, 1 ch, 3 dc in same sp. *Ch 1, skip 3 sts from round 2, 3 dc in next sp, 1 ch, skip 3 dc from round 2, 3 dc, 3 ch, 3 dc into next sp. Repeat from * once. Ch 1, skip 3 st from round 2, 3 dc into next sp, 1 ch, join with a ss into third ch of 3 ch. Fasten off, weave in ends.

When joining to 3 completed squares

Hold the unfinished square against the finished squares, RS facing (one square above, one square to the left of that square, one square to the left of this square).

ROUND 3 Join new color and work between the posts/stitch of the stitches of round 2 throughout. Ch 3 (counts as a double), 2 dc into same place. Ch 1, 1 ss join into 3-ch corner sp of completed square above, 1 ch, 3 dc into same place (forms a corner). 1 ss join into next 1-ch sp of completed square above, skip 3 sts from round 2, 3 dc in next sp, 1 ss join into next 1-ch sp of completed square above, skip 3 sts from round 2, 3 dc in next sp, 1 ss join into 3-ch corner sp of completed square above, 1 ss join into 3-ch corner sp of completed square to top left, 1 ss join into 3-ch corner sp of completed square to left, 3 dc in same sp. 1 ss join into next 1-ch sp of completed square to left, skip 3 sts from round 2, 3 dc in next sp, 1 ss join into next 1-ch sp of completed square to left, skip 3 dc from round 2, 3 dc in next sp, 1 ch, 1 ss join into 3-ch corner sp of completed square to left, 1 ch, 3 dc into same sp. Ch 1, skip 3 sts from round 2, 3 dc in next sp, 1 ch, skip 3 sts from round 2, 3 dc, 3 ch, 3 dc in next sp, 1 ch, skip 3 sts from round 2, 3 dc into next sp, 1 ch, join with a ss into third ch of 3 ch. Fasten off and weave in ends.

Edging

ROW 1 With yarn B, or your choice of color, join in any 3-ch corner sp. Ch 3, 2 dc, 3 ch, 3 dc. 1 dc in each dc along each edge, 1 dc in each 1-ch sp and 2 dc into each 3-ch corner sp from square below. 3 dc, 3 ch, 3 dc in each 3-ch corner sp. Join with a ss and fasten off.

ROW 2 With yarn A, join in any 3-ch corner sp. Ch 3, 2 dc, 3 ch, 3 dc. 1 dc in each dc along each edge. 3 dc, 3 ch, 3 dc in each 3-ch corner sp. Join with a ss and fasten off.

Each granny square, or motif, starts with a foundation ring. Turn to page 26 for more information about how to use slip stitches to form a foundation ring.

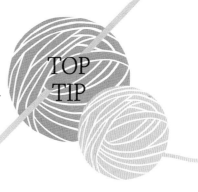

Practise joining motifs with some sample squares.

TOP TIP

Chevron pillow

Working chevrons in stripes produces a striking fabric with little effort. Regular shaping creates the peaks and troughs, while the crisp cotton makes for well-defined zigzags.

PROJECTS
For more striped patterns
>> *go to pages 174, 206, and 246*

Essential information

DIFFICULTY LEVEL Easy

SIZE Approx 13¾ x 13¾in (35 x 35cm)

YARN Any DK yarn will substitute here. This uses cotton, but try a wool mix as an alternative

A x 1   **B** x 1   **C** x 1

CROCHET HOOK G/6 US (4mm) hook

NOTIONS Yarn needle
14in (35cm) square pillow form
2 black buttons

GAUGE Exact gauge is not essential

<< This pillow is made with Casacade Yarns Ultra Pima DK, 220yds/201m/50g, in A: White (3728), B: Lipstick red (3755), and C: True black (3754).

Pattern
With yarn A, work 73 ch.
ROW 1 1 sc into second ch from hook, 1 sc in each ch to end. Turn. (72sts)
ROW 2 Ch 1, 1 sc into same st, 7 sc, skip next 2 sc, 7 sc, *2 sc in each of next 2 sts, 7 sc, skip next 2 sc, 7 sc; rep from * to last st, 2 sc in last st. Turn.
Row 2 forms pattern, rep for desired length of fabric, changing color after every 4 rows in this order:
Yarn A
Yarn B
Yarn C
When fabric measures approx 30in (75cm), ending with four rows of yarn A, fasten off yarn and weave in ends.

Finishing
Block piece lightly to shape.
Wrap piece around pillow form, with an overlap halfway down the back of the pad. Make sure that the starting edge of the piece is on top, and is overlapping the bottom of the piece. Sew up bottom two side seams of the pillow, then sew down the top two side seams, overlapping the bottom seam. Fasten the opening of the pillow by sewing buttons on the bottom edge of the piece, corresponding to the skipped sc sts next to the end of each point. These will form the buttonholes.

To ensure that the crochet doesn't stretch after the pillow form is inserted, make a couple of whipstitches under the buttons to join the two white zigzags on the flap and the backing of the pillow cover.

Granny pillow

This chic update on the humble granny square is quick to make but has high impact. The pattern produces a stylish pillow that is simple even for beginners.

PROJECTS

For more granny square patterns
>> *go to pages 234 and 288*

Essential information

DIFFICULTY LEVEL Easy

SIZE 16in (40cm) square

YARN You can substitute any DK weight yarn for this project

A x 2   **B** x 2   **C** x 4   **D** x 2

CROCHET HOOK F/5 US (3.75mm) hook

NOTIONS Yarn needle
16 x 16in 40 x 40cm) pillow form

GAUGE Rounds 1-3 measure 3in (8cm)

The open nature of this giant granny square means that the pillow form will show through the crochet fabric. The white pillow form shown here works well because the main color is white. However, if you prefer to make your pillow in different shades, you may wish to choose a colored insert or cover the pillow form before placing it inside the crocheted cover.

Pattern (make 2)

Always work with RS facing.

With yarn A, 4 ch, ss in first ch to form a ring.

ROUND 1 Ch 4 (counts as 1 dc and 1 ch), *3 dc into ring, 1 ch, rep from * twice, 3 dc into ring, join with a ss to third of 4 ch. Fasten off A.

ROUND 2 Join B into any ch sp, 3 ch (counts as first dc), 2 dc, 2 ch, 3 dc in same ch sp, 1 ch, *3 dc, 2 ch, 3 dc in next ch sp, 1 ch; rep from * twice, join with a ss in top of initial 3 ch. Fasten off B.

ROUND 3 Join C into any corner ch sp, 3 ch (counts as first dc), 2 dc, 2 ch, 3 dc in same ch sp, 1 ch, 3 dc in next ch sp, 1 ch, *3 dc, 2 ch, 3 dc in next ch sp, 1 ch, 3 dc in next ch sp, 1 ch; rep from * twice, join with a ss in top of initial 3 ch. Fasten off C.

ROUND 4 Join D into any corner ch sp, 3 ch (counts as first dc), 2 dc, 2 ch, 3 dc in ch sp, 1 ch, 3 dc in next ch sp, 1 ch, 3 dc in next ch sp, 1 ch, *3 dc, 2 ch, 3 dc in next ch sp, 1 ch, 3 dc in next ch sp, 1 ch, 3 dc in next ch sp, 1 ch; rep from * twice, join with a ss in top of initial 3 ch. Fasten off D.

Continue working each round in color sequence as follows, working as round 4; each round will have 1 extra 3 dc in ch sp worked on each side of the square, corners remain the same.

ROUNDS 5 AND 6 Yarn C.

ROUND 7 Yarn A.

ROUNDS 8 AND 9 Yarn C.

ROUND 10 Yarn B.

ROUNDS 11 AND 12 Yarn C.

ROUND 13 Yarn D.

ROUND 14 Yarn C.

ROUND 15 Yarn A.

Where two rounds are worked consecutively in C, you may prefer to ss to next corner space instead of fastening off and rejoining yarn. Fasten off yarn, weave in ends.

Finishing

Press front and back according to ball band instructions. Place front and back with wrong sides together, rejoin A to top left corner space, and working through front and back, join on three sides as follows: 1 sc in ch sp, *1 sc in top of each of next 3 dc, 1 sc in ch sp; rep from * to corner, 3 sc in corner ch sp; rep from * to next corner sp, 3 sc in corner ch sp; rep from * to top right-hand corner. Leaving the top of the pillow open, insert pillow form and close by continuing in sc to first st, ss into top of first sc.
Fasten off yarn, weave in ends.

>> This pillow is made with Debbie Bliss Cotton DK, 92yds/84m/50g, in A: Fuchsia (58), B: Aqua (61), C: Cream (02), and D: Periwinkle (62).

Owl pillow

This colorful toy owl is made in Tunisian Simple stitch. You can practice the technique, which uses a long crochet hook, on a sample square before attempting the shaping used for this project.

PROJECTS

For another Tunisian stitch pattern
>> *go to page 124*

Essential information

DIFFICULTY LEVEL Difficult

SIZE 15 x 12¼in (38 x 31cm)

YARN You can use any DK weight yarn for a similar look to this project

A x 3   **B** x 1   **C** x 1   **D** x 1

E small amount   **F** small amount

CROCHET HOOK G/6 US (4mm) and H/8 US (5mm) hook I/9 US (5mm) Tunisian hook

NOTIONS Yarn needle
20in (50cm) cotton fabric suitable for a pillow form
Approx 8oz (220g) polyfill

GAUGE 17 sts x 16 rows to 4in (10cm)

<< This owl is made with Rowan Handknit Cotton, 93yds/85m/50g, in A: Linen (205), B: Ecru (251), C: Raspberry (356), D: Blue John (365), E: Ochre (349), and F: Black (252).

SPECIAL ABBREVIATIONS (SEE P.124)

TSS: Tunisian Simple stitch: Chain any number to length desired.

FOUNDATION ROW:

Forward pass: Insert hook into first ch sp from hook. Yo and pull up a loop. *Insert into next, yo and pull up a loop. Repeat from * keeping all loops on hook.
Return pass: Yo and pull back through one loop. * Yo and pull through two loops. Repeat from * until one loop remains on hook.

ROWS:

Forward pass: Working forward again, *insert hook from side to side under next vertical bar (behind front bar and in front of back bar), yo and draw up a loop. Repeat from * to last, keeping all loops on hook. Pull up a loop from the last st.
Return pass: Yo and pull back through one loop. * Yo and pull through two loops. Repeat from * until one loop remains on hook.
Repeat the second row. In the pattern, the pickup and takeoff are written as one row.

INCREASE: On the forward pass, put your hook under the horizontal bar between the normal vertical pickup points. Yo, and pull the new loop on the hook, inc complete.

DECREASE: On the forward pass, put your hook under two vertical loops, yo, and pull through both loops, dec complete.

TYING IN COLORS: This is done on the return pass of the row. When you have the last loop of yarn A on the hook, put your yarn over color B so the yarns are twisted, then take off as normal in B.

Front

ROW 1 With the Tunisian hook and yarn A, 25 ch; pick up the loops (25 loops on hook), work return pass.

ROW 2 Pick up a st (2 loops on the hook) inc, pick up the next 21 st, inc, pick up last 2 st (27 loops on hook). Return pass.

ROW 3 As row 2, inc between the second and third st, and between third and second st at the other end (29 loops). Return pass.

ROW 4 As row 2. (31 loops)

ROW 5 As row 2. (33 loops)

ROW 6 START WINGS Divid yarn C in half so you have two balls of yarn C. Take yarn A off the hook, with yarn C make a slip knot and 3 ch, pick up 2 loops. (3 loops of yarn C on hook) pick up the loop in yarn A, pick up the rest of the row in yarn A. In yarn C, make a slip knot and 3 ch, pick up 2 st. (3 yarn C sts on hook). (3C, 33A, 3C = 39 sts). Return pass.
See "tying in colors" instructions (left) for this and subsequent rows when taking off loops.

ROW 7 With yarn C, pick up 3 loops (4 loops on hook), pick up 31 loops of A, and 4 in C (4C, 31A, 4C = 39 sts). Work return pass in color sequence from now on.

ROW 8 With yarn C, pick up a loop, inc, pick up 2 more loops in C, 31 in A, 2 in C, inc, pick up last 2 loops.(5C, 31A, 5C = 41 sts). Fasten off A.

ROW 9 Pick up so you have 6C on the hook, 29D and 6C. (41sts)

ROW 10 Inc between second and third st, and third and second st at the other end. Pick up so you have 7C, 29D, and 7C. (43sts)

ROW 11 Pick up 8C, 27D, and 8C. (43sts)

ROW 12 Inc as row 10, 10C, 25A, 10C. (45sts)

From now on you will be given the color sequence needed on the hook for each row, and inc as row 10.

ROW 13 C10, A25, C10. (45sts)

ROW 14 Inc row C12, A23, C12. (47sts)

ROW 15 Inc row C13, A23, C13. Fasten off A. (49sts)

ROW 16 C13, D23, and C13. (49sts)

ROW 17 C13, D23, and C13. (49sts)

ROW 18 Inc row C14, D23, C14. Fasten off D. (51sts)

ROW 19 C14, A23, C14. (51sts)

ROW 20 C14, A23, C14. (51sts)

ROW 21 Inc row C15, A23, C15. (53sts)

ROW 22 C15, A23, C15. Fasten off A. (53sts)

ROW 23 C15, D23, C15. (53sts)

ROW 24 As row 23.

ROW 25 C14, D25, C14. Fasten off D. (53sts)

ROW 26 C13, A27, C13. (53sts)

ROW 27 C13, A27, C13. (53sts)

ROW 28 C13, A27, C13. (53sts)

ROW 29 C12, A29, C12. Fasten off A. (53sts)

ROW 30 C12, D29, C12. (53sts)

ROW 31 C12, D29, C12. (53sts)

ROW 32 Start dec at outer edges, (see "decrease" instructions, p.157). The end of the row dec is done 3 sts from the end, then pick up the last st as usual. In C pick up first st, dec, pick up 8 more sts in C, 31 in D, 8 in C, dec, pick up last st. (C10, D31, C10 = 51 sts). Fasten off D.

ROW 33 C10, A31, C10. (51sts)

ROW 34 Dec either end as before, C8, A33, C8. (49sts)

ROW 35 C8, A33, C8. (49sts)

ROW 36 You will now be starting the head. Dec either end. C6, A10, B15, (start with a second ball of A) A10, C6. (47sts)

ROW 37 C5, A9, B19, A9, C5. (47sts)

ROW 38 Dec either end C3, A8, B23, A8, C3. (45sts)

ROW 39 Dec either end C2, A6, B27, A6, C2. (43sts)

Return pass: you will also be working dec on this part of the row. Yo, and pull through 2 loops, take off in the normal manner until you have 3 loops on the hook, yo and in C pull through all 3 loops. Fasten off C. (41sts)

ROW 40 With yarn A, pull a loop through the

last C st, A5, B31, A5. (41sts)

ROW 41 Dec either end, A2, B35, A2. Fasten off A. (39sts)

ROW 42 Put your hook under the edge A loop and pull B loop through, dec, pick up 33 loops in B, dec, pick up last loop. (37sts)

ROW 43 Dec either end. (35sts)

ROW 44 Dec either end. (33sts)

ROW 45 Dec either end. (31sts)

ROW 46 Dec either end. (29sts)

ROWS 47–53 TSS. (29sts)

ROW 54 Inc either end. (31sts)

ROW 55 Inc either end. (33sts)

ROW 56 START EARS Pick up 12 st (13 loops on hook). Return pass. (13sts)

ROW 57 Pick up 7 loops (8 loops on hook). Return pass.

ROWS 58–63 Pick up one less st each row (2 sts left on row 63).

Change to H/8 US (5mm) hook and, putting hook under vertical bars, work in ss down the ear and across the head until there are 12 sts left on row 56. Change back to Tunisian hook and pick up the rest of the row (12sts). Return pass.

ROW 57 Ss across 4 loops, pick up so you have 8 loops on the hook. Return pass.

ROWS 58–63 Work a dec at the beginning of each row. Fasten off B. Weave in all ends.

Back (work completely in A)

ROWS 1–5 As front.

ROW 6 Ch 3, pick up 2 loops, then 33 loops from body, with a spare length of A, 3 ch, pick up these loops (39 loops on the hook). Return pass.

ROWS 7–38 Work as for front, inc and dec where stated. You will have the total number of loops on the hook for each row.

ROW 39 Dec either end, work return pass as normal. (43sts)

ROW 40 Dec either end. (41sts)

ROW 41 Dec either end. (39sts)

ROW 42 Dec either end. (37sts)

ROWS 43–63 As front, fasten off, weave in ends.

Eyes (make 2)

With yarn F and G/6 US (4mm) hook, make a slip knot from the tail, 3 ch, 12 dc into the

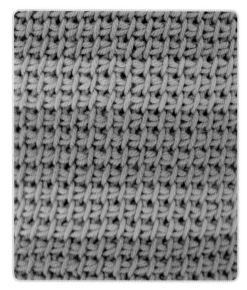

Neat stripes in blue and oatmeal represent this owl's chest plumage. For more information on changing yarn color, turn to page 39; for more colorwork techniques, refer to pages 118-121.

first ch, fasten off with an invisible join, leaving a 6in (15cm) tail for sewing onto the face. Pull up the tail so there is no hole in the center of the eye and sew firmly. With yarn B, add a V shape in the center of each eye.

Beak

With yarn E and G/6 US (4mm) hook.

ROW 1 Make a slip knot and 2 ch, sc in the first ch turn. (1 sc)

ROW 2 Ch 1, 2 sc in sc. (2sts)

ROW 3 Ch 1, 2 sc in the first sc, sc in the next sc. (3sts)

ROW 4 Ch 1, 2 sc in the first sc, sc in next 2 sts. (4sts)

NEXT ROW Working down the side of the triangle, Ch 1, 5 sc down the first side, 2 ch, 5 sc down the second side, 1 ch, sc in each sc. (14 sc)

Fasten off with an invisible join leaving an 8in (20cm) tail for sewing the beak to the face. Sew the eyes and the beak to the head.

Feet (make 2)

With yarn B and G/6 US (4mm) hook.

ROW 1 Make a slip knot and 7 ch, sc in second

ch from the hook, sc in the rest of the ch.
Turn. (6 sc)

ROW 2 Ch 1, 2 sc in the first sc, sc in the next 4
sts, 2 sc in the last sc. Turn. (6sts)

ROW 3 Ch 3, dc in the same st, dc in the next
2 sts, 2 dc in each of the next 2 sts, dc in the
next 2 sts, 2 dc in the last st. (12sts)

ROW 4 FIRST CLAW Ch 2, dc in the same st, dc
in next 2 sts, turn. (3sts)

ROW 5 Ch 2, dc dec, fasten off.

2ND CLAW Join yarn to next st on row 3.

ROW 4 Ch 3, dc dec twice, dc in the next st,
turn. (3sts)

ROW 5 Ch 2, dc dec, fasten off.

3RD CLAW Join yarn to the next st on row 3.

ROW 4 Ch 3, dc in next st, 2 dc in top of 3 ch,
turn. (3sts)

ROW 5 Ch 2, dc dec, fasten off.

DC ROUND CLAW Start at foundation ch, work
10 sc up the first side, 2 ch, 5 sc down second
side, ss into next st.

MIDDLE CLAW Sc 6 up the first side, 2 ch, 6 sc
down other side, ss into next st.

3RD CLAW Sc 5 up first side, 2 ch, 10 sc down
second side, 1 ch, sc along foundation ch, ss
into first sc, fasten off leaving a 6in (15cm)
tail for sewing to the body.

Making the pillow form

Using the front of the owl as a guide, draw
around the owl, cut out the template ¹/₂in
(1cm) larger than the outline. Cut two pieces
of material to the correct shape and sew
together, stuffing the pillow before you sew
the bottom closed.

Finishing

With H/8 US (5mm) hook and the
appropriate color, put the wrong sides of the
owl together with the front facing you, and
starting at the bottom of the wing, sc all
around, putting in the pillow form before you
sc the bottom of the pillow. Sew feet to the
bottom of the pillow.
Fasten off yarn, weave in ends.

The dense effect of Tunisian Simple stitch makes
this owl appear very neat and compact, with his raspberry
pink wings folded into his body. His feet are worked in
regular crochet stitches and sewn on.

Home and gifts

Desktop storage pots

An ideal project for beginners, these colorful and practical storage pots are quick and easy to make and can be used for storing anything from pens and stationery to jewelry. The pots are worked in a spiral and vary in size.

PROJECTS
For more storage projects
>> *go to pages 164 and 166*

For double strength, each storage pot is made rigid by working with double strands of yarn. When your pot has reached the diameter you require, begin working upward and end at your preferred height.

<< These pots are made with Shibui Knits Linen, 246yds/225m/50g, in A: Cascade (2033) and B: Lime (2024).

NOTE Place a stitch marker in the first stitch of each round, moving the marker up as each round is completed.

Tall pot
With yarn A, work 2 ch, 6 sc in second ch from hook.
ROUND 1 2 sc in each st. (12sts)
ROUND 2 *2 sc in next st, sc in next st; rep from * to end. (18sts)
ROUND 3 *2 sc in next st, sc in next 2 sts; rep from * to end. (24sts)
ROUND 4 *2 sc in next st, sc in next 3 sts; rep from * to end. (30sts)
ROUND 5 Working in back loops only, sc in each st to end.
Continue working even rounds through both loops (1 sc in each st to end) until piece measures 4in (10cm) from round 5. With yarn B, work even rounds for 3 rounds or until work reaches desired height.
Fasten off, weave in ends.

Small pot
With yarn B, work as for tall pot to end of round 5.
Continue working even rounds through both loops (1 sc in each st to end) until piece measures 2in (5cm) from round 5, or desired height.
Fasten off, weave in ends.

Wide pot
With yarn B, work as for tall pot to end of round 4.
ROUND 5 *2 sc in next st, sc in next 4 sts; rep from * to end. (36sts)
ROUND 6 *2 sc in next st, sc in next 5 sts; rep from * to end. (42sts)
ROUND 7 *2 sc in next st, sc in next 6 sts; rep from * to end. (48sts)
ROUND 8 Working in back loops only, sc in each st to end.
Continue working even rounds through both loops (1 sc in each st to end) for 4 rounds. With yarn A, work even rounds for 4 rounds or until work reaches desired height.
Fasten off, weave in ends.

Essential information

DIFFICULTY LEVEL Easy

SIZE Large: approx 8 x 6¾in (20 x 17cm)
Medium: approx 6 x 6in (15 x 15cm)
Small: approx 5½ x 4in (14 x 10cm)

YARN Any super bulky yarn will work here. You
can even try making your own yarn from old
T-shirts or jersey fabric

A x 3   **B** x 3

CROCHET HOOK P US (12mm) hook

NOTIONS Stitch marker
Large-eyed yarn needle

GAUGE Exact gauge is not essential

Structured baskets

Using such bulky yarns means these baskets work up quickly. The yarn is recycled so can vary from cone to cone. Adjust your hook as necessary for the thickness of the yarn, and crochet tightly for a rigid fabric.

PROJECTS

For more basket projects
>>go to pages 162, 174, and 176

For stylish storage, these three baskets stack neatly inside each other. Easy-to-grasp handles are crocheted into the larger two baskets for carrying.

<< These baskets are made with Lion Brand Zpaghetti yarn, 55yds/50m/340g, in A: Beige and B: Pinky red.

NOTE These baskets are worked in spirals. Do not join rounds, but place a marker at the first stitch of the round, moving it up as each round is completed.

Large basket

With yarn A, work 2 ch and work 6 sc into second ch from hook, join round with a ss to first st.

ROUND 1 Ch 1, work 2 sc in each st around, do not join round, place marker. (12sts)

ROUND 2 *2 sc in next st, 1 sc in next st, rep from * to end. (18sts)

ROUND 3 *2 sc in next st, 1 sc in next 2 sts, rep from * to end. (24sts)

ROUND 4 *2 sc in next st, 1 sc in next 3 sts, rep from * to end. (30sts)

ROUND 5 *2 sc in next st, 1 sc in next 4 sts, rep from * to end. (36sts)

ROUND 6 *2 sc in next st, 1 sc in next 5 sts, rep from * to end. Join round with a ss. (42sts)

ROUND 7 Ch 1, 1 sc TBL into each st around. Join with ss.

ROUND 8 Ch 1, 1 sc into each st around. Do not join round.

Work last round 5 times.

ROUND 14 Ch 3, dc into bottom of same st, skip next st, *2 dc into next st, skip next st; rep from * to end of round, join to top of first ch with a ss.

Work 1 round as round 8.

ROUND 16 Ch 1, 7 sc, 7 ch, skip next 7 sc, 14 sc, 7 ch, skip next 7 sc, sc to end.

ROUND 17 Ch 1, (sc to 7-ch sp, 7 sc into ch sp) twice, sc to end, join round with a ss. Fasten off yarn, weave in ends.

Medium basket

With yarn A, work as for large basket to round 5. (36sts)

ROUND 6 Ch 1, 1 sc TBL into each st around. Join with ss.

ROUND 7 Ch 1, 1 sc into each st around. Do not join round.

Work last round 3 times, then change to yarn B and work 2 rounds.

ROUND 13 Ch 1, 6 sc, 6 ch, skip next 6 sc, 12 sc, 6 ch, skip next 6 sc, sc to end.

ROUND 14 Ch 1, (sc to 6 ch sp, 6 sc into ch sp) twice, sc to end, join round with a ss. Fasten off yarn, weave in ends.

Small basket

With yarn B, work as for large basket to round 4. (30sts)

ROUND 5 Ch 1, 1 sc TBL into each st around. Join with ss.

Change to yarn A.

ROUND 6 Ch 1, 1 sc into each st around. Do not join round.

Work last round 4 times. Join round with a ss. Fasten off yarn, weave in ends.

Hanging toy basket

This pretty accessory will brighten up any child's playroom. Constructed in spirals using single crochet, it can easily be tackled by a beginner. Instructions are given for a medium and large toy basket.

PROJECTS
For more spiral patterns
>> *go to pages 170 and 174*

Essential information

DIFFICULTY LEVEL Easy

SIZE 9¾ (12) x 15¾ (17¾)in/25 (30) x 40 (45)cm

YARN Any aran weight or cotton blend can be used here

A x 1   **B** x 1   **C** x 1

CROCHET HOOK E/4 US (3.5mm) hook

NOTIONS Stitch marker
Yarn needle

GAUGE 14 sts x 16 rows per 4in (10cm)

NOTE Worked in the round in a spiral, do not turn and do not join at end of each round.

Pattern
With yarn A, ch 4 and join with a ss to form a ring.
ROUND 1 Ch 1 (does not count as stitch), 6 sc into ring, place marker to indicate last st of round (move marker up at end of each round, so it always indicates last st). (6sts)
ROUND 2 2 sc into each st. (12sts)
ROUND 3 *1 sc in next st, 2 sc in next st, rep from * to end. (18sts)
ROUND 4 *1 sc in next 2 sts, 2 sc in next st, rep from * to end. (24sts)
ROUND 5 *1 sc in next 3 sts, 2 sc in next st, rep from * to end. (30sts)
ROUND 6 *1 sc in next 4 sts, 2 sc in next st, rep from * to end. (36sts)
ROUND 7 *1 sc in next 5 sts, 2 sc in next st, rep from * to end. (42sts)
ROUND 8 *1 sc in next 6 sts, 2 sc in next st, rep from * to end. (48sts)
ROUND 9 *1 sc in next 7 sts, 2 sc in next st, rep from * to end. (54sts)
ROUND 10 *1 sc in next 8 sts, 2 sc in next st, rep from * to end. (60sts)
ROUND 11 *1 sc in next 9 sts, 2 sc in next st, rep from * to end. (66sts)
ROUND 12 *1 sc in next 10 sts, 2 sc in next st, rep from * to end. (72sts)
ROUND 13 *1 sc in next 11 sts, 2 sc in next st, rep from * to end. (78sts)
ROUND 14 *1 sc in next 12 sts, 2 sc in next st, rep from * to end. (84sts)
ROUND 15 *1 sc in next 13 sts, 2 sc in next st, rep from * to end. (90sts)

ROUND 16 *1 sc in next 14 sts, 2 sc in next st, rep from * to end. (96sts)

LARGE SIZE ONLY
NEXT ROUND *1 sc in next 15 sts, 2 sc in next sc, rep from * to end. (102sts)
Continue without shaping until piece measures 6¼in (16cm) for small size and 7in (18cm) for large size from round 1.

LARGE SIZE ONLY
NEXT ROUND *1 sc in next 15 sts, dc2tog, rep from * to end. (96sts)

BOTH SIZES
NEXT ROUND *1 sc in next 14 sts, dc2tog, rep from * to end. (90sts)
NEXT ROUND *1 sc in next 13 sts, dc2tog, rep from * to end. (84sts)
NEXT ROUND *1 sc in next 12 sts, dc2tog, rep from * to end. (78sts)
NEXT ROUND *1 sc in next 11 sts, dc2tog, rep from * to end. (72sts)
Change to B and work 6 (8) rounds in sc as set.
Change to C and work 2 (2) rounds in sc as set.

Hanging loop
At start of next round, make 20 ch, skip 12 sts, sc to end of round. (60sts and 20ch)
NEXT ROUND 1 sc in each ch and 1 sc in each st to end of round. (80sts)
Work 4 (5) rounds in sc as set.
FINAL ROUND 1 ss in each sc to end.
Fasten off yarn, weave in ends. Block lightly according to instructions on ballband.

>> This hanging toy basket is made with Berroco Weekend. 205yds/187m/50g, in A: Turquoise (5966), B: Taffy (5925), and C: Ambrosia (5920).

Essential information

DIFFICULTY LEVEL Intermediate

SIZE 10½in (27cm) diameter

YARN Any aran weight, preferably superwash wool, will give a similar texture and finish

A x 1   **B** x 1   **C** x 1   **D** x 1

E x 1   **F** x 1

CROCHET HOOK 7 US (4.5mm) hook

NOTIONS Yarn needle

GAUGE Rounds 1–3 measure 4in (10cm) diameter

Round stool cover

The vibrant colors of this stool cover add interest to a practical project. Worked in the round using doubles and single crochet, this is an ideal project for someone with some experience of crochet.

PROJECTS

For more circular patterns
>> go to pages 60, 186, and 198

Pattern

With yarn A, work 4 ch, join with a ss to form a ring (see p.56).

ROUND 1 Ch 3, 1 dc, *1 ch, 2 dc, rep from * four times, (6 dc pairs made), fasten off A.

ROUND 2 Join B into any ch sp, 3 ch, 1 dc, 1 ch, 2 dc in first ch sp, *1 ch, 2 dc, 1 ch, 2 dc in next ch sp, rep from * four times, join with a ss into top of 3 ch. (6-dc pairs and 12-ch sp). Fasten off B.

ROUND 3 Join C into any ch sp, 3 ch, 2 dc into same ch sp, *1 ch, 3 dc into next ch sp, rep from * to end, join with a ss into top of 3 ch, fasten off C. (12 3-dc and 12-ch sp)

ROUND 4 Join D into any ch sp, work as for round 3, fasten off D. (12 3-dc and 12-ch sp)

ROUND 5 Join E into any ch sp, work as for round 2, fasten off E. (12-dc pairs and 24-ch sp)

ROUND 6 Join F into any ch sp, work as for round 3, fasten off F. (24 3-dc and 24-ch sp)

ROUND 7 Join A into any ch sp, work as for round 3, fasten off A. (24 3-dc and 24-ch sp)

ROUND 8 Join B into any ch sp, work as for round 3, fasten off B. (24 3-dc and 34-ch sp)

ROUND 9 Join C into any ch sp, work as for round 3, but work 2 ch between each 3 dc, fasten off C. (24 3-dc and 24-ch sp)

ROUND 10 Join D into any ch sp, 1 ch, * work 1 sc into top of each dc, 1 sc in ch sp, repeat from * to end, join with a ss into top of 1 ch (96 sc), do not turn work, do not fasten off yarn. Continue to work in rounds decreasing as follows:

ROUND 11 Ch 1, *1 sc in each of next 6 sc, sc2tog, repeat from * to end, join with a ss in top of 1 ch. (84sts)

ROUND 12 Ch 1, 1 sc in each sc to end of round, join with a ss in top of ch 3.

ROUND 13 As round 12.

ROUND 14 Ch 1, *1 sc in each of next 5 sc, sc2tog, repeat from * to end, join with a ss in top of 1 ch. (72sts)

ROUND 15 As round 12.

ROUND 16 Ch 1, * 1 sc in each of next 4 sc, sc2tog, repeat from * to end. (60sts)

ROUND 17 As round 12. Fasten off yarn, weave in ends.

Double crochet gives a lovely openwork finish to the top of this cover, but the underneath is much more dense because it is worked in single crochet. This will ensure that the cover fits snugly over the stool, preventing it from slipping.

<< This stool cover is made with Rowan Pure Wool Aran, 186yds/170m/100g, in A: Burnt (700), B: Vert (686), C: Splash (701), D: Marine (683), E: Burlesque (689), and F: Ember (679).

Rustic ottomans

These simple ottomans are a great way to bring a touch of color into your home. The size is simple to adjust by working more, or fewer, increase rounds.

PROJECTS

For more patterns in chunky yarns
>> go to pages 164 and 174

Essential information

DIFFICULTY LEVEL Easy

SIZE Large: 16in (40cm) diameter
Small: 12in (30cm) diameter

YARN A super bulky cotton or stretchy jersey fabric yarn will be suitable for this project

A x 4   **B** x 5

CROCHET HOOK L/11 US (8mm) hook

NOTIONS Stitch marker
Large-eyed yarn needle
2 round box pillows, approx 16in x 2in
(40cm x 5cm) and 12in x 2in (30cm x 5cm);
or a low-tog comforter to fill the large ottoman

GAUGE Rounds 1–3 measures approx 5in
(12cm) diameter

NOTE The top of each ottoman is made first, then the sides. The base is made as a separate piece and sewn on. This allows the pillow filling to be removed for washing.

Top

With L/11 US (8mm) hook, work 6 ch, ss in the first ch to form a ring.
ROUND 1 6 sc into ring, do not join, continue working in a spiral using stitch marker to indicate the last st of each round (remove and replace after last sc of each round). Do not turn, continue to work in a spiral with RS facing. (6sts)
ROUND 2 2 sc in each sc. (12sts)

Stretchy jersey or cotton yarn, such as the Hooplayarn used here (a by-product of the textile industry), is growing in popularity with crocheters. Its chunkiness means that your ottomans will grow rapidly, while its texture creates a pretty knotted effect.

ROUND 3 (1 sc, 2 sc in next sc) to end. (18sts)
ROUND 4 (2 sc, 2 sc in next sc) to end. (24sts)
Continue increasing as set, working 1 more sc between each increase, making 6 increases evenly on each round until work measures 12 (16)in/30 (40)cm. Make a note of the stitch count, since this will be needed for making the base of the ottoman.
NEXT ROUND 1 sc TBL in each sc to end.
NEXT AND SUBSEQUENT ROUNDS 1 sc in each st to end, continue to work in a spiral, without increasing until the sides measure 3 (6)in/ 8 (15)cm. Fasten off yarn and weave in ends. It is advised that all loose ends of yarn are sewn securely in place as, due to the nature of the yarn, they can work loose over time and may fray.

Base

Work as for top, increasing as set until stitch count matches stitch count noted for top. Fasten off yarn, weave in ends.

Finishing

Fill the ottoman with a pillow form or comforter. Attach bottom to sides by sewing through last round of sides and last round of bottom to secure. Weave in loose ends securely. Shape gently to give a rounded appearance.

>> These ottomans are made with Hooplayarn, 109yds/100m/500g, in A: Sparkling embers and B: Warm ginger. Lion Brand Zpagetti also works well.

for *Summer tunic dress*
go to page 246

Cat basket

This colorful cat basket makes good use of the increasingly popular T-shirt yarn, which is a by-product of the clothing industry. It is satisfying to make, since the thickness of the yarn allows you to get very quick results.

PROJECTS

For more single crochet projects
>> *go to pages 166, 194, and 266*

Essential information

DIFFICULTY LEVEL Easy

SIZE Approx 17½in (44cm) diameter

YARN You can use super bulky weight T-shirt yarn, cotton, or felted wool to achieve a similar effect. You may need to hold yarn double to make it rigid

A x 1   **B** x 1   **C** x 1

CROCHET HOOK N/15 US (10mm) hook

NOTIONS Stitch marker
Large-eyed yarn needle
Circular pillow, optional

GAUGE Exact gauge is not essential

SPECIAL ABBREVIATIONS
ADJUSTABLE RING: See p. 132
CRAB STITCH: See p. 144

NOTE The basket is worked in a spiral. Do not join at end of round. Mark the first stitch of each round with a stitch marker or length of colored yarn, in order to keep track of rounds and stitches.

Pattern

With yarn A, make an adjustable ring and work 6 sc into ring. (6sts)

ROUND 1 2 sc in each sc to end. (12sts)

ROUND 2 *1 sc in next st, 2 sc in next st, rep from * to end. (18sts)

ROUND 3 With yarn B, *1 sc in next 2 sts, 2 sc in next st, rep from * to end. (24sts)

ROUND 4 With yarn A, *1 sc in next 3 sts, 2 sc in next st, rep from * to end. (30sts)

ROUND 5 *1 sc in next 4 sts, 2 sc in next st, rep from * to end. (36sts)

ROUND 6 With yarn B, *1 sc in next 5 sts, 2 sc in next st, rep from * to end. (42sts)

ROUND 7 With yarn A, *1 sc in next 6 sts, 2 sc in next st, rep from * to end. (48sts)

ROUND 8 *1 sc in next 7 sts, 2 sc in next st, rep from * to end. (54sts)

ROUND 9 With yarn B, *1 sc in next 8 sts, 2 sc in next st, rep from * to end. (60sts)

ROUND 10 With yarn A, *1 sc in next 9 sts, 2 sc in next st, rep from * to end. (66sts)

ROUND 11 *1 sc in next 10 sts, 2 sc in next st, rep from * to end. (72sts)

ROUND 12 With yarn B, *1 sc in next 11 sts, 2 sc in next st, rep from * to end. (78sts)

ROUND 13 With yarn A, *1 sc in next 12 sts, 2 sc in next st, rep from * to end. (84sts)

ROUND 14 *1 sc in next 13sts, 2 sc in next st, rep from * to end. (90sts)

ROUND 15 1 sc TBL in each st to end.

ROUND 16 1 sc in each st (front and back loops) to end.

ROUND 17 With yarn B, 1 sc in each st to end.

ROUNDS 18–19 With yarn A, 1 sc in each st to end.

ROUND 20 With yarn B, 1 sc in each st to end.

ROUNDS 21–22 With yarn A, 1 sc in each st to end.

ROUND 23 With yarn C, crab st in each st to end. Ss at end of round to join.
Fasten off, weave in ends.
Place a circular pillow inside (optional).

>> This cat basket is made with Lion Brand Zpagetti, 765yds/700m/850g, in A: Marina, B: Beige, and C: Red.

TOP TIP

Work stitches tightly to make a rigid basket.

Keeping it simple with a single crochet stitch gives a pleasing, even effect. The yarn needs to be as non-stretchy as possible to keep the basket rigid, and the diameter and height can be adjusted by adding or subtracting increases and rounds.

Fruit bowl

A very simple yet elegant bowl for storage, and perfect for holding fruit, this project is worked in the round, with one "through back loop only" round used to create the crisp rim from which the sides rise.

PROJECTS
For more storage patterns
>> go to pages 162, 164, and 166

Essential information

DIFFICULTY LEVEL Easy

SIZE Approx 11 x 2in (28 x 5cm)

YARN Use any aran weight, preferably cotton, yarn held double or a chunky yarn held singly

A x 3   **B** x 1

CROCHET HOOK H/8 US (5mm) hook

NOTIONS Stitch marker
Yarn needle

GAUGE Exact gauge is not essential, but gauge is worked tightly for rigidity

NOTE Work in spirals. Do not join rounds, but place a marker at first stitch of the round, moving it each round to mark the beginning of a round. Yarn is used as a double strand.

Pattern
With yarn A, work 2 ch and 6 sc into second ch from hook, join round with a ss to first st.
ROUND 1 Ch 1, work 2 sc in each st around, do not join round, place marker. (12sts)

When crocheting into the back of one loop (written in the pattern as sc TBL) rather than working both loops of a double crochet stitch, you will create a horizontal bar across your fabric. This creates a firm rim line between the base and the sides.

ROUND 2 (2 sc in next st, 1 sc in next 1 st) around. (18sts)
ROUND 3 (2 sc in next st, 1 sc in next 2 sts) around. (24sts)
ROUND 4 (2 sc in next st, 1 sc in next 3 sts) around. (30sts)
ROUND 5 (2 sc in next st, 1 sc in next 4 sts) around. (36sts)
ROUND 6 (2 sc in next st, 1 sc in next 5 sts) around. (42sts)
Continue in this way, working one extra st between increases each round until you have worked 19 rounds and have 120 sts. If you want a larger bowl, you can continue increasing in this way until the desired size is achieved. Join round with a ss.
ROUND 20 Ch 1, 1 sc TBL into each stitch around.
ROUND 21 Ch 1, 1 sc into each st around. Repeat round 21 until work measures approx 1$\frac{1}{4}$in (3cm) from base. Join round with a ss. Change to yarn B and work as round 21 until side measures 2in (5cm) from base. Join round with a ss.
Fasten off yarn, weave in ends.

>> This bowl is made with Berroco Weekend, 207yds/187m/100g, in A: Oats (5903) and B: Taffy (5925).

For extra strength and rigidity, hold the yarn double.

TOP TIP

A stitch marker is essential when working in the round in sc because it allows you to keep track of the start of each round. By working the stitches accurately, you will create this lovely spiral pattern on the base of your bowl. Turn to page 20 for details on stitch markers.

Filigree bookmarks

A very simple, quick-to-make project, these delicate bookmarks are perfect for using up ends of yarn. Use the thicker yarn for a bookmark for a coffee-table book and the finer one for a bookmark for a novel.

PROJECTS
For more crochet cotton patterns
>> go to pages 184 and 306

Essential information

DIFFICULTY LEVEL Easy

SIZE Approx 7in x ³⁄₄in (18 x 2cm), with a 7in (18cm) tassel

YARN Try small amounts of fine crochet cotton yarn for this project—the bookmark will get slightly bigger or smaller, depending on the thickness

A x 1   B x 1

CROCHET HOOK 5 steel US (2mm) and B/1 US (2.5mm) hooks

NOTIONS Yarn needle, Assorted beads, if desired

GAUGE Exact gauge is not essential

Pattern
With the 5 steel US (2mm) hook, if working with the finer yarn, or the B/1 US (2.5mm) hook, if using the thicker yarn, work 42 ch.

ROUND 1 6 sc into second ch from hook, skip next ch, 1 sc into next ch, skip next ch, *6 sc into next ch, skip next ch; 1 sc into next sc, skip next ch; rep from * to last ch, work (6 sc, 1 ch, 6 sc) into last ch, do not turn. Now rotate your work 180 degrees and continue

The main strip is worked in the round by crocheting into both sides of the starting chain. Note the difference between the sizes of the bookmarks—this is achieved by using different thicknesses of crochet yarn and sizes of hook.

working back into the unworked loop of each ch as follows: *skip next ch, sc into next ch, skip next ch, 6 sc into next ch; rep from * to end, 1 ch, ss to first sc to join round.

ROUND 2 Ch 4 (counts as 1 dc, 1 ch), dc into second sc from the first round, (1 ch, 1 dc) into each of next 3 sc, skip next 3 sc, *(dc, 1 ch) into each of next 3 sc, 1 dc into next sc, skip 3 sc; rep from * to last 6 sc group, (dc, 1 ch) into each of next 4 sc, dc into next sc, 3 ch, **(dc, 1 ch) into each of next 4 sc, dc into next sc, skip next 3 sc; rep between * and **, join round with a ss. Fasten off, weave in ends.

Finishing
Cut two lengths of yarn 14in (36cm) long and fold in half. Insert loop through the 3-ch sp at one end of the bookmark. Push the end of the lengths through the loop, braiding the yarn if desired, and pull tight to make tassel. Thread assorted beads onto the ends of the tassel and secure with a knot.

>> The small bookmark is made with Size 8 Pearl Cotton, 95yds/90m/10g, in A: Kingfisher blue (806) and the large bookmark is made with Rowan Siena 4 Ply, 153yds/140m/50g, in B: Greengage (661).

Fish and starfish garland

A fun project for a child's room, this marine garland can be worked in separate parts that are assembled at the end. Add as many fish and starfish as you like.

PROJECTS
For more chain stitch projects
>> *go to pages 28 and 30*

Essential information

DIFFICULTY LEVEL Easy

SIZE 67in (170cm) long; each motif measures approx 4in (10cm)

YARN You can use any cotton DK yarn for a similar look to this project

A x 1   B x 1   C x 1   D x 1

E x 2   F x 1

CROCHET HOOK G/6 US (4mm) hook

NOTIONS Yarn needle
Embroidery needle

GAUGE Exact gauge is not essential

SPECIAL ABBREVIATIONS
SC2TOG: Insert hook into stitch specified, yo, bring yarn through stitch from back to front, insert hook into next stitch, yo, bring yarn through stitch from back to front, yo and pull through all 3 loops on the hook.

NO-CHAIN DOUBLE CROCHET FOUNDATION: Ch 3, yo, insert hook into first chain, yo and pull through first chain (this will be referred to as an extra chain later on and you will have 3 loops on hook) yo, pull through 1, yo, pull through 2, yo pull through 2.

To repeat, yo, insert the hook into "extra chain", yo, pull yarn through (3 loops on hook) then yo through 1, yo through 2, yo through 2.
SLIP STITCH JOIN: Put hook into stitch, yo, bring yarn through stitch and loop on hook. Chain 258 using a no-chain double foundation (see left).
ADJUSTABLE RING: See p.132

NOTE Working in a spiral, mark the last stitch in each round with a stitch marker.

Fish (make 3 of each)
Use the following colors: F with B, D with C, and A with E, using first color for main body.
FOUNDATION Work Ch 4, ss into first ch to form a ring.
ROUND 1 (RS) Ch 1, 6 sc into ring, mark last stitch with a stitch marker.
ROUND 2 2 sc into first sc made in round 1 (1 sc into next st, 2 sc into next st) repeat to end. (9sts)
ROUND 3 (1 sc into next 2 sts, 2 sc into next st) repeat to end. (12sts)
ROUND 4 4 sc into next 4 sts, 2 sc into next 6 sts. (13sts)
ROUND 5 (5 sc into next 5 sts, 2 sc into next st) twice, sc into last st. (15sts)
ROUND 6 (6 sc into next 6 sts, 2 sc into next st) twice, sc into last st. (17sts)
ROUND 7 (7 sc into next 7 sts, 2 sc into next st) twice, sc into last st. (19sts)
ROUND 8 1 sc into each st. (19sts)
ROUND 9 (sc into next 7 sts, sc2tog) twice, sc into last st. (17sts)
ROUND 10 (sc into next 6 st, sc2tog) twice, sc into last st. (15sts)
ROUND 11 (sc into next 5 sts, sc2tog) twice, sc into last st. (13sts)

ROUND 12 (sc into next 4 sts, sc2tog) twice, sc into last st. (11sts)
ROUND 13 Dc into next 4 sts, sc2tog, sc into next 5 st. (10sts)
ROUND 14 Dc into each st. (10sts)
Flatten the body of the fish keeping the working loop on the hook to the right (left if you are left-handed).
Remove stitch marker as you will now be working in rows.
ROW 1 Dc into next 4 sts, through both front and back body panels, turn. (4sts)
ROW 2 Ch 1 (does not count as a stitch), sc into next 3 sts, 2 sc into last st, turn. (5sts)
ROW 3 Ch 1, sc into next 4 sts, 2 sc into last st, turn. (6sts)
ROW 4 Ch 1, sc into next 5 sts, 2 sc into last st, turn. (7sts)
ROW 5 Ch 2 (counts as a hdc), dc into next 3 sts, ss into next st, dc into next 2 sts, 1 dc and 1 hdc into last stitch.
Fasten off yarn, weave in ends.

Finishing
Use second color for edge and face.
Join color 2 where the tail meets the body (with fish facing to the left) and sc evenly around the edge of the fish body and tail.
Put 2 sc into the tail points and the fish nose.
In the same color, embroider the eye and the mouth. Fasten off yarn, weave in ends.

>> This garland is made with Tahki Yarns Cotton Classic DK, 108yds/100m/50g, in A: Wheat (3253), B: Magenta (3420), C: Tangerine (3405), D: Turquoise (3805), E: Dark royal (3873), and F: Leaf green (3724).

Starfish (make 6)

Make 3 starfish using colors A and B, and 3 more using C and D.
Use first color for main body.
FOUNDATION RING Use the adjustable ring method for starting, then work 11 sc into ring. (11sts). Pull the tail end to close the hole.
ROUND 1 Ch 1, 1 sc into st at the base of the 1 ch. (1 sc into next st, 2 sc into next st) to end. Join with a ss to first sc made. (16sts)
ROUND 2 *Ch 7, 1 sc into second ch from hook, hdc into next 2 ch, dc into next 2 ch, dtr into next ch, skip 2 sts on round 1, ss into next st on round 1. Repeat from * 4 more times. Ss in first ch on round 1. Do not fasten off. (5 star points)

Finishing

Dc evenly around the arms of the starfish (6 sc per side) putting 1 sc, 1 ch, 1 sc into the same st at the point of the arm.
Fasten off yarn, weave in ends.
Make second star in same color.
Using second color to edge and for face, place both stars with WS together and sc evenly around the edges joining both stars as you go putting 1 sc, 1 ch, 1 sc into each point. Join with a ss. Fasten off, weave in ends.
Embroider facial features on all starfish.

Garland

Work 258 ch using a no-chain dc foundation.
ROW 1 With yarn A, turn, 1 ch, sc into each st, turn. (258sts)
ROW 2 (Make sure not to twist the chain) Ch 1, 16 sc, 7 ch—join first starfish with a ss join. Working back up the chain toward the garland header, 6 ss along the 7 ch, 1 sc to join to garland header.
15 sc (along garland base), 34 ch—join first fish with a ss join. Working back up the chain toward garland header, 33 ss along the 34 ch, 1 sc to join to garland header.
15 sc (along garland base), 15 ch—join second fish with a ss join. Working back up the chain toward garland header, 14 ss along the 15 ch, 1 sc to join to garland header.
15 sc (along garland base), 38 ch—join second

starfish with a ss join. Working back up the chain toward garland header, 37 ss along the 38 ch, 1 sc to join to garland header.
15 sc (along garland base), 12 ch—join third fish with a ss join. Working back up the chain toward the garland header, 11 ss along the 12 ch, 1 sc to join to garland header.
15 sc (along garland base), 3 ch—join fourth fish with a ss join. Working back up the chain toward garland body, 2 ss along the 3 ch, 1 sc to join to garland.
15 sc (along garland base), 19 ch—join third starfish with a ss join. Working back up the chain toward garland body, 18 ss along the 19 ch, 1 sc to join to garland.
15 sc (along garland base), 28 ch—join fourth starfish with a ss join. Working back up the chain toward garland body, 27 ss along the 28 ch, 1 sc to join to garland.
15 sc (along garland base), 15 ch—join fifth fish with a ss join. Working back up the chain toward garland body, 14 ss along the 15 ch, 1 sc to join to garland.
15 sc (along garland base), 21 ch—join sixth fish with a ss join. Working back up the chain toward garland body, 20 ss along the 21 ch, 1 sc to join to garland.
15 sc (along garland base), 42 ch—join

seventh fish with a ss join. Working back up the chain toward garland body, 41 ss along the 42 ch, 1 sc to join to garland.
15 sc (along garland base), 2 ch—join fifth starfish with a ss join. Working back up the chain toward garland body, 1 ss along the 2 ch, 1 sc to join to garland.
15 sc (along garland base), 20 ch—join eighth fish with a ss join. Working back up the chain toward garland body, 19 ss along the 20 ch, 1 sc to join to garland.
15 sc (along garland base), 24 ch—join sixth starfish with a ss join. Working back up the chain toward garland body, 23 ss along the 24 ch, 1 sc to join to garland.
15 sc (along garland base), 8 ch—join ninth fish with a ss join. Working back up the chain toward garland body, 7 ss along the 8 ch, 1 sc to join to garland.

Finishing

Dc to end of garland (17 sc), fasten off yarn, weave in ends.

Pairs of happy starfish bob around between the row of fish on this fun garland. Use French knots for the eyes and a row of six chain stitches for the smiling mouth. Do not place your garland within reach of small children because it could be a choking hazard.

Flower pin cushion

This colorful pin cushion is worked in spirals for the base, and the use of different stitches creates pretty patterns with minimal fuss.

PROJECTS

For more projects worked in the round
>> go to pages 194, 196, and 204

Essential information

DIFFICULTY LEVEL Easy

SIZE Approx 3in (8cm) in diameter

YARN Any small amount of crochet thread will substitute here

A x 1　**B** x 1　**C** x 1　**D** x 1　**E** x 2

CROCHET HOOK B/1 US (2.5mm) hook

NOTIONS Stitch marker
Yarn needle
Polyfill

GAUGE Exact gauge is not essential

NOTE Do not join rounds, but place a marker at the first stitch of the round, moving it up as each round is completed to mark the beginning of each round.
Ch 1 at beg of non-spiral rounds does not count as a stitch.

TOP TIP A little patience may be required if new to crochet cotton.

Pattern

With yarn A, work 2 ch.
ROUND 1 6 sc into second ch from hook, join round with a ss.
ROUND 2 Ch 1, 2 sc into each st around, join round with a ss. (12sts)
ROUND 3 Ch 1, 1 sc in each st around, join round with a ss. (12sts)
ROUND 4 Ch 1, 1 sc, (3 dc into next st, 1 sc) 5 times, 3 dc into last st, join round with a ss. Fasten off.
Change to yarn B, attaching to any central dc of 3-dc group.
ROUND 5 Ch 1, *3 sc into dc, 1 dc into next dc, 1 tr into sc, 1 dc into next dc; rep from * to end of round. Join round with a ss. (36sts)
ROUND 6 Ch 1, 1 sc, (2 sc into next st, 5 sc) to end of round, ending with 4 sc only, join round with a ss. Fasten off. (42sts)
Change to yarn C, attaching to the first sc of a pair.
ROUND 7 Ch 1, (1 sc, 1 ch, 1 sc, 1 hdc, 1 dc, 3 dc into next st, 1 dc, 1 hdc) around. Join round with a ss, fasten off. (54sts)
Change to yarn D, attaching yarn to central dc of any 3-dc group.
ROUND 8 Ch 1, *3 sc into central dc, 1 sc, 1 hdc, 1 dc, skip 1 sc, 1 tr in ch sp, skip 1 sc, 1 dc, 1 hdc, 1 sc; rep from * to end of round. (60sts)
ROUND 9 Ch 1, 1 sc into each st to end of round. Work the next round TFL of every stitch.
ROUND 10 2 ss, 1 ch, *2 sc, 1 hdc, 1 dc, 3 dc into next st, 1 dc, 1 hdc, 2 sc, 1 ss; rep from * to end of round. Fasten off.

Change to yarn E, attaching to the back loop of any stitch from round 9.
ROUND 11 Ch 1, 1 sc TBL into each st around. (60 sc TBL)
Work 6 rounds straight in regular sc, working in spirals, placing a marker at the beg of each round and moving it up as you go.
NEXT ROUND (8 sc, sc2tog) around. (54sts)
NEXT ROUND (7 sc, sc2tog) around. (45sts)
NEXT ROUND (6 sc, sc2tog) around. (36sts)
Continue in this way, decreasing 6 stitches per round by working one fewer sc in between decreases, until there are 6 sts left. Stuff the cushion before the hole gets too small.
Fasten off yarn, thread through remaining stitches, and pull up tight to close hole. Weave in all ends.

To crochet in the round, you will first need to make a foundation row that is joined into a ring. Refer to page 26 for more information about working slip stitch and using slip stitches to form a foundation ring.

>> This pin cushion is made with Rowan Siena 4 Ply, 153yds/140m/50g, in A: Tandoori (676), B: Mariner (672), C: Beacon (668), D: Green (661), and E: Frost (653).

Chunky rug

This stylish rug is worked in rounds and makes an eye-catching addition to any room. The chunky yarn is soft and warm underfoot and works up quickly on a large crochet hook.

PROJECTS

For more chunky patterns
>> go to pages 30, 206, and 226

Essential information

DIFFICULTY LEVEL Intermediate

SIZE 35½in (90cm) diameter

YARN Any super chunky yarn with a high synthetic content is suitable

x 4

CROCHET HOOK P US (12mm) hook

NOTIONS Yarn needle

GAUGE Rounds 1-2 measure 6in (15cm) diameter

SPECIAL ABBREVIATIONS

Clusters worked as follows, depending on pattern instruction:

HDCCL: half double crochet cluster. Hook into st, yarn over, draw through, yo and draw through 1 loop, insert hook into st, yo, draw through, yo and draw through all 3 loops on hook.

DCCL: double crochet cluster. Yo, insert hook into st, yo, draw through, yo and draw through 2 loops, yo, insert hook into st, yo, draw through, yo and draw through 2 loops, yo and draw through remaining 3 loops on hook.

TRCL: treble cluster. Yo twice, insert hook into st, yo, draw through, yo and draw through 2 loops twice, yo twice, insert hook into st, yo, draw through, yo and draw through 2 loops twice, yo and draw through rem 3 loops on hook.

DOUBLE CLUSTER PAIR: dccl, 1 ch, dccl all in the same ch sp.

Pattern

Work 4 ch, ss into first ch to make a ring.

ROUND 1 Ch 2, 1 hdc into ring, 1 ch, *hdccl into ring, 1 ch, repeat from * 6 more times, ss into top of first hdc to close round. (8 hdccl)

ROUND 2 Ss into next ch sp, 3 ch, 1 dc into ch sp, 2 ch, *dccl in next ch sp, 2 ch, repeat from * to end of round, ss into top of first dc to close round. (8 dccl)

ROUND 3 Ss into next ch sp, 3 ch, 1 dc into ch sp, 1 ch, dccl in same ch sp, 1 ch, *dccl, 1 ch, dccl, in next ch sp, 1 ch, repeat from * to end, ss into top of first dc to close round. (8 dccl pairs)

ROUND 4 Ss into next ch sp, 3 ch, 1 dc into ch sp, 1 ch, *dccl in next ch sp, 1 ch, repeat from * to end, ss into top of first dc to close round. (16 dccl)

ROUND 5 Ss into next ch sp, 3 ch, 1 dc into ch sp, 1 ch, dccl into same ch sp, 1 ch, *dccl, 1 ch, dccl in next ch sp, 1 ch, repeat from * to end, ss into top of first dc to close round. (16 dccl pairs)

ROUND 6 Ss into next ch sp, 3 ch, 1 dc into ch sp, 1 ch, *dccl in next ch sp, 1 ch, repeat from * to end, ss into top of first dc to close round. (32 dccl)

ROUND 7 Ss into next ch sp, 3 ch, 1 dc into ch sp, 1 ch, dccl into same ch sp, 1 ch, dccl in next ch sp, ch 1 *dccl, 1 ch, dccl in next ch sp, 1 ch, dccl in next ch sp, 1 ch, repeat from * to end, ss into top of first dc to close round. (16 dccl and 16 dc cluster pairs)

ROUND 8 As round 6. (48 dccl)

ROUND 9 Ss into next ch sp, 5 ch, *1 tr in next ch sp, 1 ch, repeat from * to end, join with a ss into fourth ch of 5 ch. (48sts)

ROUND 10 Ss into next ch sp, 3 ch, 1 dc into ch sp, 1 ch, dccl into same ch sp, 1 ch, trcl in next ch sp, 1 ch, *dccl, 1 ch, dccl in next ch sp, 1 ch, trcl in next ch sp, 1 ch, repeat from * to end, ss into top of first dc to close round. (24 dc cluster pairs and 24 large dccl made)

ROUND 11 As round 6. (72 dccl)

ROUND 12 Ch 1, *1 sc in top of dccl, 1 sc in ch sp, repeat from * to end, ss into 1 ch to close round.

Finishing

Weave in all ends securely on wrong side. Pin rug to a flat surface and spray lightly with water, shape to a flat circle, and let dry. A nonslip backing can be sewn to the reverse of the rug, if desired.

>> This rug is made with Lion Brand Hometown USA, 81yds/74m/140g, in Houston cream (98).

The clusters in this project create an attractive mesh pattern toward the outside of the rug and this contrasts well with the tighter stitches at the edge, and the nice neat finish given by the final row of single crochet.

Hats
and scarves

Baby bonnet

This bonnet has a simple construction—a rectangle folded and sewn to make a cute pixie point at the back. Create your own stripe sequence and textures by changing stitches for each stripe, as here, or use the same stitch all the way up.

PROJECTS

For more double stitch patterns
>>*go to pages 44 and 186*

Essential information

DIFFICULTY LEVEL Easy

SIZE To fit a baby, 0–3 (3–6) months

YARN Any DK weight yarn will substitute here. Baby yarns are preferable for their softness and easy-to-wash fibers

A x 1   B x 1   C x 1

CROCHET HOOK G/6 US (4mm) hook

NOTIONS Yarn needle
1/2in (15mm) pink button

GAUGE 18 sc to 4in (10cm) square

Pattern

With yarn A, work 56 (62) ch.
ROW 1 1 hdc in third ch from hook, 1 hdc in each ch to end. (54(60)hdc)
ROW 2 Ch 2, 1 hdc in each st to end.
ROW 3 As row 2.
Change to yarn B.
ROW 4 Ch 1, 1 sc in each st to end of row.
ROWS 5–7 As row 4.
Change to yarn C.
ROW 8 Ch 3, 1 dc in each st to end of row.
ROW 9 As row 8.
ROWS 10–18 Rep rows 1–9 stripe sequence.
Change to yarn A.
ROWS 19–21 Ch 2, 1 hdc in each st to end.
Change to yarn B and work straight in sc until piece measures approx 6(6^1/$_4$)in/15(16)cm.

Finishing

Fold piece in half lengthwise to create the bonnet, sewing along top seam, which will become the back of bonnet, to close it.
ROUND 1 With yarn C, work 20 ch for chin strap, attach chain to bottom corner of the hat and work evenly in sc all around face opening, working 3 sc into corner sp to get round, then work in sc evenly along bottom of the bonnet for neck opening, join round with a ss.
ROUND 2 Work 1 sc into each ch of chin strap, working 3 sc into last ch, then turn work around 180 degrees and work back into unworked bottom loops of chain. Complete the face opening evenly in sc, then work (sc2tog, 1 sc) along the neck opening to decrease, work 1 sc into each sc along chin

Turn to pages 70–71 for seam techniques. Use the same colored yarn for finishing as the surrounding yarn of the seam, so that the seam does not show.

strap, to center sc of 3 sc, 3 ch, skip next sc, sc in each sc to end of chin strap. Fasten off yarn and weave in all ends.
Sew button to bottom corner of bonnet, corresponding to buttonhole of chin strap.

>> This bonnet is made with Debbie Bliss Baby Cashmerino, 137yds/125m/50g, in A: Ecru (101), B: Candy pink (006), and C: Hot pink (060).

Child's hat with ears

This hat is the cutest headgear ever—worked in the round as one dome, the ears are then crocheted in two pieces and sewn on.

PROJECTS

For more patterns in the round
>> go to pages 266 and 274

Essential information

DIFFICULTY LEVEL Easy

SIZE To fit a child, age 1–5 years

YARN You can use any wool or wool-mix DK yarn for this project

A x 1   **B** x 1

CROCHET HOOK 7 US (4.5mm) hook

NOTIONS Stitch marker
Yarn needle

GAUGE 15 hdc x 12 rows per 4in (10cm)

Pattern

With yarn A, work 3 ch and 8 hdc into third ch from hook, ss into first st to join.
ROUND 1 Work 2 hdc into each hdc, join round with a ss to first st. (16sts)
ROUND 2 Ch 2, *work 2 hdc into next st, 1 hdc into next st, rep from * to end of round, join round with a ss to first st. (24sts)
ROUND 3 Ch 2, *work 1 hdc in next st, 2 hdc into next st, 1 hdc into next st, rep from * to end of round, join round with a ss to first st. (32sts)
ROUND 4 Ch 2, *work 1 hdc in next 2 sts, 2 hdc into next st, 1 hdc into next st, rep from * to end of round, join round with a ss to first st. (40sts)
ROUND 5 Ch 2, *work 1 hdc in next 3 sts, 2 hdc into next st, 1 hdc into next st, rep from * to end of round, join round with a ss to first st. (48sts)
Continue in this way, working extra sts between each inc until there are 72 sts.
Work straight without increasing (1 hdc in each st) for approx 4in (10cm).
Fasten off yarn. Join yarn B to bottom round of hat crown and work 1 row of sc all around, join round with a ss.
Fasten off yarn, weave in ends.

Ears (make 2)

With yarn A, work in spirals, placing a marker at end of each round, moving it up each round. Work 2 ch and 6 sc into second ch from hook, join round with a ss to first st. Continue in spirals for remainder of ear piece.

ROUND 1 Ch 1, 2 sc into each sc, do not join round. (12sts)
ROUND 2 *1 sc in next sc, 2 sc in next sc, rep from * to end of round. (18sts)
ROUND 3 *1 sc in next 2 sc, 2 sc in next sc, rep from * to end of round. Join round with a ss. (24sts)
Fasten off yarn. With yarn B, make two more ears the same up to round 2.

Finishing

Block hat pieces lightly.
Sew each yarn A ear piece to a yarn B ear piece, with wrong sides facing each other and yarn B at front.
Sew an ear to each side of the hat crown.

Make a tight ring at the center of each ear piece for a neat finish. Turn to page 56 for more details about crocheting flat circles.

>> This hat is made with Rowan Kid Classic, 153yds/140m/50g. in A: Bitter sweet (866) and Rowan Pure Wool DK. 50g/125m/137yds, in B: Pier (006).

Men's beanie hat

This classic beanie-style hat is made in the round, from crown to rim. Made entirely in single crochet, the stripes add classic style. The ribbing at the edge is made by working around the single crochet posts on the round below.

PROJECTS

For more hat patterns
>> go to pages 190, 192, 196, and 198

Essential information

DIFFICULTY LEVEL Intermediate

SIZE To fit an adult male

YARN You can use any aran weight wool or wool mix yarn to achieve a similar effect

A x 1   **B** x 1   **C** x 1

CROCHET HOOK 7 US (4.5mm) and H/8 US (5mm) hook

NOTIONS Stitch marker
Yarn needle

GAUGE 17 sts x 20 rows per 4in (10cm)

SPECIAL ABBREVIATIONS

RSCF: raised single crochet front. At the front of the work, insert hook from right to left, around the post of the sc on the previous row, yarn over hook, draw through, yarn over hook, draw through 2 loops on hook, therefore making a sc.

RSCB: raised single crochet back. At the back of the work, insert hook from right to left, around the post of the sc on the previous row, yarn over hook, draw through, yarn over hook, draw through 2 loops on hook, therefore making a sc.

NOTE Do not join rounds, but place a marker at the first stitch of the round, moving it up as each round is completed to mark the beginning of each round.

Pattern

With yarn A and H/8 US (5mm) hook, work 2 ch.
ROUND 1 9 sc in second ch from hook, place marker. (9sts)
ROUND 2 2 sc in each sc to marker. (18sts)
ROUND 3 *1 sc, 2 sc in next sc, rep from * to marker. (27sts)
ROUND 4 *2 sc, 2 sc in next sc, rep from * to marker. (36sts)
ROUND 5 *3 sc, 2 sc in next sc, rep from * to marker. (45sts)

Combining colors as stripes is more challenging than crocheting in just one color, but it's well worth the effort and easy once you've mastered the technique. Turn to page 39 for more details.

ROUND 6 Sc in each st to marker.
ROUND 7 *4 sc, 2 sc in next sc, rep from * to marker. (54sts)
ROUND 8 Sc in each st to marker.
ROUND 9 *5 sc, 2 sc in next sc, rep from * to marker. (63sts)
ROUND 10 Sc in each st to marker.
ROUND 11 *6 sc, 2 sc in next sc, rep from * to marker. (72sts)
ROUND 12 Sc in each st to marker.
ROUND 13 *7 sc, 2 sc in next sc, rep from * to marker. (81sts)
Work straight in continuous rounds of sc until hat measures $4\frac{1}{4}$in (10.5cm).
With yarn B, work 2 rounds in sc.
With yarn C, work 2 rounds in sc.
With yarn B, work 2 rounds in sc.
With yarn A, work 3 rounds in sc.
With yarn B, work 2 rounds in sc.
With yarn C, work 2 rounds in sc.
With yarn B, work 2 rounds in sc.
With yarn A, work 2 rounds in sc.
NEXT ROUND With yarn B and 7 US (4.5mm) hook, sc2tog, sc in each st to end. (80sts)
NEXT ROUND *rscf, rscb, rep from * to end, ss in next 2sts.
Fasten off, weave in ends.

>> This beanie is made with Debbie Bliss Bluefaced Leicester British Wool, 82yds/75m/50g, in A: Duck egg (12), B: Red (08), and C: Denim (13).

Essential information

DIFFICULTY LEVEL Easy

SIZE To fit a child, age 3–4 (4–5:5–6)

YARN Any DK weight yarn with a high merino wool content will achieve a similar effect

A x 2   **B** x 1

CROCHET HOOK E/4 US (3.5mm) hook

NOTIONS Yarn needle
Two circles cut from cardboard, with an outer diameter of 2¼in (6cm) and a ring cut from the middle with a diameter of 1in (2.5cm) to make the pompom

GAUGE 19 sts x 8 rows per 4in (10cm)

SPECIAL ABBREVIATIONS
ADJUSTABLE RING: See p. 132

Child's hat with earflaps

This simple and fun project will keep your little one warm all winter. Worked in the round from the top, the hat uses half double stitches to give warmth. The hat circumferences measure $17^3/4$in (45cm), $18^1/2$in (47cm), and 19in (48cm).

PROJECTS

For more children's patterns
>> go to pages 210, 212, and 246

Pattern

ROUND 1 Using the adjustable ring method of starting and yarn A, work 2 ch and then 6 hdc into the ring. Gently close the ring and join into a round with a ss. (7sts)

ROUND 2 Ch 2, 1 hdc into same st, 2 hdc into each st to end, join into a round with a ss. (14sts)

ROUND 3 Ch 2, *2 hdc into next st, 1 hdc into next st; rep from * to last st, 2 hdc into next st, join into a round with a ss. (21sts)

ROUND 4 Ch 2, *2 hdc into next st, 1 hdc into each of next 2 sts; rep from * to last 2 sts, 2 hdc into next st, 1 hdc into next st, join into a round with a ss. (28sts)

Continue in this way, increasing 7 sts on each round until 9 rounds in total have been worked. (63sts)

ROUND 10 Ch 2, 1 hdc into each st to end, join into a round with a ss.

ROUND 11 Ch 2, *2 hdc into next st, 1 hdc into each of next 8 sts; rep from * to last 8 sts, 2 hdc into next st, 1 hdc into each of next 7 sts, join into a round with a ss. (70sts)

ROUND 12 Ch 2, *2 hdc into next st, 1 hdc into each of next 9 sts; rep from * to last 9 sts, 2 hdc into next st, 1 hdc into each of next 8 sts, join into a round with a ss. (77sts)

ROUND 13 Ch 2, 1 hdc into each st to end, join into a round with a ss.

ROUND 14 Ch 2, *2 hdc into next st, 1 hdc into each of next 10 sts; rep from * to last 10 sts, 2 hdc into next st, 1 hdc into each of next 9 sts, join into a round with a ss. (84sts)

MEDIUM AND LARGE SIZES ONLY

ROUND 15 Ch 2, 1 hdc into each st to end, join into a round with a ss.

ROUND 16 Ch 2, *2 hdc into next st, 1 hdc into each of next 11 sts; rep from * to last 11 sts, 2 hdc into next st, 1 hdc into each of next 10 sts, join into a round with a ss. (91sts)

LARGE SIZE ONLY

ROUND 17 Ch 2, 1 hdc into each st to end, join into a round with a ss.

ROUND 18 Ch 2, *2 hdc into next st, 1 hdc into each of next 12 sts; rep from * to last 12 sts, 2 hdc into next st, 1 hdc into each of next 11 sts, join into a round with a ss. (98sts)

ALL SIZES

Work straight (as per round 10) until the depth of the hat measures 6 ($6^1/4$:$6^3/4$)in/ 15 (16:17)cm from the beginning.

NEXT ROUND With yarn B, 1 ch, 1 sc into each st to end, join into a round with a ss.

NEXT ROUND With yarn A, 2 ch, 1 hdc into each st to end, join into a round with a ss.

NEXT ROUND With yarn B, 1 ch, 1 sc into each st to end, join into a round with a ss. Break off yarn B.

NEXT ROUND With yarn A, 2 ch, 1 hdc into each st to end, join into a round with a ss. Break off yarn A.

Making the earflaps

Rejoin yarn A at 15 (15:16) sts after the end of the last round. 2 ch, 1 hdc into each of the next 14 (15:16) sts. Turn.

ROW 1 Ch 2, hdc2tog, work 1 hdc into each st to the last 2 sts, hdc2tog. 12 (13:14) sts. Turn. Repeat row 1 until 2 (1:2) sts remain. Fasten off yarn.

Make the second earflap on the other side of the hat to match.

Edging

Join yarn B to the end of the last complete round worked.

Work 1 ch. 1 sc into each st.

At the first earflap, work 2 sc into each end of row to the point of the earflap.

Work 26 ch, then turn and, starting from the third ch from hook, work 1 sc into each ch.

Work 2 sc into each end of row.

Work 1 sc into each st along the base of the hat.

Work the second earflap in the same way as the first.

Work 1 sc into each st to the end of the round. Join with a ss. Fasten off yarn.

Finishing

Make a 2in (5cm) pom-pom in yarn B and attach to the top of the hat. Weave in all ends.

Essential information

DIFFICULTY LEVEL Intermediate

SIZE To fit an adult female

YARN You can use any DK weight silk/wool blend for a similar effect

A x 1 **B** x 1 **C** x 1

CROCHET HOOK G/6 US (4mm) hook

NOTIONS Yarn needle

GAUGE 8 bobbles per 4in (10cm)

SPECIAL ABBREVIATIONS

BEG BOBBLE: Ch 3, (yo and insert hook in st, yo and draw a loop through, yo and draw through first 2 loops on hook) 3 times all in the same st, yo and draw a loop through all 4 loops on hook.

BOBBLE STITCH: (yo and insert hook in st, yo and draw a loop through, yo and draw through first 2 loops on hook) 4 times all in the same st, yo and draw a loop through all 5 loops on hook.

DEC 1 BOBBLE: (yo and insert hook in st, yo and draw a loop through, yo and draw through first 2 loops on hook) 4 times all in the same st, rep in next st, yo and draw a loop through all 10 loops on hook.

CRAB STITCH: See p. 144

Women's beret

The beret is quick and easy to make and will make a perfect gift for a friend. The beret is worked in the round starting at the center and then adding each row.

PROJECTS
For more crab stitch patterns
>> go to pages 144, 174, and 240

Pattern

With yarn A, work 4 ch, ss in last ch from hook to form ring.

ROUND 1 Ch 3, 11 dc into center ring. (12sts)

ROUND 2 Ch 3, (yo and insert hook in first st, yo and draw a loop through, yo and draw through first 2 loops on hook) 3 times all in the same st, yo and draw a loop through all 4 loops on hook, (counts as first bobble), *1 bobble in next st; rep from * 10 times, ss in top of 3 ch. Fasten off. (12 bobbles)

ROUND 3 With B, join yarn in any ch sp, beg bobble, 1 bobble in same ch sp, *2 bobbles in next ch sp; rep from * 10 times, ss in top of 3 ch. Fasten off. (24 bobbles)

ROUND 4 With C, join yarn in any ch sp, beg bobble, 1 ch, *1 bobble in next ch sp, 1 ch; rep from * 22 times, ss in top of 3 ch. Fasten off. (24 bobbles)

ROUND 5 With A, join yarn in any ch sp, beg bobble, 1 bobble in same ch sp, 1 bobble in next ch sp, *2 bobbles in next ch sp, 1 bobble in next ch sp; rep from * 10 times, ss in top of 3 ch. Fasten off. (36 bobbles)

ROUND 6 With B, join yarn in any ch sp, beg bobble, 1 ch, *1 bobble in next ch sp, 1 ch; rep

from * 34 times, ss in top of 3 ch. Fasten off. (36 bobbles)

ROUND 7 With C, join yarn in any ch sp, beg bobble, 1 bobble in same ch sp, 1 bobble in next 2-ch sp, *2 bobbles in next ch sp, 1 bobble in next 2-ch sp; rep from * 10 times, ss in top of 3 ch. Fasten off. (48 bobbles)

ROUND 8 With A, join yarn in any ch sp, beg bobble, 1 ch, *1 bobble in next ch sp, 1 ch; rep from * 46 times, ss in top of 3 ch. Fasten off. (48 bobbles)

ROUND 9 With B, join yarn in any ch sp, beg bobble, 1 bobble in same ch sp, 1 bobble in next 3-ch sp *2 bobbles in next ch sp, 1 bobble in next 3-ch sp; rep from * 10 times, ss in top of 3 ch. Fasten off. (60 bobbles)

ROUND 10 With C, join yarn in any ch sp, beg bobble, 1 ch, *1 bobble in next ch sp, 1 ch; rep from * 58 times, ss in top of 3 ch. Fasten off. (60 bobbles)

ROUND 11 With A, rep round 10.

ROUND 12 With B, rep round 10.

ROUND 13 With C, rep round 10.

ROUND 14 With A, join yarn in any ch sp, 3 ch, (yo and insert hook in same ch sp, yo and draw a loop through, yo and draw through first 2 loops on hook) 3 times all in the same ch sp, (yo and insert hook in next ch sp, yo and draw a loop through, yo and draw through first 2 loops on hook) 4 times all in the same ch sp, yo and draw a loop through all 10 loops on hook, (dec 1 bobble), 1 ch, (1 bobble in next ch sp, 1 ch) 3 times, *dec 1 bobble, 1 ch (1 bobble in next ch sp, 1 ch) 3 times; rep from * 10 times, ss in top of 3 ch. Fasten off. (48 bobbles)

ROUND 15 With B, join yarn in any ch sp, beg bobble, 1 ch, *1 bobble in next ch sp, 1 ch; rep

The lovely bobble stitches used in this hat make it a very tactile and attractive project.

from * 46 times, ss in top of 3 ch. Fasten off. (48 bobbles)

ROUND 16 With C, join yarn in any ch sp, 3 ch, (yo and insert hook in same ch sp, yo and draw a loop through, yo and draw through first 2 loops on hook) 3 times all in the same ch sp, (yo and insert hook in next ch sp, yo and draw a loop through, yo and draw through first 2 loops on hook) 4 times all in the same ch sp, yo and draw a loop through all 10 loops on hook, (dec 1 bobble), 1 ch, (1 bobble in next ch sp, 1 ch) twice, *dec 1 bobble, 1 ch (1 bobble in next ch sp, 1 ch) twice; rep from * 10 times, ss in top of 3 ch. (36 bobbles)

ROUND 17 With A, join yarn in any ch sp, 1 ch, work 1 sc in the top of each bobble and each 1 ch around, ss in top of ch. (72sts)

ROUNDS 18–19 Repeat round 17.

ROUND 20 1 ch, work in crab stitch around, ss in ch.
Fasten off, weave in ends.

Lacy scarf

This pretty and very feminine scarf uses multiple increases to create ruffles. The pattern is worked in a round, but working into both sides of the starting chain. It can easily be adapted for a longer or shorter scarf.

PROJECTS

For more scarf projects
>> go to pages 40, 204, and 206

Essential information

DIFFICULTY LEVEL Easy

SIZE Approx 59 x 4in (150 x 10cm)

YARN For the same light and airy feel, use any fine mohair but you can use any lace weight yarn with varying effect

x 3

CROCHET HOOK 7 US (4.5mm) hook

NOTIONS Yarn needle

GAUGE Exact gauge is not essential

Pattern

Make a length of chain approx 4in (10cm) shorter than desired scarf.

For this 59in (150cm) long scarf, a chain of approx 55in (140cm) was worked. Now work 3 ch extra (counts as first treble on round 1).

ROUND 1 2 dc into fourth ch from hook, 1 dc in each ch to end, do not join or turn, work 3 dc into the last ch, then turn your work 180 degrees and work 1 dc into the unworked bottom loop of each ch to end, join round with a ss to top of first ch.

ROUND 2 Ch 3, 1 dc into bottom of ch, 3 dc into central dc of 3-dc group of round 1, 2 dc into each dc to other end of scarf, work 3 dc into central dc, then 2 dc into each st to end, join round with a ss to top of first ch.

ROUND 3 Ch 4, 1 tr into bottom of ch, * 2 tr into each dc to center dc of 3-dc group of round 2, work 3 tr into central dc; rep from *, then 2 tr into each st to end, join round with a ss to top of first ch.

ROUND 4 Ch 5 (counts as 1 tr, 1 ch), (1 tr, 1 ch), all into bottom of ch, * (1 tr, 1 ch) into each tr to center tr of 3-tr group of round 3, work (1 tr, 1 ch, 1 tr, 1 ch, 1 tr) into central tr; rep from * then (1 tr, 1 ch) into each st to end, join round with a ss to top of first ch.

You can now continue to make rounds in the same way if you wish—work an increase round working 2 dc into each st or ch sp, or work a plain round or whatever type of ruffle round you wish until the desired width of ruffle is reached.

Fasten off, weave in ends. Do not block the scarf as it may flatten the ruffle.

Work additional stitch increases in each round for a more highly ruffled scarf, or work plain rows in between increases for a less ruffled one.

>> This scarf is made with Rowan Kidsilk Haze, 230yds/210m/25g. in Dewberry (600).

Broomstick lace shawl

What better accessory for a wedding or summer garden party than this delicate, threadlike shawl? Crocheted with a long broomstick and using gossamer fine yarn, the stunning result hides how easy it is to make.

PROJECTS

For more openwork patterns
>> go to pages 116, 200, and 254

Essential information

DIFFICULTY LEVEL Easy

SIZE Approx 23½ x 59in (60 x 150cm)

YARN Any lace weight mohair yarn will give a similar effect. This pattern can also be made with any DK yarn for a more solid shawl. Non-fluffy yarns will produce a robust shawl

x 5

CROCHET HOOK 7 US (4.5mm) hook

NOTIONS 8mm x 14 or 16in (20 x 35 or 40cm) long broomstick or knitting needle
Yarn needle

GAUGE 6 groups of 4 loops (24 sc) and 4 rows to 4in (10cm)

NOTE The shawl is a straight piece of broomstick lace, but half of it is worked on one side of the foundation row of single crochet, referred to here as the "spine," and half of it is worked on the other side. This gives a symmetrical look to the finished shawl. If you find it hard to insert the hook into the top of the sc to put the next loop on the broomstick, use a smaller, pointed-ended hook—remember to use the 7 US (4.5mm) hook to work the sc sts.

Construction pattern

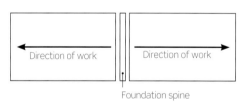

Foundation spine

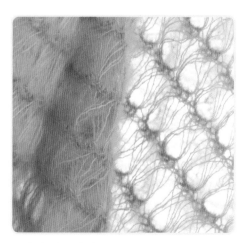

Work the foundation row of single crochet into the back bump only of the initial chain, to provide balanced loops to work each side of the shawl outward, from the center back foundation "spine."

Foundation spine and first side

Work 144 ch making sure they are kept nice and loose. Leave a long tail in case you miscount and need to make a few extra chains to get the right number of stitches on the foundation row.
Insert hook under back bump only of first ch, 1 sc. Insert hook in same way, 1 sc in each ch to end. (144 sc)

Pattern row

Pick up a loop onto the broomstick in each sc across. (144 loops)
Take off loops in groups of 4, placing 4 sc in each group. (144 sc = 36 groups)
Rep pattern row for half of required length. Fasten off.

Second side

Join yarn to end of initial spine of sc farthest away from the tail of yarn and work pattern row as for first side.

Finishing

Weave in all ends.
Avoid heavy blocking of this shawl or you will flatten the beautiful, fluffy texture of the yarn. Pin out to the required size, lightly spritz with water, and allow to dry naturally.

>> This shawl is made with Rowan Kidsilk Haze, 230yds/210m/25g, in Meadow (581).

Tweed stitch cowl

This warm and wooly cowl is made in the round using the shape of a Möebius strip. By making one twist, the loop appears never-ending and each round of crochet increases both the top and the bottom of the piece.

PROJECTS
For more scarf patterns
>> go to page 116, 200, and 206

Essential information

DIFFICULTY LEVEL Easy

SIZE 36 x 7in (92 x 18cm)

YARN Any aran weight yarn with high wool content will produce a similar effect

. x 4

CROCHET HOOK I/9 US (5.5mm) hook

NOTIONS Stitch marker
Yarn needle

GAUGE 16 sts x 18 rows per 4in (10cm)

Pattern
Work 148 ch.

FOUNDATION ROW Starting in the third ch from hook, *1 sc into next st, 1 ch, skip next st; rep from * to last st, 1 sc into last st. Join with a ss into the last ch from hook (i.e., the base of the first st), making 1 twist (which means that round 1 will be worked in the base of the sts on the foundation row).
Mark the first st with the stitch marker or safety pin. (This is purely to help you see easily where the round has started; the double-sided nature of the cowl and the fabric can sometimes make this tricky.)

ROUND 1 Ch 1, *work 1 sc into the ch sp on the row below, 1 ch, skip next st; rep from * to end, join with a ss.

ROUND 2 Ch 3, *skip next st, work 1 sc into the ch sp on the row below, 1 ch; rep from * to last st, work 1 sc into the last st, join with a ss.
Repeat these 2 rows 7 more times (16 rows in total).
Fasten off, weave in ends.

Tweed stitch is an easy crochet stitch that is also known as seed stitch. It creates a dense-textured fabric, which is ideal for a winter warmer.

>> This cowl is made with Rowan Felted Tweed Aran, 95yds/87m/50g, in Plum (731).

Men's chunky scarf

This striped scarf is made lengthwise in half double crochet worked between the stitches, with added length provided by the addition of tassels. Turn to pages 24–25 and pages 38–39 for details about the stitches used in this project.

PROJECTS

For more patterns for men
>> go to pages 194 and 226

Essential information

DIFFICULTY LEVEL Easy

SIZE 6¾ x 90½in (17 x 230cm)

YARN You can use any chunky weight, merino wool yarn to achieve a similar effect

A x 2   **B** x 2   **C** x 2   **D** x 2

CROCHET HOOK K/10½ US (6.5mm) hook

NOTIONS Yarn needle

GAUGE 8 sts x 9.5 rows per 4in (10cm)

By working half double crochet in the spaces between stitches to create tiny "pockets," and by using chunky yarn, this scarf is sure to keep the wearer toasty warm by trapping warm air within the scarf.

Pattern

With yarn A, work 182 ch.
ROW 1 1 hdc in third ch from hook, hdc in each ch to end, turn.
ROW 2 Ch 2, *hdc in the space between the first 2 sts, rep from * to end, turn.
With yarn B, rep row 2 twice.
With yarn C, rep row 2 twice.
With yarn D, rep row 2 twice.
With yarn A, rep row 2 twice.
With yarn B, rep row 2 twice.
With yarn C, rep row 2 twice.
With yarn D, rep row 2 twice.
Fasten off, weave in ends.

Tassels

With matching yarn, place 1 tassel at the end of each row on both ends of the scarf as follows:
Cut four 10in (25cm) long pieces of yarn, fold in half, feed loop through end of row, bring ends through loop, pull to fasten in place (see p. 74).

>> This scarf is made with Debbie Bliss Rialto Chunky, 66yds/60m/50g, in A: Navy (12), B: Ecru (03), C: Duck egg (10), and D: Camel (06).

Weave in the yarn ends as you work along the rows.

TOP TIP

Gloves, socks, and slippers

Child's wrist warmers

Worked in single crochet, these simple striped wrist warmers are an ideal way to practice changing colors. With no shaping, the thumb slit is worked by leaving part of the seam open when sewing up.

PROJECTS

For more striped patterns
>> *go to pages 260, 278, and 306*

Essential information

DIFFICULTY LEVEL Easy

SIZE To fit a child, age 8–10 years

YARN Any DK weight wool-blend yarn, preferably machine washable, can be substituted here

A x 1   **B** x 1   **C** x 1

CROCHET HOOK G/6 US (4mm) hook

NOTIONS Yarn needle

GAUGE 14 sts x 16 rows per 4in (10cm)

NOTE When working color changes, yarn should be changed on last yo of last sc in the row; yarn should be cut and not "carried."

Pattern *(make 2)*

With yarn A, work 21 ch.
ROW 1 (WS) Sc into second ch from hook, 1 sc in each st to end, change to B. (20sts)
ROW 2 (RS) Ch 1, sc to end, turn.
ROW 3 As row 2, change to C at end of row.
Continue working in single crochet in the following color sequence:
ROWS 4 AND 5 Yarn C.
ROWS 6 AND 7 Yarn A.
ROWS 8 AND 9 Yarn B.
ROWS 10 AND 11 Yarn C.
ROWS 12 AND 13 Yarn A.
ROWS 14 AND 15 Yarn B.
ROWS 16 AND 17 Yarn C.
ROWS 18 AND 19 Yarn A.
ROWS 20 AND 21 Yarn B.
Fasten off yarn, weave in all ends.
Rejoin C to top right-hand corner of row 1, work shell trim as follows:
sc in first st, ss in next sc, *5 hdc in next sc, skip 1 sc, ss in next sc, rep from * to end.
Fasten off C (6 hdc shells made).
Turn work 180 degrees and rejoin C to top right-hand edge, repeat shell trim.

Finishing

With RS facing, fold piece in half and sew a seam along row edge, leaving ³/₄in (2cm) unworked for thumb slit.
Weave in any remaining ends.
Turn right side out, join C to any row on thumb slit and work sc evenly around.
Fasten off, weave in ends.
Press according to ball band instructions.

The cuff of each wrist warmer is decorated with half double shells. Refer to pages 38–39 for information about half double crochet and simple stripes.

>> These wrist warmers are made with Berroco Vintage DK, 288yds/263m/50g, in A: Fondant (2110), B: Pool party (21107), and C: Magenta (21108).

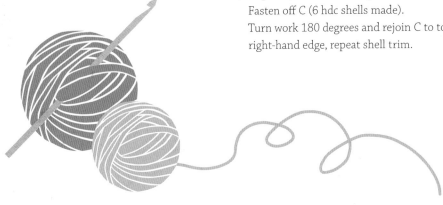

Child's mittens with string

Simple stitches in bright colors create the perfect accessory for a little boy or girl. Constructed in spirals of single crochet, these mittens work up in next to no time and are ideal for beginners.

PROJECTS

For more beginner patterns
>> go to pages 28, 36, and 64

Essential information

DIFFICULTY LEVEL Easy

SIZE To fit a child, age 6–10 years

YARN You can use any soft 4-ply to DK weight yarn with a synthetic content for durability to achieve a similar effect

A x 1   **B** x 1   **C** x 1

CROCHET HOOK D/3 US (3.25mm) hook

NOTIONS Stitch marker
Yarn needle

GAUGE Exact gauge is not essential

NOTE You may find it useful to mark the last st of first 4 rounds with a stitch marker. Do not join rounds, but place a marker at the first stitch of the round, moving it up as each round is completed to mark the beginning of each round.

Pattern (make 2)

With yarn A, work 4 ch, ss in first ch to form a ring.

ROUND 1 6 sc into ring. (6sts)

ROUND 2 2 sc in each st. (12sts)

ROUND 3 *1 sc in first st, 2 sc in next st, rep from * to end of round. (18sts)

ROUND 4 *1 sc in next 2 sts, 2 sc in next st, rep from * to end of round. (24sts)

ROUND 5 ONWARD Continue to work in sc until piece measures 3in (8cm).

The joining string is 100 chain stitches long, but you can lengthen or shorten it to suit the height of your child by simply adding or omitting stitches.

Thumb opening

NEXT ROUND Ch 6, miss 6 sc, sc to end of round (this is first of 6 ch).

NEXT ROUND 1 sc in each of 6 ch, sc to end. Work sc in each st for 3 further rounds. Fasten off A.

Join B into any sc, work 2 rounds of sc in B, fasten off B.

Join C into any sc, work 2 rounds of sc in C, fasten off C.

Rejoin A to any sc, work 3 rounds of sc in A. Fasten off yarn, weave in ends.

Thumb

Join A to any point around thumb opening. Work 12 sc evenly around gap.

Working in sc, continue to work in a spiral until thumb measures 1³⁄₈in (3.5cm).

NEXT ROUND sc2tog to end of round. (6sts)

Cut off yarn leaving a long tail, thread tail onto a yarn needle then thread through remaining stitches, pull tight, and fasten off. Join A into a sc on last round of first mitten, make 100 ch (or to desired length), ss into any st on last round of second mitten. Fasten off yarn, weave in ends.

>> These mittens are made with Debbie Bliss Baby Cashmerino, 137yds/125m/50g, in A: Sky (340032), B: Rose (340054), and C: Lime (340018).

Ladies' wrist warmers

These vibrant and practical wrist warmers have a pretty, three-dimensional texture created by puff stitches and a crochet rib using raised doubles.

PROJECTS
For more puff stitch patterns
>> *go to page 142*

Essential information

DIFFICULTY LEVEL Intermediate

SIZE Approx 8 (8³/₄:9¹/₂)in (20 [22:24])cm

YARN Any DK weight yarn will substitute here

x 2

CROCHET HOOK E/4 US (3.5mm) hook

GAUGE 18 dc to 4in (10cm) square

NOTIONS Yarn needle

SPECIAL ABBREVIATIONS
RDCF: raised double front: At the front of the work, yo, insert hook from right to left, around the post of the double stitch on the previous row, yo, draw through, yo, draw through 2 loops on hook, yo, draw through last 2 loops on hook, therefore making a double stitch.
RDCB: raised double back. At the back of the work, yo, insert hook from right to left, around the post of the double stitch on the previous row, yo, draw through, yo, draw through 2 loops on hook, yo, draw through last 2 loops on hook, therefore making a double stitch.
PUFF STITCH: *yo, insert into st, yo and draw loop through the stitch, drawing loop up to the height of the sts in the row; rep from * 4 times into the

These wrist warmers are made from two basic rectangles sewn together with gaps left for thumb holes. Turn to pages 70-71 for details about seams.

same st. 9 loops on hook, yo, and draw loop through all loops on hook. Puff completed.

Pattern
Work 32 (35:40) ch.
ROW 1 1 dc into third ch from hook and into each ch to end. Turn. (29 (33:37)sts)
ROW 2 Ch 3 (counts as first RdcB), *1 RdcF, 1 RdcB; rep from * to end of row.
ROW 3 Ch 3 (counts as first RdcF), *1 RdcB, 1 RdcF; rep from * to end of row.
Rep last two rows until rib measures approx 3in (8cm), or desired length.

Right glove
ROW 1 (RS) Ch 2, 1 hdc in each st to end, turn.
Rep last row twice more.
ROW 4 Ch 3, (1 puff, 1 dc) 8 times, hdc to end of row, turn.

Rep row 1 three times.
ROW 8 Ch 3, (1 dc, 1 puff) 7 times, hdc to end of row, turn.
Rep row 1 three times.
ROWS 12–18 As rows 4–11.
ROW 19 As row 1.
Fasten off yarn, leaving long end for sewing up seam.

Left glove
ROW 1 (RS) Ch 2, 1 hdc in each st to end, turn.
Rep last row twice more.
ROW 4 Ch 3, hdc to last 16 sts, (1 puff, 1 dc) 8 times, turn.
Rep row 1 three times.
ROW 8 Ch 3, hdc to last 15 sts, (1 puff, 1 dc) 7 times, 1 dc into last st, turn.
Rep row 1 three times.
ROWS 12–18 As rows 4–11.
ROW 19 As row 1.
Fasten off yarn, leaving long end for sewing up seam.

Finishing
Fold each glove in half lengthways so that right sides face each other, then sew up side seam 2in (5cm) down from top, fasten off yarn, and reattach approx 2¹/₂in (6cm) further down the seam, to allow space for thumb, checking that the distance is correct to fit your hand. Sew up remainder of seam down to bottom of rib.

>> These wrist warmers are made with Classic Elite Yarns Inca Alpaca, 109yds/100m/50g, in Morning glory (1163).

Baby girl's booties

These little shoes make the perfect baby shower gift. They are worked up in a single piece in a round, from the middle of the sole and up to the sides, with the strap added afterward. A contrasting-color trim and a button complete the look.

PROJECTS

For more patterns in the round
>> go to pages 176, 192, and 198

Essential information

DIFFICULTY LEVEL Easy

SIZE To fit a baby, age 3–6 months

YARN Any DK weight yarn with some cotton content for added structure will be perfect here

A x 1   **B** x 1

CROCHET HOOK E/4 US (3.5mm) hook

NOTIONS Yarn needle

GAUGE 10 sts x 2in (5cm)

Pattern

After completing round 7, measure the length of the sole—it should be approx 4–4¹⁄₄in (10–11cm) long. Ss into starting ch at end of each round.

Sole

With yarn A, work 9 ch, starting in second ch from hook.
ROUND 1 7 sc, 3 sc in next st, do not turn, continue in back loops of foundation ch, 6 sc, 2 sc in last st, ss in first st. (18sts)

ROUND 2 Ch 1, 2 sc in next st, 6 sc, 2 hdc in next st 3 times, 6 sc, 2 sc in next 2 sts, ss in first st. (24sts)

ROUND 3 Ch 1, 1 sc, 2 sc in next st, 6 sc, *1 hdc, 2 hdc in next st; rep from * 2 more times, 6 sc, **1 sc, 2 sc in next st; rep from ** 1 more time, ss in first st. (30sts)

ROUND 4 Ch 1, 2 sc, 2 sc in next st, 6 sc, *2 hdc, 2 hdc in next st; rep from * 2 more times, 6 sc, **2 sc, 2 sc in next st; rep from ** 1 more time, ss in first st. (36sts)

ROUND 5 Ch 1, 3 sc, 2 sc in next st, 6 sc, *3 hdc, 2 hdc in next st; rep from * 2 more times, 6 sc, **3 sc, 2 sc in next st; rep from ** 1 more time, ss in first st. (42sts)

ROUND 6 Ch 1, 4 sc, 2 sc in next st, 6 sc, *4 hdc, 2 hdc in next st; rep from * 2 more times, 6 sc, **4 sc, 2 sc in next st; rep from ** 1 more time, ss in first st. (48sts)

ROUND 7 Ch 1, 5 sc, 2 sc in next st, 6 sc, *5 hdc, 2 hdc in next st; rep from * 2 more times, 6 sc, **5 sc, 2 sc in next st; rep from ** 1 more time, ss in first st. (54sts)

Sides

ROUND 8 Ch 2 (counts as first st), 53 hdc, ss into second ch (for smaller shoe size, replace all hdc stitches with sc stitches). (54sts)

ROUND 9 Ch 2 (counts as first st), 12 hdc, hdc2tog, 17 hdc, hdc2tog, 15 hdc, hdc2tog, 3 hdc, ss into second ch. (51sts)

ROUND 10 Ch 2 (counts as first st), 12 hdc, hdc2tog, 16 hdc, hdc2tog, 14 hdc, hdc2tog, 2 hdc, ss into second ch. (48sts)

ROUND 11 Ch 2 (counts as first st), 12 hdc, hdc3tog, 14 hdc, hdc3tog, 12 hdc, hdc2tog, 1 hdc, ss into second ch. (43sts)

ROUND 12 Ch 1 (does not count as st), 13 sc, sc3tog, 12 sc, sc3tog, 10 sc, sc2tog, ss into first st. (38sts)
Fasten off.

Straps

For the right shoe, count 3 sts from the left side sc3tog from row 12, then attach yarn A. For the left shoe, count 1 st from the right side sc3tog from row 12, then attach yarn A.
ROW 1 Ch 1, 2 sc. (2sts)
ROWS 2–12 Turn work, 1 ch, 2 sc.
ROW 13 8 ch, ss into last st to make a loop.
Fasten off.

Trim

With yarn B, work an even trim of reverse single crochet, or crab stitch, (see p. 144) along the top edge of the shoe, going all around the strap.

Button (make 2)

With yarn B, make an adjustable ring (see p. 132).
ROUND 1 6 sc into the ring, pull ring tight. (6sts)
ROUND 2 2 sc in each st. (12sts)
ROUND 3 sc in each st.
ROUND 4 sc2tog across all sts. (6sts)
Sew up button opening and sew to shoes. Weave in loose ends.

>> These booties are made with Rowan Wool Cotton DK, 124yds/113m/50g, in A: Flower (943) and B: Tender (951).

For a smaller shoe to fit a 0-3 month old, measuring 3½ x 2½in (9 x 6cm), swap the hdc stitches for sc stitches where pattern indicates. Alternatively, stop making the sole part when you get to the length you need, and go on to make sides, matching the number of decreases in each round.

Essential information

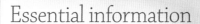

DIFFICULTY LEVEL Easy/Intermediate

SIZE To fit a child, age 3–6 months
For a smaller shoe, see caption on page 217

YARN You can use any DK weight yarn with some cotton content for structure

A x 1   **B** x 1

CROCHET HOOK E/4 US (3.5mm) hook

NOTIONS Yarn needle
2 small pieces of Velcro®
Sewing needle and thread

SPECIAL ABBREVIATIONS
RAISED SINGLE CROCHET BACK (RSCB):
See p. 194

GAUGE 10 sts per 2in (5cm)

Baby boy's booties

These booties are worked in a round, with a raised contrast color strip separating sole from sides and a chunky strap to keep them on tiny feet. Using Velcro® to fasten makes them really easy to put on and take off, too!

PROJECTS

For more shoe patterns
>> go to pages 216, 220, and 222

For a rigid shoe, use a cotton-based yarn that will create a stiff fabric. For a softer feel, try a pure merino yarn. Refer to page 50 for instructions on how to work single crochet increases.

<< These booties are made with Rowan Wool Cotton DK, 124yds/113m/50g, in A: Ship shape (955) and B: Clear (941).

Pattern

Measure the length of the sole after completing round 7—it should be approx 4–4¼in (10–11cm).

Sole

With yarn A, work 9 ch, starting in second ch from hook.

ROUND 1 7 sc, 3 sc in next st, rotate through 180 degrees and continue along the back loop of the chains, 6 sc, 2 sc in last st, ss in first st. (18sts)

ROUND 2 Ch 1, 1 sc inc, 6 sc, 3 dc inc, 6 sc, sc inc in each of last 2 sc, ss in first st. (24sts)

ROUND 3 Ch 1, 1 sc, 1 sc inc, 6 sc, *1 dc, 1 dc inc; rep from * 2 more times, 6 sc, **1 sc, 1 sc inc; rep from ** 1 more time, ss in first st. (30sts)

ROUND 4 Ch 1, 2 sc, 1 sc inc, 6 sc, *2 dc, 1 dc inc; rep from * 2 more times, 6 sc, **2 sc, 1 sc inc; rep from ** 1 more time, ss in first st. (36sts)

ROUND 5 Ch 1, 3 sc, 1 sc inc, 6 sc, *3 dc, 1 dc inc; rep from * 2 more times, 6 sc, **3 sc, 1 sc inc; rep from ** 1 more time, ss in first st. (42sts)

ROUND 6 Ch 1, 4 sc, 1 sc inc, 6 sc, *4 dc, 1 dc inc; rep from * 2 more times, 6 sc, **4 sc, 1 sc inc; rep from ** 1 more time, ss in first st. (48sts)

ROUND 7 Change to yarn B, 1 ch, 5 sc, 1 sc inc, 6 sc, *5 dc, 1 dc inc; rep from * 2 more times, 6 sc, **5 sc, 1 sc inc; rep from ** 1 more time, ss in first st. (54sts)

Sides

ROUND 8 Ch 1, 54 rscb, ss into first st.

ROUND 9 Ch 1, 54 rscb, ss into first st.

ROUND 10 Change to yarn A, 1 ch, 54 sc, ss into first st.

ROUND 11 Ch 1, 54 sc, ss into first st.

ROUND 12 Ch 1, 13 sc, *dc2tog, 3 dc; rep from * 3 more times, dc2tog, 17 sc, sc2tog. (48sts)

ROUND 13 Ch 1, 13 sc, *dc2tog, 2 dc; rep from * 3 more times, dc2tog, 15 sc, sc2tog. (42sts)

ROUND 14 Ch 1, 13 sc, *dc2tog, 1 dc; rep from * 3 more times, dc2tog, 13 sc, sc2tog. (36sts)

ROUND 15 Ch 1, 13 sc, 5 dc2tog, 13 sc, ss into first st. (31sts)
Fasten off.

Straps

With yarn A, work 9 ch, starting in second ch from hook.

ROW 1 8 sc. (8sts)

ROWS 2–12 turn work, ch 1, 8 sc.

ROW 13 sc2tog, 4 sc, sc2tog. (6sts)

ROW 14 sc2tog, 2 sc, sc2tog. (4sts)

ROW 15 2 sc2tog. (2sts) Fasten off.

Add some surface crochet stripes in chain stitch on the rounded edge for decoration, in yarn B.

Finishing

Sew the straps onto the shoes. Cut two small squares of Velcro® and sew on to secure the rounded edge of the strap down.
Weave in loose ends.

Child's edged slippers

These cuffed slippers are worked in the round, then crocheted flat before rejoining to create the slipper shape. The foot length is adjustable and, because the slipper is worked from the toe, it is easy to custom-fit.

PROJECTS

For more single crochet patterns
>> go pages 194, 216, and 278

Essential information

DIFFICULTY LEVEL Easy

SIZE To fit a child, age 2-3 (4-5:6-7) years

YARN Any aran weight yarn would suit this project

A x 2   **B** x 1

CROCHET HOOK E/4 US (3.5mm) and 7 US (4.5mm) hooks

NOTIONS 2 stitch markers
Yarn needle

<< These slippers are made from Valley Yarns Valley Superwash, 97yds/89m/50g, in A: Colonial blue (502) and Berroco Comfort, 178yd/165m/50g, in B: Chalk (2700).

Pattern (make 2)

With 7 US (4.5mm) hook and yarn A, work 4 ch, join with a ss to form a ring.
ROUND 1 6 sc into ring, do not join, continue working in a spiral using stitch marker to indicate the last st of each round (remove and replace after last sc of each round). Do not turn, continue to work in a spiral with RS facing.
ROUND 2 Work 2 sc in each sc. (12sts)
ROUND 3 *1 sc in next 2 sts, 2 sc in next st, rep from * to end. (18sts)

MEDIUM AND LARGE SIZES ONLY
ROUND 4 *1 sc in next 2 sts, 2 sc in next st, rep from * to end. (24sts)

LARGE SIZE ONLY
ROUND 5 *1 sc in next 3 sts, 2 sc in next st, rep from * to end. (30sts)

ALL SIZES
At the end of round 3 (4:5), continue to work in a spiral without increasing until toe measures $2^{1}/_{2}$ ($2^{3}/_{4}$:3)in/6 (7:8)cm. Turn. Remainder of the sole is worked flat.
ROW 1 Ch 1, sc in second ch from hook, sc to last 6 (6:8) sc, turn 12 (18:22) sc.
ROW 2 Dc to end.
Continue to work in sc until sole measures 5 ($5^{1}/_{2}$:$6^{1}/_{4}$)in/12 (14:16)cm from round 1.
Fasten off A.
With RS facing, sew heel seam.
Turn slipper right way out and continue with RS facing.
With 7 US (4.5mm) hook, rejoin A to center of heel seam, 1 ch (does not count as a st),

working in sc, work 1 row evenly around top piece of slipper, working 1 st into each row and each st across front of toe, ss into top of first sc to join.
NEXT ROW Place markers in center 2 toe stitches. Ch 1 (does not count as st), sc to first marker, turn 1 ch, sc to second marker. Continue working back and forth in sc, leaving the center two stitches unworked. Continue until cuff measures $^{3}/_{4}$ (1:$1^{1}/_{4}$)in/ 2 (2.5:3cm). For a longer cuff, work more rows here.
FINAL ROW Dc to first marker, remove markers, sc2tog, sc to end. Fasten off yarn.

Trim

With E/4 US (3.5mm) hook and B, join yarn to wrong side of top edge, work 2 rows of sc to finish. Fasten off yarn, weave in all ends. Fold over cuff and sew in place.

The approximate foot length for each of the three sizes of slipper measures 5in (12cm), $5^{1}/_{2}$in (14cm), and $6^{1}/_{4}$in (16cm).

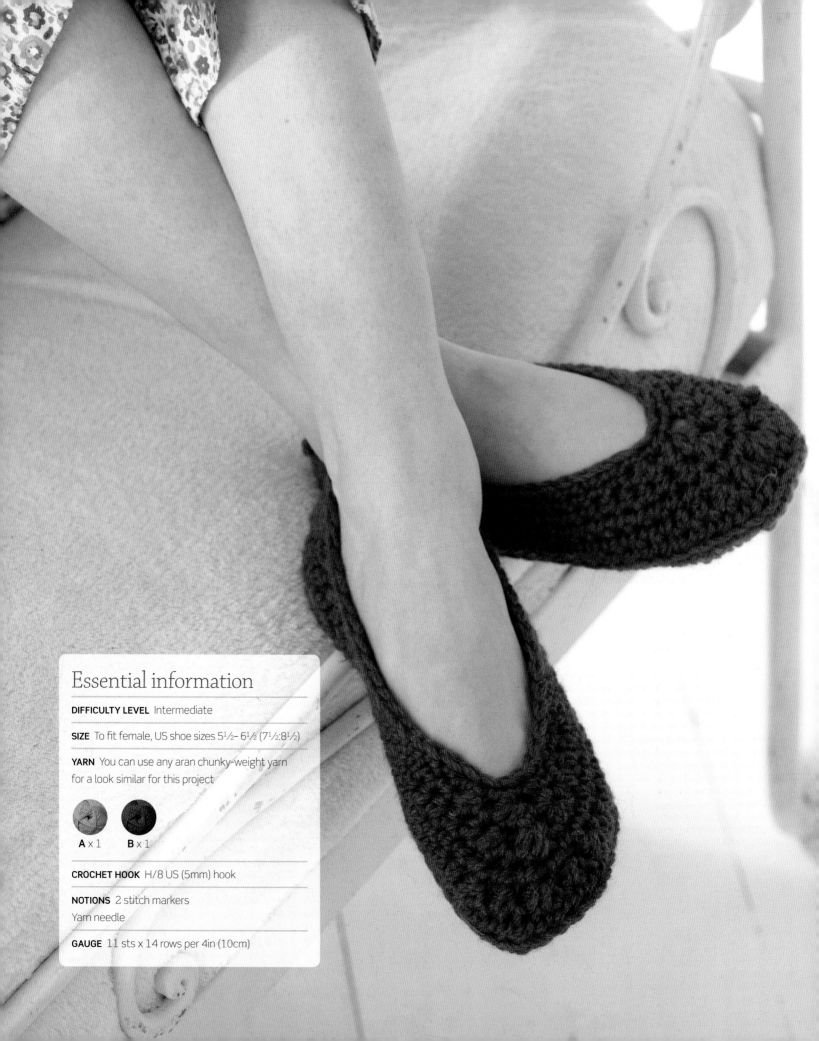

Essential information

DIFFICULTY LEVEL Intermediate

SIZE To fit female, US shoe sizes 5½- 6½ (7½:8½)

YARN You can use any aran chunky-weight yarn for a look similar for this project

A x 1   **B** x 1

CROCHET HOOK H/8 US (5mm) hook

NOTIONS 2 stitch markers
Yarn needle

GAUGE 11 sts x 14 rows per 4in (10cm)

Ladies' soft slippers

A simple but stylish way to keep your toes cozy indoors. Play with color and brighten up dull days with a splash of neon or choose neutral shades for understated elegance.

PROJECTS
For more half double crochet patterns
>> *go to pages 40 and 206*

Pattern

The sole is worked in spirals; do not join at end of each round and do not turn. When the sole is completed, yarn A is fastened off and yarn B joined into the same stitch to make the upper.

Sole (make 2)

ROUND 1 With yarn A, work 18 (20:22) ch, 3 sc in third ch from hook, 10 (12:14) sc, 4 dc, 5 dc into last ch, place marker in top of third dc (remove and replace this marker on subsequent rounds as indicated), do not turn but work into the opposite side of the foundation ch for rem sts, 4 dc, 10 (12:14) sc, 2 sc in same st as initial 3 sc. Do not join and do not turn, place a second marker in last st (remove and replace on subsequent rounds to mark last st). (38 (42:46)sts)

ROUND 2 3 hdc, sc to first before first marker, 2 hdc into next st, 3 dc into next st (remove and replace marker in center dc), 2 hdc into next st, sc to last 2 sts, 2 hdc, do not join or turn, place marker in last hdc. (42 (46:50)sts)

ROUND 3 3 hdc into next st, 2 hdc into next st, 3 hdc, sc to 2 sts before marker, 1 hdc, 2 dc into next st, remove marker, 3 dc into next st (replace marker in center dc), 2 dc into next st, 1 hdc, sc to last 4 sts, 3 hdc, 2 hdc in next st. Do not join and do not turn. (50 (54:58)sts)

ROUND 4 1 hdc, 3 hdc into next st, 1 hdc in next st, 2 hdc in next st, 3 hdc, sc to 6 sts before marker, 3 hdc, (2 hdc into next st) 2 times, 2 dc into next st, remove marker, 3 dc into next st (replace marker in center st), 2 dc into next st, (2 hdc into next st) 2 times, 3 hdc, sc to last 4 sts, 3 hdc, 2 hdc in next st. Do not join and do not turn. (62 (66:70)sts) Ss into next 3 sts, fasten off A.

Upper (make 2)

Join B into last ss.

ROUND 1 1 sc in each st to end, join with a ss to top of first sc. (62 (66:70)sts)

ROUND 2 Ch 1 (does not count as a stitch), 1 sc TBL in each sc to end, join to top of first sc. (62 (66:70)sts)

ROUND 3 Ch 2 (counts as first hdc), 6 (7:8) hdc, 16 sc, 2 (3:4) hdc, (hdc2tog) 2 times, hdc3tog place marker to indicate center toe stitch, (hdc2tog) 2 times, 2 (3:4) hdc, sc to last 8 (9:10) sts, 8 (9:10) hdc, join to top of first hdc. (56 (60:64)sts)

ROUND 4 Ch 1 (does not count as a st), 1 sc in same sp as 1 ch, 2 sc, (dc2tog) 3 times, sc to last 8 sts, (dc2tog) 3 times, sc to end (remove and replace marker when you reach it), join with a ss to top of first sc. (50 (54:58)sts)

ROUND 5 Ch 1 (does not count as st), sc to 7 sts before marker, 4 hdc, hdc2tog, hdc3tog, (remove and replace marker), hdc2tog, 4 hdc, sc to end, join to top of first sc. (46 (50:54)sts)

ROUND 6 Ch 1 (does not count as a st), 3 sc, (dc2tog) 2 times, sc to 3 sts before marked stitch, hdc2tog, hdc3tog, hdc2tog, sc to last 5 sts, (dc2tog) 2 times, sc to end. Join to top of first sc. (38 (42:46)sts)

SHOE SIZES 7½ AND 8½ ONLY

ROUND 7 Ch 2 (counts as stitch), hdc to first before marker, hdc3tog, hdc to end. (40 (44)sts)

ALL SIZES

ROUND 8 Dc to end.

ROUND 9 (optional for narrow feet) Work 1 ss into each sc to end.
Fasten off yarn, weave in ends.
Block lightly by spraying with water and stuffing with cotton to create shape.

These slippers are designed to be snug at first because the yarn will "give" with wear. If in doubt about which size to make, opt for the smaller size. Choose a dark color for the sole, since it's more practical than a lighter shade.

<< Use Berroco Ultra Alpaca. 215yds/198m/100g. in A: Salt and pepper (6207) and B: Cyclamen (6258).

Essential information

DIFFICULTY LEVEL Intermediate

SIZE To fit female, US shoe sizes $6^1/_2$–$9^1/_2$

YARN You can substitute any DK-weight sock yarn for this project, preferably with nylon

x 1

CROCHET HOOK B/1 US (2.5mm) and C/2 US (3mm) hooks

NOTIONS 2 stitch markers, yarn needle

GAUGE 23 sts x 22 rows per 4in (10cm)

Ladies' ankle socks

These pretty, comfortable socks are worked in the round from the cuff down, using an alternating pattern of single crochet and double crochet stitches. The tip of the toe and the heel are reinforced by using single crochet.

PROJECTS
For more single crochet patterns
>> go to pages 34, 162, and 260

Pattern (make 2)
Work the cuff-ribbing sideways.

Cuff-ribbing (worked sideways)
With B/1 US (2.5mm) hook, work 10 ch.
ROW 1 1 hdc in third ch from hook, 1 hdc in each ch to end, turn. (8sts)
ROW 2 1 hdc TBL in each st to end, turn.
Rep row 2 a further 28 times. (30 rows)
Using ss all along row, join first row to last row to form a large ring.

Cuff to heel
Turn ribbing 90 degrees, so you are working into the sides of the rows on the cuff.
ROUND 1 With C/2 US (3mm) hook, work 45 sc evenly around the cuff, place marker to indicate end of round.
You are now working in continuous rounds.
ROUND 2 *1 sc, 1 dc, rep from * to marker, 1 sc.
ROUND 3 *1 dc, 1 sc, rep from * to marker, 1 dc.
Rep rounds 2 and 3 until sock measures 7¹/₂in (19cm), making sure to end on a round 3.

Heel
ROW 1 22 sc, turn.
ROW 2 1 ch, 22 sc, turn.

<< These socks are made with Regia Angora Merino 4-ply, 219yds/200m/50g, in Aqua (07082).

Work in rows of sc until heel flap measures 2in (5cm).

Turn the heel
ROW 1 Ch 1, 13 sc, sc2tog, 1 sc, turn.
ROW 2 6 sc, sc2tog, 1 sc, turn.
ROW 3 Dc to 1 st from end of prev row, sc2tog (your second st of the sc2tog will be the next sc, which is 2 rows below), 1 sc, turn.
Rep row 3, 5 times. (14sts)

Foot
ROUND 1 14 sc, evenly work 10 sc in side of heel rows, place marker, 1 sc, *1 dc, 1 sc, rep from * across to other side of heel, 1 dc, place marker, evenly work 12 sc into sides of heel rows, place marker to indicate end of round. (59sts)
ROUND 2 20 sc, (sc2tog) twice, 1 dc, *1 sc, 1 dc, rep from * to marker, 1 sc, (sc2tog) twice, sc to end marker. (55sts)
ROUND 3 (1 sc, 1 dc) 9 times, sc2tog, dc2tog, 1 sc, *1 dc, 1 sc, rep from * to marker, 1 sc, dc2tog, sc2tog, (1 dc, 1 sc) twice, 1 dc. (51sts)
ROUND 4 (1 dc, 1 sc) 8 times, dc2tog, sc2tog, 1 dc, *1 sc, 1 dc, rep from * to marker, 1 dc, sc2tog, dc2tog, (1 sc, 1 dc) twice. (47sts)
Remove all but ending marker.
ROUND 5 *1 sc, 1 dc, rep from * to last st, 1 sc.
ROUND 6 *1 dc, 1 sc, rep from * to last st, 1 dc.
Rep last 2 rounds until sock measures 9in (23cm).

Toe
ROUND 1 16 sc, sc2tog, place marker, 1 sc, sc2tog, 23 sc, place marker, sc to end of round. (46sts)
ROUND 2 *sc to 3 sts from marker, sc2tog,

Adjust the size of these socks by adding or subtracting stitches in multiples of two, in the round, to change the foot circumference, or by working the foot longer or shorter to adjust the length.

1 sc, slip marker (put it into the new loop on your hook to mark the start of the next round), 1 sc, sc2tog, rep from * once, sc to end of round. (42sts)
Rep round 2, 3 times. (On the last round there will be no sc after the last sc2tog). (30sts)
Remove end marker.
ROUND 3 *sc to 3 sts from marker, sc2tog, 1 sc, slip marker, 1 sc, sc2tog, rep from * once. (26sts)
ROUND 4 Rep round 3. (22sts)
Fasten off, leaving a long end.

Finishing
Turn sock inside out and using the end left from fastening off, ss across both thicknesses of toe sts to seam together. Weave in ends.

Essential information

DIFFICULTY LEVEL Intermediate

SIZE To fit a male, US shoe sizes 9–12

YARN You can use any DK-weight wool/
acrylic blend yarn to achieve a similar effect

A x 1   **B** x 1

CROCHET HOOK B/1 US (2.5mm) and D/3 US
(3mm) hooks

GAUGE 19 sts x 14 rows per 4in (10cm)

NOTIONS 2 stitch markers
Yarn needle

SPECIAL ABBREVIATIONS

LHDC: linked half double. On starting st,
insert hook into second ch of starting ch, yo,
draw through, insert hook into st, yo, draw
through st, yo, draw through all loops on
hook. For each st after that as follows:
insert hook into horizontal bar in st before,
yo, draw through, insert hook into st, yo, draw
through st, yo, draw through all loops on hook.

LHDC2TOG: linked half double 2 together.
Insert hook into horizontal bar in st before,
yo, draw through, insert hook into next st,
yo, draw through st, insert hook into next
st, yo, draw through st, yo, draw through
all loops on hook.

Men's chunky socks

These warm socks are made in the round, worked from the cuff down, with a contrasting color used on the ribbing, heel, and toe, and worked in stripes to add extra detailing.

PROJECTS
For more single crochet patterns
>> *go to pages 64 and 176*

Socks (make 2)
Adjust the size by adding or subtracting stitches in the round to change the circumference, or by working the foot longer or shorter to adjust the length.

Cuff ribbing (worked sideways)
With B/1 US (2.5mm) hook and yarn B, 1 hdc in each ch to end, turn. (12sts)
ROW 2 1 hdc TBL in each st to end, turn.
Rep row 2 a further 46 times. (48 rows)
Using ss all along row, join first row to last row to form a large ring.

Cuff to heel
Turn ribbing 90 degrees, so you are working into the sides of the rows on the cuff.
ROUND 1 With D/3 US (3mm) hook and yarn A, 2 ch, 1 lhdc in each row side to end, change to yarn B, join, place stitch marker to indicate end of round. (48sts)
ROUND 2 Ch 2, lhdc in each st to end, change to yarn A, join.
ROUND 3 Ch 2, lhdc2tog, lhdc in each st to 2sts from marker, lhdc2tog, change to yarn B, join. (46sts)

ROUND 4 Rep round 2, change to yarn A.
ROUND 5 Rep round 2, change to yarn B.
ROUND 6 Rep round 3. (44sts)
ROUND 7 Rep round 2, change to yarn A.
ROUND 8 Rep round 2, do not join.
From now on, work in continuous rounds throughout.
ROUND 9 1 lhdc, lhdc2tog, lhdc in each st to 2 sts from marker, lhdc2tog. (42sts)
Work straight in continuous rounds of lhdc until sock measures 6¾in (17cm) from cuff edge.

Heel
ROW 1 22 lhdc (do NOT fasten off yarn A, as you will pick this up again later on the foot).
With yarn B, 20 sc, turn.
ROW 2 Ch 1, 1 sc in each sc to end, turn.
Rep row 2 until heel measures 2½in (6cm).

Turn the heel
ROW 1 Ch 1, 12 sc, sc2tog, 1 sc, turn.
ROW 2 Ch 1, 6 sc, sc2tog, 1 sc, turn.
ROW 3 Sc to 1 st from end of prev row, sc2tog (your second st of the sc2tog will be the next sc which is 2 rows below), 1 sc, turn.
Rep row 3 until you reach the end of the heel stitches, there will be no sc after the sc2tog at the end of your last 2 rows. (12sts)
Fasten off.

Foot
ROUND 1 With yarn A, left in place at beginning of heel, 2 ch, work 8 lhdc evenly up the side of the heel, 1 lhdc in each of the sts from the heel turn and 8 lhdc evenly placed down the other side of the heel flap; place

marker, work lhdc in each lhdc across the front of foot, place marker. (50sts)
You are now working in continuous rounds of lhdc again.
ROUND 2 Lhdc2tog, 1 lhdc, lhdc2tog, 18 lhdc, lhdc2tog, 1 lhdc, lhdc2tog, slip marker, lhdc in each st to next marker. (46sts)
ROUND 3 Lhdc2tog, 1 lhdc, lhdc2tog, 14 lhdc, lhdc2tog, 1 lhdc, lhdc2tog, remove marker, lhdc in each st to next marker. (42sts)
ROUND 4 Lhdc in each st to end of round.
Work in continuous rounds of lhdc until sock measures 10in (25cm) from heel.

Toe
ROUND 1 With yarn B, 21 sc, place marker, sc to end of round.
ROUND 2 Sc2tog, *sc to 2 sts from marker, sc2tog**, slip marker, sc2tog, rep from * between * and **. (38sts)
Rep round 2, 6 times. (14sts)
Fasten off, leaving a long end.

Finishing
Turn sock inside out and using the end left from fastening off, ss across both thicknesses of toe sts to seam together.
Weave in ends.

What to wear

Baby's crossover cardigan

This sweet, wrap-around cardigan is worked in half double crochet and crosses over from left to right, as well as right to left. The crocheted ties can be altered as your child grows, to extend the life of your lovingly made garment.

PROJECTS

For more half double crochet patterns
>> go to pages 40 and 206

Essential information

DIFFICULTY LEVEL Easy

SIZE To fit a child, age 12–18 months

YARN You can use any wool or wool mix, 4-ply to sportweight yarn for this project

x 4

CROCHET HOOK G/6 US (4mm) hook

GAUGE 18 sts x 13 rows to 4in (10cm)

NOTIONS Safety pins
Yarn needle

SPECIAL ABBREVIATIONS

HALF DOUBLE DECREASE: yo, put hook in next st, and pull through yarn (3 loops on the hook), yo, insert hook in the next st, and pull through yarn (5 loops on the hook), yo, and pull through all loops.

<< This cardigan is made with Debbie Bliss Baby Cashmerino, 137yds/125m/50g, in Baby blue (340204).

Pattern

The fronts and back of this cardigan are worked in one piece.

Front and back

ROW 1 Work 150 ch, hdc into the third ch from the hook, hdc into the rest of the ch. (148 hdc, 2 ch)
ROW 2 Ch 2, hdc in each hdc, no hdc into top of 2 ch. (148 hdc)
ROW 3 Ch 2, hdc2tog, hdc in the rest of the hdc, no hdc into top of 2 ch. (146 hdc)
Repeat row 3 until you have 108 hdc.
Start dividing, first front, keep in pattern.

First front

ROW 23 Ch 2, hdc2tog, hdc in the next 24 sts. (25sts)
ROW 24 Ch 2, hdc to end, no hdc into top of 2 ch. (24sts)
ROW 25 Ch 2, hdc2tog, hdc into each hdc, hdc into 2 ch. (23sts)
Repeat rows 24–25 until you have 11 sts.
ROW 38 Ch 2, hdc in the same place as 2 ch, hdc to end, not in top of 2 ch. (11sts)
Fasten off leaving a 12in (30cm) tail for sewing up.

Back

Skip 4 st on row 22 from edge of first front. Rejoin yarn.
ROW 23 Ch 2, hdc in the same st, hdc in the next 48 sts, turn. (49sts)

ROW 24 Ch 2, hdc in the same st, hdc to the end, no hdc into the top of the 2 ch. (49sts)
ROWS 25–38 Rep row 24.

Neck shaping

ROW 39 Ch 2, hdc in the same st, and hdc in the next 9 hdc. (10sts)
Fasten off.
Skip 29 hdc, rejoin yarn.
Ch 2, hdc in the same st, hdc in the next 9 sts.
Fasten off.

Half double crochet makes a thick, dense fabric that is perfect for clothes. Lightweight, soft baby yarn, as used here, also makes this cardigan both a great summer and winter cover-up.

The beauty of crocheting the ties on this cardigan is that you won't need to sew on ribbons or strips of fabric that tiny fingers might pull off. Work your chain stitches with an even tension (see pp. 24–25) for a neat finish.

Second front

Skip 4 sts on row 22 from edge of back. Rejoin yarn.

ROW 23 Ch 2, hdc in the same st, hdc to end. (25sts)

ROW 24 Ch 2, hdc2tog, hdc to end, no hdc into top of 2 ch. (23sts)

ROW 25 Ch 2, hdc in the same st, hdc to end. (23sts)

Repeat rows 24–25 until you have 11 sts.

ROW 38 Ch 2, hdc in the next 10 hdc. (10sts) Fasten off leaving a 12in (30cm) tail for sewing up.

Sleeves (make 2)

ROW 1 Make 31 ch, hdc in third ch from the hook, hdc in each ch, turn. (29sts)

ROW 2 Ch 2, hdc in same st, hdc in each hdc, **do not hdc in top of 2 ch throughout**. (29sts)

ROW 3 As row 2. (29sts)

ROW 4 Ch 2, 2 hdc in same st (inc made), hdc in each hdc to end. (30sts)

Repeat rows 2–4 until you have 35 hdc.

ROW 20 Rep row 2. (35sts)

ROW 21 As row 20. (35sts)

ROW 22 Ch 2, 2 hdc in same st, hdc in each hdc to last st, 2 hdc in last st. (37sts)

Repeat rows 20–22 once. (39sts)

ROW 26 Rep row 2. (39sts)

ROW 27 1 ch, ss across 6 st, 2 ch, hdc in next 27 hdc, turn. (27sts)

ROW 28 Ch 2, hdc2tog, hdc in each hdc to last 2 sts, hdc2tog, turn. (24sts)

Repeat row 28 until you have 12 hdc. Fasten off.

Finishing

Sew the shoulder seams together using backstitch. Whipstitch the sleeve seams together. With safety pins, pin the sleeve into the arm hole. The first pin should have the sleeve seam between the missed st on row 23 and the middle of the sleeve cap in line with the shoulder seam. Ease the rest of the sleeve in place, then whip st the two pieces together. Repeat for the other sleeve.

Edging

Join the yarn to the center back of the neck and work sc all around the garment, working 3 sc to 2 rows of hdc on the fronts, joining to the first sc with a ss.

Work sc round the bottom of the sleeve joining to the first sc with a ss.

Ties

Attach yarn to first st on the bottom of the garment, work 40 ch, fasten off, weave in ends. Repeat at the last st. Make a 40-ch tie 10in (25cm) from the beginning ch and 10in (25cm) from the other end, and also on row 20, where fronts cross over.

Block the garment lightly before sewing up.

TOP TIP

Child's poncho

A giant granny square makes a colorful and cozy poncho with a square in the middle to go over the head. For more information about crocheting a granny square, turn to pages 102–103.

PROJECTS

For more granny square patterns
>> *go to pages 154, 168, and 302*

Essential information

DIFFICULTY LEVEL Easy

SIZE To fit a child, age 4–9 years

YARN You can use any DK yarn for a similar look to this project

A x 1   B x 1   C x 1   D x 1

E x 2   F x 2

CROCHET HOOK 7 US (4.5mm) hook

NOTIONS 4 stitch markers
Yarn needle

GAUGE 4 x 3 dc groups to 4in (10cm), 9 rows to 4in (10cm)

Pattern

ROW 1 With yarn A, make a slip knot 4in (10cm) from the end of the yarn, work 75 ch, dc into the fourth ch from the hook (first 4 ch count as a dc st), dc in the next ch, *1 ch, dc in the next 3 ch, repeat from * to the end (24 x 3 dc groups), 1 ch, ss to the top of the 3 ch. Make sure you do not twist the row, fasten off and weave in end. With the 4in (10cm) tail, join to the fourth ch and sew in end.
Put stitch markers in first, 7th, 13th, and 19th ch sp leaving 5-ch sp between each 2 markers. These mark where the corners will be.

ROW 2 Join yarn B at first marked ch sp, work (3 ch, 2 dc, 3 ch, 3 dc) in same ch sp to make the first corner, 1 ch, *(3 dc in next ch sp, 1 ch) 5 times**, (3 dc, 3 ch, 3 dc) in next ch sp, 1 ch; repeat from * twice, then from * to ** once, ss into the top of the 3 ch at the beginning of the round, fasten off and sew in ends. (20 x 3 dc groups and 4 corner groups)

ROW 3 Join yarn C to 3-ch corner sp, work (3 ch, 2 dc, 3 ch, 3 dc) in same ch sp, 1 ch, *(3 dc in next ch sp, 1 ch) to next corner**, (3 dc, 3 ch, 3 dc) in 3-ch corner sp, 1 ch; rep from * twice, then from * to ** once, ss to top of 3 ch

and fasten off. Weave in ends. (6 x 3 dc groups between corners)

ROWS 4–16 Repeat row 3 in following colors. You will have one more 3 dc group on each side of the square on each row.

ROW 4 Yarn D. (7 x 3 dc)
ROW 5 Yarn E. (8 x 3 dc)
ROW 6 Yarn A. (9 x 3 dc)
ROW 7 Yarn B. (10 x 3 dc)
ROW 8 Yarn F. (11 x 3 dc)
ROW 9 Yarn C. (12 x 3 dc)
ROW 10 Yarn E. (13 x 3 dc)
ROW 11 Yarn A. (14 x 3 dc)
ROW 12 Yarn D. (15 x 3 dc)
ROW 13 Yarn B. (16 x 3 dc)
ROW 14 Yarn C. (17 x 3 dc)
ROW 15 Yarn E. (18 x 3 dc)
ROW 16 Yarn F. (19 x 3 dc)

ROWS 17–32 Repeat color sequence again.

ROW 33 With yarn A, work in sc all around the edges, working 5 sc at the corners, fasten off with an invisible join.

>> This poncho is made with Berroco Vintage DK, 288yds/263m/100g, in A: Dewberry (2167), B: Pool party (21107), C: Bubble (21107), D: Fondant (2110), E: Mushroom (2104), and F: Minty (2112).

Using a yarn that is 100 percent wool makes this a warm and snuggly garment for a child. Choose colors carefully for a harmonious effect and use the same color for the neckline and the single crochet edging along the bottom to give a coherent feel.

Striped sweater

This versatile garment is made in the round, working from the bottom up. The sleeves are then joined to the body and the yoke is shaped using raglan style decreases (see pp. 52–53).

PROJECTS

For more patterns in the round
>> go to pages 174 and 184

Essential information

DIFFICULTY LEVEL Intermediate

SIZE To fit a child, age 3-4 (4-5:6-7) years

YARN You can use any DK weight merino-mix yarn to achieve a similar effect

A x 3 (3:5)   **B** x 1 (1:1)   **C** x 1 (2:2)

CROCHET HOOK E/4 US (3.5mm) and G/6 US (4mm) hooks

NOTIONS 4 stitch markers
Yarn needle

GAUGE 16 sts x 8.5 rows per 4in (10cm)

<< This sweater is made with Debbie Bliss Baby Cashmerino DK, 137yds/125m/50g, in A: Royal (70), B: Pool (71), and C: White (100).

Pattern

This garment is given in three sizes, with the smallest size first. The larger sizes are shown in parentheses.

Body

With yarn A and larger hook, work 108 (112:116) ch, being careful not to twist, join first ch to last ch with ss to create a large ring.

ROUND 1 With E/4 US (3.5mm) hook, 1 ch, 1 sc in each ch to end, join to top of ch 1 with ss, place stitch marker to indicate end of round. (108(112:116)sts)

ROUND 2 Ch 1, 1 sc in each st to end, join. Rep round 2 until piece measures $1^{1}/_{4}$in (3cm).

NEXT ROUND Ch 3, 1 dc, in each st to end of round, join.

Rep last round another 2 (4:4) times. Continuing to work in straight rounds of dc, work as follows:

1 round in yarn B.
2 rounds in yarn C.
1 round in yarn B.
6 (7:7) rounds in yarn A.
1 round in yarn B.
2 rounds in yarn C.
1 round in yarn B.
1 (1:2) rounds in yarn A.
Fasten off.

Sleeves (make 2)

With yarn A and G/6 US (4mm) hook, work 28 (29:29) ch, being careful not to twist, join first ch to last ch with ss, to create a large ring.

ROUND 1 Using smaller hook, 1 ch, 1 sc in each ch to end, join. (28 (29:29)sts)

To check whether this sweater will fit your child, the exact measurements are as follows: to fit chest size 23 (24:25)in/58.5 (61:63.5)cm, and with a sleeve length of $15^{1}/_{4}$ ($16^{1}/_{4}$:17)in/39 (41:43)cm.

The attractive neckline, worked in dense single crochet, contrasts beautifully with the much more open double crochet used in the body of the sweater.

ROUND 2 Ch 1, 1 sc in each st to end, join. Rep round 2 until piece measures 1¼in (3cm).

Main sleeve

Place stitch marker at start of round, and move it up for each row.

ROUND 1 Ch 3, 1 dc in each st to end, join.

ROUND 2 Ch 3, 2 dc in next st, 1 dc in each st to 2 sts from marker, 2 dc in next st, 1 dc, join. (30 (31:31)sts)

Rep last 2 rounds once. (32 (33:33)sts)

Rep round 1.

With yarn B, rep round 2. (34 (35:35)sts)

With yarn C, rep rounds 1 and 2. (36 (37:37)sts)

With yarn B, rep round 1.

With yarn A, rep round 2. (38 (39:39)sts)

Rep rounds 1 and 2, 2 (3:3) times. (42 (45:45)sts)

SIZE 3–4 YEARS ONLY

Rep round 1.

ALL SIZES

With yarn B, rep round 1.

With yarn C, rep round 2. (44 (47:47)sts)

With yarn C, rep round 1.

With yarn B, rep round 2. (46 (49:49)sts)

With yarn A, rep round 1.

SIZE 6–7 YEARS ONLY

Rep round 2. (51sts)

ALL SIZES

Fasten off.

Joining sleeves to body

From fasten off point on body, count 4 sts and place marker in the next st, from marker count 8 (9:9) sts counterclockwise and place marker (leaving 8 (9:9) sts between markers). From first marker placed, count 44 (45:47) sts and place marker (leaving 44 (45:47) sts between markers), from this 3rd marker, count 8 (9:9) sts and place marker (leaving 8(9:9) sts between markers).

Around the body you should now have marked st, 44 (45:47) sts, marked st, 8 (9:9)

sts, marked st, 44 (45:47) sts, marked st, 8 (9:9) sts.

From fasten off point on each sleeve, count 4 sts to the right and place marker in next st, from marker count 8 (9:9) sts counterclockwise and place marker in next st. (8 (9:9) sts between markers.)

Joining round

Line up the right sleeve to the right underarm of the body, with a beg slipknot on the hook, insert hook in marked stitches of both the body and the sleeve together at the back of the sweater and ss to join, 3 ch (counts as dc), dc in each st across the back of the body to 2nd marked stitch, *inserting hook through both layers of marked sts of body and other sleeve, work 1 dc, dc across sts of sleeve* to marker, working through both layers, 1 dc in marked sts of sleeve and body, dc across front to next marker, rep between * and * and ss to top of ch 3 to join. Remove underarm st markers. (164 (170:178)sts)

ROUND 1 Ch 3, dc2tog, 40 (41:43) dc, dc2tog, 1 dc, place marker, *1 dc, dc2tog, 30 (32:34) dc, dc2tog, 1 dc, ** place marker, 1 dc, dc2tog, 40 (41:43) dc, dc2tog, 1 dc, place marker, rep from * to **, join. (156 (162:170)sts)

ROUND 2 Ch 3, (dc2tog) twice, dc to 5 sts from marker, (dc2tog) twice, 1 dc, *slip marker, 1 dc, (dc2tog) twice, dc to 5 sts from marker, (dc2tog) twice, 1 dc, rep from * to end of round. (140 (146:154)sts)

ROUND 3 Ch 3, dc2tog, dc to 3 sts from marker, dc2tog, 1 dc, *slip marker, 1 dc, dc2tog, 1 dc to 3 sts from marker, dc2tog, 1 dc, rep from * to end of round. (132 (138:146)sts)

Rep last 2 rounds twice. (84 (90:98)sts)

Rep round 3, 2 (2:3) times. (68 (74:74)sts)

NEXT ROUND Ch 1, 1 sc in each st to end. Rep last round until sc rounds measure 1¼in (3cm).

Fasten off.

Finishing

Seam together the underarm sts using ss on the inside of the garment.

Weave in all ends.

Child's hoodie

This cozy hooded jacket, for a small person in your life, is worked straight and then seamed. The edging in crab stitch gives a neat detail for a practical jacket.

PROJECTS

For more crab stitch patterns
>> go to pages 144 and 174

Essential information

DIFFICULTY LEVEL Intermediate

SIZE To fit a child, age 3–4 (4–5:6–7) years

YARN Any fingering-weight yarn with a high wool content will produce a similar effect

A x 7(7:8)   **B** x 1(1:2)

CROCHET HOOK D/3 US (3mm) hook

NOTIONS Yarn needle
5 toggles, 1¼in (3cm) long

GAUGE 21 sts x 17 rows per 4in (10cm) square

SPECIAL ABBREVIATIONS
1 sc worked at the start of a row counts as a sc stitch.
3 sc worked at the start of a row counts as a dc stitch.
CRAB STITCH: See p. 144.

Pattern

The first size given is for a small hoodie, with the medium and large sizes in parentheses.

Back

With yarn B, work 68 (72:76) ch.
FOUNDATION ROW Starting in the third ch from hook, work 1 sc into each st to end. Break off yarn B and join yarn A. (67 (71:75)sts)
ROW 1 Work 3 ch (for the first dc), work 1 dc into each st to end.
ROW 2 Work 1 ch, work 1 sc into each st to end.
These two rows form the pattern.
Repeat these rows until the piece measures 8 (9½:11)in/20 (24:28)cm from beginning, ending with a row 2.

Shape for armholes

Keep in pattern throughout.
NEXT ROW Ch 1, work 1 ss into each of the first 4 (5:6) st of the row. 3 ch (for first dc), work 1 dc into each stitch to the last 3 (4:5) sts. Turn. (61 (63:65)sts)
Keeping in pattern, work straight until the piece measures 5½ (6:6½)in/ 13.5 (15:16.5)cm from armhole.

Shape shoulders and neck

NEXT ROW Ch 1, work 1 ss into each of the next 9 (9:8) sts, work 1 sc into each of the next 9 sts, work 1 ss into each of the next 25 (27:31) sts, work 1 sc into each of the next 9 sts, work 1 ss into each of the last 9 (9:8) sts. Fasten off yarn.

Left front

With yarn B, work 34 (36:38) ch.
FOUNDATION ROW Starting in the third ch from hook, work 1 sc into each st to end. (33 (35:37)sts)
Break off yarn B and join yarn A.
ROW 1 Work 3 ch (for the first dc), work 1 dc into each st to end.

Neat wooden toggles look appropriate for this hoodie and finish it off with a lovely detail. They are easier for small hands to do up, although buttons can be substituted if preferred.

>> This hoodie is made with Rowan Pure Wool 4-ply, 175yds/160m/50g, in A: Kiss (436) and B: Porcelaine (451).

ROW 2 Ch 1, 1 sc into each st to end. Repeat these rows until the piece measures 8 (9½:11)in/20 (24:28)cm from beginning, ending with a row 2.

Shape for armholes

Keep in pattern throughout.
NEXT ROW (RS) Ch 1, work 1 ss into each of the first 4 (5:6) st of the row. 3 ch (for first dc), work 1 dc into each stitch to end. (30 (31:32)sts)
Keeping in pattern, work straight until the piece is 6 rows shorter than the back (not including the shoulder shaping row) ending on a wrong side row.

Shape neck

NEXT ROW Ch 3 (for first dc), work 1 dc into each st until 9 (9:11) sts to end, turn. (21 (22:21)sts)
NEXT ROW Ch 3 (for first dc), dc2tog, work 1 dc into each st to end. (20 (21:20)sts)
NEXT ROW Ch 3 (for first dc), work 1 dc into each st to the last 2 sts, dc2tog. (19 (20:19) sts)
NEXT ROW Ch 3 (for first dc), dc2tog, work 1 dc into each st to end. (18 (19:18)sts)
Work 2 rows straight.

Shape shoulder

NEXT ROW (RS) Ch 1, work 1 ss into each of the next 8 (9:8) sts, work 1 sc into each of the st to end. Fasten off yarn.

Right front

Make as per left front, but reverse the shaping.

Sleeves (make 2)

With yarn B, work 30 (32:35) ch.
FOUNDATION ROW Starting in the third ch from hook, work 1 sc into each st to end. (29 (31:34) sts)
Break off yarn B and join yarn A.
ROW 1 Work 3 ch (for the first dc), work 1 dc into each st to end.
ROW 2 Work 1 ch, work 1 sc into each st to end.
ROW 3 Work 3 ch (for the first dc), work 2 dc into next st, work 1 dc into each st to last

3 sts, work 2 dc into next st, 1 dc into the last st. (31 (33:36)sts)
ROW 4 Work 1 ch, work 1 sc into each st to end.
ROW 5 Work 3 ch (for the first dc), work 1 dc into each st to end.
ROW 6 Work 1 ch, work 2 sc into next st, work 1 sc into each st to last 2 sts, work 2 sc into next st, work 1 sc into last st. (33 (35:38)sts)
Continue in this way, increasing every third row, until there are 53 (61:66) sts.
Work straight until the sleeve measures 10¼ (12:13½)in/26 (30:34)cm).
Fasten off yarn.

Pockets (make 2)

With yarn A, work 19 (23:25) ch.
FOUNDATION ROW Starting in the third ch from hook, work 1 sc into each st to end. (18 (22:24)sts)
Working in patt as for back, work 13 rows.
ROW 14 Ch 1, work 1 ss into each of the next 3 sts, work 1 sc into each st to end. (15 (19:21)sts)
ROW 15 Ch 3 (for first dc), work 1 dc into each st to end.
ROW 16 Ch 1, work 1 ss into each of the next 2 sts, work 1 sc into each st to end. (13 (17:19)sts)
ROWS 17-21 Work in patt, decreasing 1 st at the shaped edge (by working 2 sts together) on each row. (9 (13:16)sts)
Work 2 rows straight.
Fasten off yarn.
Block all pieces.

Buttonhole band

ROW 1 Join yarn A to the top of the left front and work 1 ch. Work in sc along the front edge, working 2 sts into each dc row end and 1 sc into each sc row end. Do not work into the contrast color at the base of the front.
ROW 2 Work 1 ch, work 1 sc into each st to end.
Repeat row 2 once more.
ROW 3 As row 2 but placing 5 buttonholes evenly along the row. Buttonholes are created by working 2 ch and skipping 2 sts.

Repeat row 2 twice more.
Fasten off yarn.

Button band

Starting at the base of the right front, work as for the buttonhole band, replacing row 3 with another row 2 repetition.
Join the shoulder seams.

Hood

With yarn A, starting at the top of the right front button band, work sc around the neck as follows: 5 across the button band, 17 (18:20) sts around the right neck, 25 (27:31) sts across the back neck, 17 (18:20) sts around the left neck, 5 across the buttonhole band. (69 (73:81)sts)
Work in patt as for back until the hood measures 9½ (10:11)in/24 (26:28)cm.
Fasten off yarn. Sew top of hood.

Edgings

SLEEVES
Join yarn B to cuff and work in crab stitch along base.
Fasten off yarn.

POCKETS
ROW 1 Join yarn B and work 1 ch. Work 15 sc evenly across the shaped edge.
ROW 2 Ch 1, work in crab stitch back across the edging.
Fasten off yarn.

BODY OF JACKET
ROW 1 Join yarn B to the base of the buttonhole band, where it joins the main jacket, and work in sc as follows: base of buttonhole band 5 sts, body and hood, 2 sts into each dc row end and 1 st into each sc row end, base of button band 5 sts.
ROW 2 Ch 1, work in crab stitch back across the edging.
Fasten off yarn.
Join sleeves to fronts and back of jacket.
Sew sleeve and side seams; sew pockets to front of jacket; sew toggles to button band.
Weave in all ends.

The contrasting pale-colored edging around the hem, hood, and sleeves gives this hoodie a professional and neat finish. Turn to pages 50–53 when working the increase and decrease stitches to shape the garment, and pages 87–89 for further details about edgings and finishings on crocheted items.

for *Child's poncho*
go to page 234

Summer tunic dress

This sweet, summer tunic dress is worked in two pieces for the front and back, which are then sewn together. The skirt is worked in the round from the top down, using increases and decreases to create a chevron effect.

PROJECTS
For an additional chevron pattern
>> *go to page 152*

Essential information

DIFFICULTY LEVEL Intermediate

SIZE To fit a child, age 1-2 (2-3:4-5) years

YARN You can use any DK-weight cotton yarn to achieve a similar effect

A x 2 (2:3)   **B** x 1   **C** x 1   **D** x 1

E x 1   **F** x 1

CROCHET HOOK E/4 US (3.5mm) hook

NOTIONS Yarn needle
2 x ¾in (2cm) buttons

GAUGE 17 sts x 12 rows per 4in (10cm) square

Pattern
With yarn A, work 51 (55:59) ch.
ROW 1 1 hdc in second ch from hook, 1 hdc in each ch to end, turn. (49 (53:57)sts)
ROW 2 Ch 2, 1 hdc in each st to end, turn.
ROW 3 Ch 2, 2 (4:2) hdc, *1 ch, skip 1 st, 3 hdc, rep from * to last 3 sts, 1 ch, skip 1 st, 2 (4:2) hdc.
ROW 4 Ch 2, 1 hdc in each st and ch sp as you come to them, turn.
Rep row 2, 1 (2:3) times.

Shape underarm
ROW 1 Ss into next 3 sts, 3 ch, 43 (47:51) hdc, turn. (43 (47:51)sts)
ROW 2 Ch 2, 1 hdc, hdc2tog, hdc to 3sts from end of row, hdc2tog, 1 hdc, turn. (41 (45:49)sts)
Rep row 2, five times. (31 (35:39)sts)
ROW 8 Ch 2, 1 hdc in each st to end.
Rep row 8 until piece measures $2^{1}/_{4}$ ($2^{1}/_{4}$:$2^{3}/_{4}$)in/ 6 (6:7)cm from underarm shaping.

Shape neckline
LEFT SIDE
ROW 1 Ch 2, 9 (10:11) hdc, turn.
ROW 2 Ch 2, skip next st, 1 hdc in each st to end, turn. (8 (9:10)sts)
ROW 3 Ch 2, hdc in each st to end, turn.
Rep last 2 rows a further 2 (3:4) times. (6sts)
Fasten off.

When crocheting a chevron design, it is really simple but you must remember to count all the stitches up one side and then count them down the other side for an even M-shape across your fabric.

RIGHT SIDE
ROW 1 Join yarn with ss to 13 (15:17)th st from edge of left side shaping, 2 ch, 1 hdc in each st across, turn. (9 (10:11)sts)
ROW 2 Ch 2, 1 hdc in each st to last 2 sts, skip next st, 1 hdc. (8 (9:10)sts)
ROW 3 Ch 2, 1 hdc in each st to end, turn.
Rep last 2 rows a further 2(3:4) times. (6sts)
Fasten off.

<< This dress is made with Debbie Bliss Eco Baby. 137yds/125m/50g, in A: Ecru (16), B: Corn (36). C: Silver (30), D: Apple (06), E: Fuchsia (32), and F: Aqua (05).

Back

Work as front to end of first row 2.

ROW 3 Ch 2, 1 hdc, *1 ch, skip 1 st, 3 hdc, rep from * to end.

Continue as front from first row 4 to row 8 of underarm shaping.

Rep row 8 until piece measures 4$^{1}/_{2}$(5:5$^{1}/_{2}$)in/ 11 (12:14)cm from underarm shaping.

Shape neckline

RIGHT SIDE

ROW 1 Ch 2, 6 hdc, turn.

Rep row 1 a further 3 times.

ROW 4 Ch 2, 2 hdc, hdc2tog, 2 hdc, turn. (5sts)

ROW 5 (BUTTONHOLE) Ch 2, 2 hdc, 1 ch, skip next st, 2 hdc, turn.

ROW 6 Ch 2, 2 hdc, hdc in ch sp, 2 hdc, turn.

ROW 7 Ch 1, 1 hdc in each st to end, turn.

Rep row 7 once.

Fasten off.

LEFT SIDE

Join yarn with ss to 19 (23:27)th st from edge of right shaping.

Work as right side.

Join front and back panels

With right sides facing, using ss, seam tog side seams under arm holes on both sides.

Skirt

With right side facing, join yarn A at right side seam.

ROUND 1 Ch 2, 2 hdc in next st, 1 hdc in each st to left seam, 2 hdc in next st, 1 hdc in each st to end of round. (96 (104:112)sts)

ROUND 2 With yarn B, 3 ch (counts as a st), 1 dc in same st as ch 3, *1 dc, (dc2tog) twice, 1 dc, (2 dc in next st)** twice, rep from * to end of round, ending last rep at **, join to top of first st with ss.

Rep round 2.

With yarn A, rep round 2.

ROUND 5 With yarn C, 3 ch, 2 dc in same st as ch 3, *1 dc, (dc2tog) twice, 1 dc, (3 dc in next st)** twice, rep from * to end of round, ending last rep at **, join. (120 (130:140)sts)

ROUND 6 Ch 3, 1 dc in same st as ch 3, *2 dc, (dc2tog) twice, 2 dc, (2 dc in next st)** twice, rep from * to end, ending last rep at **, join.

ROUND 7 With yarn A, rep round 6.

ROUNDS 8–9 With yarn D, rep round 6.

ROUND 10 With yarn A, rep round 6.

ROUNDS 11–12 With yarn E, rep round 6.

ROUND 13 With yarn A, 3 ch, 2 dc in same st as ch 3, *2 dc, (dc2tog) twice, 2 dc, (3 dc in next st)** twice, rep form * to end of round, ending last rep at **, join. (144 (156:168)sts)

ROUND 14 With yarn F, 3 ch, 1 dc in same st as ch-3, *3 dc, (dc2tog) twice, 3 dc, (2 dc in next st)** twice, rep from * to end of round, ending last rep at **, join.

ROUND 15 Rep round 14.

ROUND 16 With yarn A, rep round 14.

ROUND 17 With yarn B, rep round 14.

SIZES 2–3 AND 4–5 YEARS ONLY

ROUND 18 Rep round 14.

SIZE 4–5 YEARS ONLY

ROUND 19 With yarn A, rep round 14.

ROUNDS 20–21 With yarn C, rep round 14.

The shoulder straps on this tunic dress are secured with tiny buttons. Choose a decorative plastic button to make a lightweight and pretty feature, or crochet your own buttons (see p. 89).

ALL SIZES

Fasten off.

Finishing

With yarn E, join to right underarm side seam, 1 ch, evenly work a round of sc all the way around the edge of the top, front, and back, join. Fasten off.

Tie

With yarn F, work 150 ch, fasten off, weave in ends. Thread tie through eyelets in row 3 of bodice and fasten with a bow at the front. Weave in ends. Sew buttons in place. Block lightly.

Use flat whipstitch to give invisible seams.

TOP TIP

This simple tie in a contrasting color is made in chain stitch and threaded through the bodice of the dress to provide a pretty bow detail at the front.

Cropped sweater

This pretty top is a great addition to a summer wardrobe. Lacy, with three-quarter length sleeves, it's perfect for layering on cold days. Worked flat in four pieces, the sweater is seamed together at the end.

PROJECTS
For more cluster patterns
>> go to page 186

Essential information

DIFFICULTY LEVEL Intermediate

SIZE To fit an adult female S (M:L)

YARN You can use any DK weight alpaca or wool yarn here. This has a slight sparkle, which you could re-create with Lurex®

x 4 (4:5)

CROCHET HOOK E/4 US (3.5mm) hook

NOTIONS Safety pin
Yarn needle

GAUGE 16 sts x 20 rows per 4in (10cm)

SPECIAL ABBREVIATIONS
2DC-CL: 2 double crochet cluster. Yo, insert in ch sp below, yo, draw through, yo, draw through 2 loops, yo, insert in next ch sp, yo, draw through, yo, draw through remaining 3 loops.
UPTURNED V STITCH: ROW 1 (working into row of sc) 3 ch, *2dc-cl (see above) (work first dc into first sc, skip 1 sc, work second dc in next sc), 1 ch, rep from * to end, 1 dc in last st.
ROW 2 Ch 3, 2dc-cl across row.
Rep row 2 for pattern.

The main body of the sweater is made up of a simple-to-follow lace repeat, with single crochet worked into the edges. Turn to pages 108–109 for more information about simple lace techniques, and pages 110–112 for lace and filet patterns.

Pattern
The following pattern will fit three bust sizes: small: 32in (81cm), medium: 36in (91cm), and large: 40in (101cm).

Front
Work 77 (85:92) ch.
ROW 1 1 sc in second ch from hook, 1 sc in each ch to end, turn. (76 (84:91) sts)
ROW 2 Ch 1, 1 sc in each st to end, turn.
Rep row 2 a further 7 times.

SMALL AND LARGE SIZES ONLY
ROW 10 Ch 1, 4 (1) sc, *2 sc in next st, 2 sc, rep from * to end. (100 (121)sts)

MEDIUM SIZE ONLY
ROW 10 Ch1, 6 sc, 2 sc in next st, 2 sc, *2 sc in next st, 1 sc, 2 sc in next st, 2 sc, rep from * to end. (115sts)

ALL SIZES
ROW 11 Work row 1 of Upturned V Stitch pattern. (33 (38:40) 2dc-cls)
ROW 12 Work row 2 of Upturned V Stitch pattern.
Rep row 12 until piece measures 12¼ (12½:13)in/31 (32:33)cm.

Shape the armholes
ROW 1 *ss into next 2dc-cl, ss in ch-1 sp, rep from * once, 3 ch, work row 2 of Upturned V Stitch pattern across to third from last ch sp (leaving 2 2dc-cls unworked). (29 (34:36) 2dc-cls)
ROW 2 Work row 2 of Upturned V Stitch pattern.
Rep row 2 until armhole measures 5½ (6:6¼)in/14 (15: 16cm from armhole shaping, ending on WS row.

Shape the neck
LEFT SIDE
ROW 1 (RS) Ch 3, *2dc-cl, 1 ch, rep from * 8 (10:10) times, 1 dc in same ch sp as last st, turn. (9 (11:11) 2dc-cls)
ROW 2 (WS) Ch 3, skip first ch-sp, *2dc-cl, 1 ch, rep from * across, turn. (8 (10:10) 2dc-cls)
ROW 3 (RS) Ch 3, *2dc-cl, 1 ch, rep from * 7

>> This sweater is made with Louisa Harding Orielle DK, 120yds/110m/50g, in Breeze (05).

(9:9) times, 1 dc in same ch sp as last st, turn. (8 (10:10) 2dc-cls)

ROW 4 (WS) Ch 3, skip first ch sp, *2dc-cl, 1 ch, rep from * across, turn. (7 (9:9) 2dc-cls)

ROW 5 (RS) Ch 3, *2dc-cl, 1 ch, rep from * 6 (8:8) times, 1 dc in same ch-sp as last st, turn. (7 (9:9) 2dc-cls)

ROW 6 (WS) Ch 3, skip first ch-sp, *2dc-cl, 1 ch, rep from * across, turn. (6 (8:8) 2dc-cls)
Fasten off.

RIGHT SIDE

ROW 1 (RS) Join yarn to 11 (12:14)-ch sp after row end for left side shaping, 3 ch, *2dc-cl, 1 ch, rep from * to end, 1 dc, turn. (9 (11:11) 2dc-cls)

ROW 2 (WS) Ch 3, *2dc-cl, 1 ch, rep from * 7 (9:9) times, 1 dc into turning ch. (8 (10:10) 2dc-cls)

ROW 3 Work row 2 of Upturned V Stitch pattern.

ROW 4 Ch 3, *2 dc-cl, 1 ch, rep from * 6 (8:8) times, 1 hdc into turning ch, turn. (7 (9:9) 2dc-cls)

ROW 5 Rep row 3.

ROW 6 Ch 3, *2dc-cl, 1 ch, rep from * 5 (7:7) times, 1 hdc into turning ch, turn. (6 (8:8) 2dc-cls)
Fasten off.

Back

Work as front to row 2 of Shape the armholes. Rep row 2 until piece measures 7$^{1}/_{2}$ (8:8$^{1}/_{2}$)in/ 19.5 (20.5:21.5)cm from armhole shaping ending on a WS row.

Shape the neck

RIGHT SIDE

ROW 1 (RS) Ch 3, *2dc-cl, 1 ch, rep from * 6(8:8) times, 1 dc in same ch sp as last st, turn. (7 (9:9 2dc-cls)

ROW 2 (WS) Ch 3, skip first ch-sp, *2dc-cl, 1 ch, rep from * across row, turn. (6 (8:8) 2dc-cls)
Fasten off.

Single crochet edging makes the garment tighter around the cuffs and waist for a better fit. Make sure that you keep an eye on the gauge so that the cuffs still contain a level of natural elasticity from the yarn.

LEFT SIDE

ROW 1 (RS) Join yarn to 15 (16:18)th 1-ch sp after end of left side shaping, 3 ch, *2dc-cl, 1 ch, rep from * to end, 1 dc, turn. (7 (9:9) 2dc-cls)

ROW 2 (WS) Ch 3, *2dc-cl, 1 ch, rep from * 5 (7:7) times, 1 dc into turning ch. (6 (8:8) 2dc-cls)
Fasten off.

Sleeves (make 2)

Work 68 (72:74) ch.

ROW 1 1 sc in second ch from hook, 1 sc in each ch to end, turn. (67 (71:73) sts)

ROW 2 Ch 1, 1 sc in each st to end, turn.

Rep row 2 a further 7 times.

ROW 10 Ch 1, 1 sc, *2 sc in next st, 1 sc, rep from * to end, turn. (100 (106:109) sts)

ROW 11 Work row 1 of Upturned V Stitch pattern. (33 (35:36) 2dc-cls)

ROW 12 Work row 2 of Upturned V Stitch pattern.

Rep row 12 until piece measures 14$^{1}/_{2}$ (15:15$^{1}/_{2}$)in/37 (38:39)cm.
Fasten off.

Finishing

Block all pieces to size.
With Front and Back body pieces RS together, seam together along the shoulder seams, using a ss.

Neckline

ROUND 1 Turn work back so RS is facing, join yarn at shoulder seam, 1 ch, work sc evenly around the neckline, front, and back, working into sides of rows where necessary, join with a ss, turn.

ROUND 2 Ch 1, 1 sc in each st around, join with a ss, turn.
Rep round 2 a further 2 times.
Fasten off.

Attaching sleeves

With RS tog, using safety pins, pin sleeves into place on body armholes, seam together using a ss.

Seam sides

Using a ss, seam together the sides and sleeves.
Weave in all ends.

TOP TIP

Crochet more length in the body for a less cropped look.

Refer to pages 70–71 for information about blocking and seaming your finished crochet garment. When blocking a textured fabric such as this double crochet cluster stitch design, it is best to wet block it.

Essential information

DIFFICULTY LEVEL Intermediate

SIZE To fit an adult female S (M: L)

YARN You can use any fine weight yarn to achieve a similar effect

x 8 (8:9)

CROCHET HOOK E/4 US (3.5mm) hook

NOTIONS Yarn needle
¾in (2cm) diameter button

GAUGE 32 sts x 14 rows per 5½in (14cm)

SPECIAL ABBREVIATIONS

DC2TOGCL: work 2 dc tog over 3 sts. (Yo and insert hook in next st, yo and draw a loop through, yo, draw through first 2 loops on hook) skip next st, (yo and insert hook in next st, yo and draw a loop through, yo draw through first 2 loops on hook), yo, and draw through all 3 loops on hook—2 st decreased.

DC4TOGCL: work 4 dc tog over the next 5 sts. Yo, insert hook in next st, yo and draw a loop through, yo and draw through first 2 loops on hook) twice, skip next st, (yo, insert hook into the following st, yo and draw a loop through, yo and draw through first 2 loops on hook) twice, yo, draw through all 5 loops—4 sts decreased.

Ladies' textured cardigan

A lightweight, three-quarter-length cardigan in a fine lace pattern, the main body of this pretty garment is worked in one piece. Adjust the length to your size by simply increasing the rows of crochet before shaping.

PROJECTS
For more openwork patterns
>> *go to pages 116 and 202*

Pattern
The sizes S (M:L) will fit bust 32 (36:40)in 81/ (91:102)cm.

Body
Work 196 (228:260) ch.

FOUNDATION ROW dc2tog, working into fifth ch from hook for first st, (1 ch, skip next ch, dc) twice, 1 ch, skip next ch, (2 dc, 1 ch, 2 dc) into the next ch, (1 ch, skip next ch, dc) twice, *1 ch, skip next ch, dc4togcl, (1 ch, skip next ch, dc) twice, 1 ch, skip next ch, (2 dc, 1 ch, 2 dc) into next ch, (1 ch, skip next ch, dc) twice, repeat from * to last 4sts, 1 ch, skip next ch, dc3tog.

ROW 1 Ch 3 (counts as a st), dc2tog, (1 ch, skip next st, dc) twice, 1 ch, skip next st, (2 dc, 1 ch, 2 dc) into the next ch, (1 ch, skip next st, dc) twice, *1 ch, skip next st, dc4togcl, (1 ch, skip next st, dc) twice, 1 ch, skip next st (2 dc, 1 ch, 2 dc) into the next ch, (1 ch, skip next st, dc) twice, repeat from * to last 4 sts, 1 ch skip next st, dc3tog.

ROWS 2–33 Repeat row 1.

Divide for arms and neck shaping
SMALL AND LARGE SIZES ONLY: RIGHT FRONT
ROW 1 Ch 3 (does not count as st), dc2tog, *(1

ch, skip next st, dc) twice, 1 ch, skip next st, (2 dc, 1 ch, 2 dc) into next ch, (1 ch, skip next st, dc) twice, 1 ch, skip next st**, dc4togcl, repeat from * 1 (2) more times, then from * to ** once, dc3tog, turn. (49 (65)sts)

Leave rem sts unworked. Place a stitch marker into base of last st in dc3tog, (these sts will be worked later for Back and Left Front).

Ch 3, dc2tog, *(1 ch, skip next st, dc into next st) twice, 1 ch, skip next st (2 dc, 1 ch, 2 dc) into next ch, (1 ch, skip next st, dc into next st) twice, 1 ch, do not work into the next st**, dc4togcl, repeat from * 1 (2) more times, then from * to ** once, ending with dc3tog, turn. (49 (65)sts)

Leave rem sts unworked, placing a stitch marker into base of dc3tog, (these sts will be divided later for Back and Left Front).

ROW 2 Ch 3, dc2tog, *(1 ch, skip next st, dc into next st) twice, 1 ch, skip next st (2 dc, 1 ch, 2 dc) into next ch, (1 ch, skip next st, dc into next st) twice**, 1 ch, skip next st, dc4togcl, repeat from * 1 (2) more times, then from * to ** once, ending with 1 ch, skip next st, dc2togcl.

ROW 3 Ch 3, skip next st, dc2tog, *(1 ch, dc into next st, skip next st) twice, 1 ch, skip next st (2 dc, 1 ch, 2 dc) into next ch, (1 ch, skip next st, dc into next st) twice, 1 ch, skip next st**, dc4togcl, repeat from * 1 (2) more times, then from * to ** once, ending with dc3tog.

ROW 4 Ch 3, dc2tog, *(1 ch, skip the next st, dc into the next st) twice, 1 ch, skip next st (2 dc, 1 ch, 2 dc) into next ch, (1 ch, skip next st, dc into next st) twice**, 1 ch, skip next st, dc4togcl, repeat from * 1 (2) more times, then from * to ** once, skip next st, dc3tog. (48 (64)sts)

ROW 5 Ch 3, skip next st, dc2tog, skip next st,

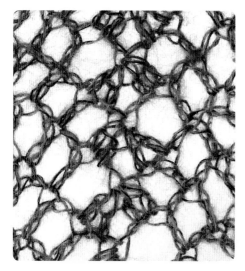

The dc2tog stitches create a series of lacey holes within the crochet, which helps the cardigan fabric to grow quite quickly. Refer to page 311 to decipher the crochet terms used in this pattern.

1 dc, 1 ch, do not work next st, *(2 dc, 1 ch, 2 dc) into next ch, (1 ch, skip next st, dc into next st) twice, 1 ch, skip next st**, dc4togcl, (1 ch, skip next st, 1 dc) twice, 1 ch, repeat from * 1 (2) times, then from * to ** ending with dc3tog. (47 (63)sts)

ROW 6 Ch 3, dc2tog, *(1 ch, skip next st, dc into the next st) twice, 1 ch, skip next st (2 dc, 1 ch, 2 dc) into the next ch**, (1 ch, skip next st, dc into the next st) twice, 1 ch, skip next st, dc4togcl, repeat from * 1 (2) more times, then from * to ** once, 1 ch, skip next st, dc into next st, skip next st, dc3tog. (46 (62)sts)

ROW 7 Ch 3, skip next st, dc2tog, 1 ch, *(2 dc, 1 ch, 2 dc) into next ch, (1 ch, skip next st, dc into next st) twice, 1 ch, skip next st**, dc4togcl, (1 ch, skip next st, 1 dc) twice, 1 ch, repeat from * 1(2) times, then from * to ** ending with dc3tog. (45 (61)sts)

ROW 8 Ch 3, dc2tog, *(1 ch, skip next st, dc into the next st) twice, 1 ch, skip next st (2 dc, 1 ch, 2 dc) into next ch**, (1 ch, skip next st, dc into next st) twice, 1 ch, skip next st, dc4togcl, repeat from * 1 (2) more times, then from * to ** once, 1 ch, skip next st, dc3tog.

ROW 9 Ch 3, dc2tog, 1 ch, *(2 dc, 1 ch, 2 dc) into next ch, (1 ch, skip next st, dc into next st) twice, 1 ch, skip next st**, dc4togcl, (1 ch, skip next st, 1 dc) twice, 1 ch, skip next st, repeat from * 1 (2) times, then from * to ** once, dc3tog.

ROW 10 Repeat row 8.

ROW 11 Repeat row 9.

ROW 12 Repeat row 8.

ROW 13 Ch 3, skip next st, dc2tog, 1 ch, 2 dc into the next ch, *(1 ch, skip next st, dc into next st) twice, 1 ch, skip next st**, dc4togcl, (1 ch, skip next st, 1 dc) twice, 1 ch, skip next st, (2 dc, 1 ch, 2 dc) into the next st, repeat from * 1 (2) times, then from * to ** ending with dc3tog. (42 (58)sts)

ROW 14 Ch 3, dc2tog, *(1 ch, skip next st, dc into next st) twice, 1 ch, skip next st (2 dc, 1 ch, 2 dc) into next ch**, (1 ch, skip next st, dc into next st) twice, 1 ch, skip next st, dc4togcl, repeat from * 1 (2) more times, (1 ch, do not work next st, dc into next st) twice, do not work next st, dc2tog. (38 (54)sts)

ROW 15 Ch 3, dc2tog, 1 ch, *dc4togcl, (1 ch, skip next st, 1 dc) twice, 1 ch, skip next st, (2 dc, 1 ch, 2 dc) into the next st, (1 ch, skip next st, 1 dc) twice, 1 ch, skip next st, repeat from * 1 (2) times, ending with dc3tog. (35 (51)sts)

ROW 16 Ch 3, dc2tog, *(1 ch, skip next st, dc

into next st) twice, 1 ch, skip next st (2 dc, 1 ch, 2 dc) into next ch**, (1 ch, skip next st, dc into next st) twice, 1 ch, skip next st, dc4togcl, repeat from * 1 (2) more times. (33 (49)sts)

ROW 17 Ch 3, dc2tog, *(1 ch, skip next st, 1 dc) twice, 1 ch, skip next st, (2 dc, 1 ch, 2 dc) into next st, (1 ch, skip next st, 1 dc) twice, 1 ch, skip next st**, dc4togcl, repeat from * to **, ending with dc3tog.

ROW 18 Ch 3, dc2tog, *(1 ch, skip next st, dc into next st) twice, 1 ch, skip next st, (2 dc, 1 ch, 2 dc) into next ch, (1 ch, skip next st, dc into next st) twice, 1 ch, skip next st**, dc4togcl, repeat from * 0 (1) times, then from * to ** once, ending with dc3tog.

LARGE SIZE ONLY

ROW 19 Repeat row 17.

ROW 20 Repeat row 18.

MEDIUM SIZE ONLY: RIGHT FRONT

ROW 1 Ch 3, dc2tog, *(1 ch, skip next st, dc into the next st) twice, 1 ch, skip next st** (2 dc, 1 ch, 2 dc) into the next ch, (1 ch, skip next st, dc into the next st) twice, 1 ch, do not work into the next st, dc4togcl, repeat from * twice, then from * to ** once, ending with 3 dc into the next ch. (57sts)

Leave rem sts unworked. Place a stitch marker into base of third dc, these stitches will be worked later for Back and Left Front.

ROW 2 Ch 3 (counts as a st), 2 dc into base st, *(1 ch, skip next st, dc into next st) twice, 1 ch, skip next st**, dc4togcl, 1 ch, skip next st, dc into next st) twice, 1 ch, skip next st, (2 dc, 1 ch, 2 dc) into next ch, repeat from * twice, then from * to ** once, dc2togcl.

ROW 3 Ch 3, skip next st, dc2tog, *(1 ch, dc into the next st, skip next st) twice, 1 ch, skip next st**, (2 dc, 1 ch, 2 dc) into next ch, (1 ch, skip next st, dc into next st) twice, 1 ch, skip next st**, dc4togcl, repeat from * twice, then from * to ** once, ending with 3 dc into last st.

ROW 4 Ch 3, 2 dc into base st, *(1 ch, skip next st, dc into the next st) twice**, 1 ch, skip next st, dc4togcl, 1 ch, skip next st, dc into next st) twice, 1 ch, skip next st (2 dc, 1 ch, 2 dc) into

next ch, repeat from * twice, then from * to ** once, dc3tog.

ROW 5 Ch 3, skip next st, dc2tog, skip next st, 1 dc, 1 ch, skip next st *(2 dc, 1 ch, 2 dc) into next ch, (1 ch, skip next st, dc into next st) twice, 1 ch, skip next st, dc4togcl, (1 ch, skip next st, 1 dc) twice, 1 ch, repeat from * 2 times, ending with 3 dc into last st.

ROW 6 Ch 3, 2 dc into base st, *(1 ch, skip next st, dc) twice, 1 ch, skip next st, dc4togcl, (1 ch, skip next st, dc) twice, 1 ch, skip next st, (2 dc, 1 ch, 2 dc) into next ch, repeat from * twice, 1 ch, skip next st, dc, skip next st, dc3tog.

ROW 7 Ch 3, skip next st, dc2tog, 1 ch, *(2 dc, 1 ch, 2 dc) into next ch, (1 ch, skip next st, dc into next st) twice, 1 ch, skip next st, dc4togcl, (1 ch, skip next st, 1 dc) twice, 1 ch, repeat from * 2 times, ending with 3 dc into last st.

ROW 8 Ch 3, 2 dc into base st, *(1 ch, skip next st, dc) twice, 1 ch, skip next st, dc4togcl, 1 ch, skip next st, dc) twice, 1 ch, skip next st (2 dc, 1 ch, 2 dc) into next ch, repeat from * twice, 1 ch, skip next st, dc3tog.

ROW 9 Ch 3, dc2tog, 1 ch, *(2 dc, 1 ch, 2 dc) into next ch, (1 ch, skip next st, dc into next st) twice, 1 ch, skip next st, dc4togcl, (1 ch, skip next st, 1 dc) twice, 1 ch, skip next st, repeat from * 2 times, ending with 3 dc into last st.

ROW 10 Repeat row 8.

ROW 11 Repeat row 9.

ROW 12 Repeat row 8.

ROW 13 Ch 3, skip next st, dc2tog, 1 ch, 2 dc into next ch, *(1 ch, skip next st, dc into next st) twice, 1 ch, skip next st, dc4togcl, (1 ch, skip next st, 1 dc) twice, 1 ch, skip next st**, (2 dc, 1 ch, 2 dc) into next ch, repeat from * once, then from * to ** ending with 3 dc into last st.

ROW 14 Ch 3, 2 dc into base st, *(1 ch, skip next st, dc) twice, 1 ch, skip next st, dc4togcl**, (1 ch, skip next st, dc) twice, 1 ch, skip next st (2 dc, 1 ch, 2 dc) into the next ch, repeat from * once, then from * to ** once, (1 ch, skip next st, dc) twice, skip next st, dc2tog.

ROW 15 Ch 3, dc2tog, 1 ch, *dc4togcl, (1 ch, skip next st, 1 dc) twice, 1 ch, skip next st**, (2 dc, 1 ch, 2 dc) into the next ch, (1 ch, skip next st, 1 dc) twice, 1 ch, skip next st, repeat

from * once, then from * to ** once, ending with 3 dc into the last st.
ROW 16 Ch 3, 2 dc into base st, *(1 ch, skip next st, dc into next st) twice, 1 ch, skip next st, dc4togcl**, (1 ch, skip next st, dc into the next st) twice, 1 ch, skip next st, (2 dc, 1 ch, 2 dc) into next ch, repeat from * once, then from * to ** once.
ROW 17 Ch 3, dc2tog, *(1 ch, skip next st, 1 dc) twice, 1 ch, skip next st**, (2 dc, 1 ch, 2 dc) into the next st, (1 ch, skip next st, 1 dc) twice, 1 ch, skip next st**, dc4togcl, repeat from * once, then from * to * once, ending with 3 dc into the last st.
ROW 18 Ch 3, 2 dc into base st, *(1 ch, skip next st, dc into the next st) twice, 1 ch, skip next st**, dc4togcl, (1 ch, skip next st, dc into the next st) twice, 1 ch, skip next st (2 dc, 1 ch, 2 dc) into the next ch, repeat from * once, then from * to ** once, dc3tog.
ROW 19 Repeat row 17.
ROW 20 Repeat row 18.

Back
With RS facing, rejoin yarn to main Body at stitch marker and work as follows:

SMALL AND LARGE SIZES ONLY
ROW 1 Ch 3 (counts as st), dc2tog, *(1 ch, skip next st, dc into next st) twice, 1 ch, skip next st, (2 dc, 1 ch, 2 dc) into next st, (1 ch, skip next st, dc into next st) twice, 1 ch skip next st**, dc4togcl, repeat from * 4 (6) times, then from * to ** once, ending with dc3tog.

MEDIUM SIZE ONLY
ROW 1 Ch 3 (counts as st), 2 dc into the base of 3 ch, *(1 ch, skip next st, dc into the next st) twice, 1 ch skip next st, dc4togcl, (1 ch, skip next st, dc into the next st) twice, 1 ch, skip next st**, (2 dc, 1 ch, 2 dc), repeat from * 5 times, then from * to ** once, ending with 3 dc into the next st.

FOR ALL SIZES
Place marker at the base of last st.
Repeat row 1 until back measures the same as the front. (18 (20:20)rows)

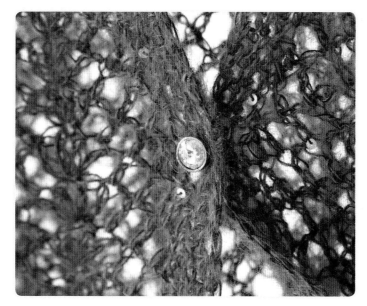

This classic-style cardigan has just one button fastening. Choose a mother-of-pearl, wood, or plastic button that will coordinate with the color of your yarn. Attach it firmly with a strand of 4-ply yarn or matching thread.

LEFT FRONT
Rejoin yarn to point at stitch marker and work as for Right Front, reversing all shaping.

Sleeves
Work 84 (100:100) ch.
FOUNDATION ROW dc2tog, working into fifth ch from hook for the first st, *(1 ch, skip next ch, dc) twice, 1 ch, skip next ch, (2 dc, 1 ch, 2 dc) into the next ch, (1 ch, skip next ch, dc) twice, 1 ch, skip next ch**, dc4togcl, repeat from * 4 (5:5) times, then from * to ** once, dc3tog. Yo, insert hook into 5th ch from hook, yo and draw through a loop, yo, insert hook into the next ch, yo and draw through a loop, yo and draw through all 3 loops on hook, *(1 ch, skip next ch, dc into the next ch) twice, 1 ch, skip next ch (2 dc, 1 ch, 2 dc) into the next ch, (1 ch, skip next ch, dc into the next ch) twice, 1 ch, skip next ch**, dc4togcl, repeat from * 3 (4) times, then from * to ** once, ending with dc3tog.
ROW 1 Ch 3 (counts as a st), dc2tog, *(1 ch, skip next st, dc into next st) twice, 1 ch, skip next st, (2 dc, 1 ch, 2 dc) into next st, (1 ch, skip next st, dc into next st) twice, *1 ch skip next st**, dc4togcl, repeat from * 4 (5:5) times, then from * to ** once ending with dc3tog.
Repeat row 1, 36 (38:40) more times.

Edging
For edging starting at the highest ripple point:
*1 ch, skip next st, 1 sc, 1 ch, skip next st, 1 hdc, 1 ch, skip next 3 sts, (2 dc, 1 ch, 2 dc) into the next st, 1 ch, skip next 3 sts, 1 hdc, 1 ch, skip next st, 1 sc, 1 ch, skip next st, ss into the next st (highest point of ripple), repeat from * to end.
For edging starting at the lowest ripple point:
3 ch, 2 dc into base of ch, 1 ch, skip next 3 sts, 1 hdc, 1 ch, skip next st, 1 sc, 1 ch, skip next st, ss into next st (highest point of ripple). Repeat as for above method to end.

Finishing
Work edging along top shoulders and back to even stitches before sewing shoulder seams. Set in sleeves. Work edging along cuffs. With wrong side facing, sc evenly along left front edge, neckline, and down right front edge, 1 ch, turn, sc along whole row again. Repeat the last row, working 1 buttonhole on right front edge of row 34 as follows: sc to buttonhole point, 2 ch, skip next 2 sc, sc. Continue in sc to end of row, 1 ch, work 1 further row. Edge bottom of cardigan. Fasten off. Weave in all ends.

Toys

Animal rattles

These bright and colorful rattles will delight any young baby. The single crochet stitch makes the toy robust and durable for lots of cheerful play. Change the character of each rattle by choosing a different animal's face.

PROJECTS
For another toy pattern
>> *turn to pages 132–135*

Essential information

DIFFICULTY LEVEL Intermediate

SIZE 5in (12cm)

YARN You can use any DK-weight cotton yarn for a similar effect

A x 1   B x 1   C x 1   D x 1   E x 1

CROCHET HOOK C/2 US (3mm) hook

NOTIONS Stitch marker
Yarn needle
Black and pink embroidery thread and needle
Polyfill
Stuffed-toy bell (to place inside the rattle)

GAUGE Exact gauge is not essential

SPECIAL ABBREVIATIONS
ADJUSTABLE RING: See p.132

NOTE Work in continuous spirals unless pattern states otherwise. Mark the end of the round with a st marker, and move it up as you work.

Dog rattle
ROUND 1 With yarn A, make an adjustable ring with 6 sc. (6sts)
ROUND 2 2 sc into each st. (12sts)
ROUND 3 *1 sc, work 2 sc into next st; rep from * around. (18sts)
ROUND 4 *2 sc, work 2 sc into next st; rep from * around. (24sts)
ROUND 5 *3 sc, work 2 sc into next st; rep from * around. (30sts)
ROUNDS 6-9 Dc around. (30sts)
ROUND 10 *3 sc, sc2tog; rep from * around. (24sts)
ROUND 11 *2 sc, sc2tog; rep from * around. (18sts)
ROUNDS 12-14 With yarn B, sc around. (18sts)
ROUNDS 15-17 With yarn C, sc around. (18sts)
ROUNDS 18-20 With yarn B, sc around. (18sts)
ROUNDS 21-23 With yarn C, sc around. (18sts)
ROUNDS 24-26 With yarn B, sc around. (18sts)
ROUND 27 With yarn A, *2 sc, work 2 sc into next st; rep from * around. (24sts)
ROUND 28 *3 sc, work 2 sc into next st; rep from * around. (30sts)
ROUNDS 29-32 Dc around. (30sts)
ROUND 33 *3 sc, sc2tog; rep from * around. (24sts)
Place a small bell in the base of the rattle and stuff the rattle firmly before continuing with the crochet.
ROUND 34 *2 sc, sc2tog); rep from * around. (18sts)
ROUND 35 *1 sc, sc2tog; rep from *around. (12sts)
ROUND 36 *sc2tog; rep from * around. (6sts)
Using a yarn needle gather the last 6 sts together. Fasten off, weave in ends.

Ears (make 2)
ROUND 1 With yarn A, make an adjustable ring with 4 sc. (4sts)
ROUND 2 2 sc into each st. (8sts)
ROUNDS 3-4 Sc around. (8sts)
ROUND 5 *2 sc, sc2tog; rep from * around. (6sts)
ROUNDS 6-7 Sc around. (6sts)
Ss to join. Fasten off, weave in ends.

Finishing
Sew ears firmly to each side of rattle head. Embroider nose and eyes with black thread.

>> These rattles are made with Takhi Yarns Cotton Classic DK, 108yds/99m/50g, in A: Light cactus (3701), B: Butter yellow (3548), C: Bubblegum (3449), D: Light blue (3449), and E: Light silver (3006).

TOP TIP

Maintain a tight gauge for a firm fabric that hides the stuffing

The mouse's ears are made from two different-colored pieces of crocheted fabric. Once both are complete, place the shapes wrong-sides together and work a series of single crochet stitches in the head color around them both to create the edging.

Keep your gauge even when working each round. This will ensure a firm, close-knit fabric. To stuff each rattle, push the polyfill gently with your finger to the base of the animal, then complete the design by crocheting its head and ears.

Each animal's eyes, nose, and mouth are sewn with six strands of black and pink embroidery thread. Bend the earflap of the dog downward and secure it with a small stitch from underneath the ear to the side of the dog's head.

Cat rattle

Repeat main pattern for rattle, replacing the colors with C, D, and B in that sequence.

Ears (make 2)

ROUND 1 With yarn C, make an adjustable ring with 4 sc. (4sts)

ROUND 2 1 sc, work 2 sc into next st); rep. (6sts)

ROUND 3 (2 sc, work 2 sc into next st); rep. (8sts)

Ss to join and fasten off. Weave in ends.

Finishing

Sew ears firmly to each side of rattle head. Embroider nose, whiskers, and eyes with black yarn.

Mouse rattle

Repeat main pattern for rattle, replacing the colors with D, E, and A in that sequence.

Ear front (make 2)

ROUND 1 With yarn A, make an adjustable ring with 8 sc. (8sts)

ROUND 2 Work 2 sc into each st. (16sts)

ROUND 3 (1 sc, work 2 sc into next st); rep around. (24sts)

Ss to join and fasten off. Weave in ends.

Ear back (make 2)

ROUND 1 With yarn D, make an adjustable ring with 8 sc. (8sts)

ROUND 2 Work 2 sc into each st. (16sts)

ROUND 3 (1 sc, work 2 sc into next st); rep around. (24sts)

Ss to join and fasten off. Weave in ends.

Finishing

Take one ear front and ear back and place wrong sides together, using yarn D and with the ear front facing, sc both sides of the ear together. Ss to join and fasten off, weave in ends. Sew ears firmly to either side of rattle head. Embroider nose with pink thread and whiskers and eyes with black thread.

Giant play ball

This cute toddler's ball is made up of hexagons and pentagons sewn together three dimensionally. If filling the ball with polyfill, first place the stuffing in a white pillowcase or lining, so that it doesn't poke through.

PROJECTS

For more color granny patterns
>> *go to pages 146, 148, and 154*

Essential information

DIFFICULTY LEVEL Intermediate

SIZE Large ball: approx 29in (74cm) circumference; small ball: approx 14in (35cm)

YARN Use any DK weight, machine-washable yarn

A x 1   B x 1   C x 1   D x 1

CROCHET HOOK G/6 US (4mm) hook

NOTIONS Yarn needle
Polyfill or foam ball

GAUGE Exact gauge is not essential

SPECIAL ABBREVIATIONS
HALF-FINISHED DOUBLE: yo, put hook through st, yo and bring back through st, yo and pull through 2 loops (2 loops left on hook).
HALF-FINISHED HDC: yo, put hook through st, yo and bring back through st (3 loops on hook).
CLUSTER: See p. 79.
PUFF: See p. 142.

NOTE Work all hexagons in stripes of random color and all pentagons in solid colors.

Hexagon *(make 20 for large ball)*
Work 4 ch, ss in first ch to form a ring.
ROUND 1 Ch 3, (yo, insert into ring, pull loop through, yo and pull through 2 loops) twice, yo, pull through all loops on hook, 2 ch, (cluster into ring, 2 ch) 5 times. (6 clusters) Change color, attaching new color to any 2-ch sp.
ROUND 2 Ch 2, (1 puff, 2 ch, 1 puff) into each 2-ch sp, join round with a ss into top of first ch. Change color, attaching new color to any 2-ch sp.
ROUND 3 Ch 3, 2 dc into 2-ch sp, *3 dc into sp between next 2 puffs, (3 dc, 3 ch, 3 dc) into next 2-ch sp; rep from * ending with (3 dc, 3 ch) back into first 2-ch sp, join round with a ss to top of third ch.
Fasten off yarn.

Pentagon *(make 12)*
Work 4 ch, ss in first ch to form a ring.
ROUND 1 Ch 3, (yo, insert into ring, pull loop through, yo and pull through 2 loops) twice, yo, pull through all loops on hook, 2 ch, (cluster into ring, 2 ch) 4 times. (5 clusters)
ROUND 2 Ch 2, (1 puff, 2 ch, 1 puff) into each 2-ch sp, join round with a ss into top of first ch.

ROUND 3 Ch 3, 2 dc into 2-ch sp, *3 dc into sp between next 2 puffs, (3 dc, 3 ch, 3 dc) into next 2-ch sp; rep from * ending with (3 dc, 3 ch) back into first 2-ch sp, join round with a ss to top of third ch.
Fasten off yarn.

Finishing
Block pieces lightly. If making a large ball, sew all pieces together three dimensionally, using whipstitch (see p. 70), with 5 hexagons around each pentagon; the ball will take shape organically, pulling into a sphere. When there are only a few shapes left to attach, stuff the ball and join remaining pieces. For a small ball, sew only 12 pentagons together in the same way as the large ball, making two sets of 5 pentagons around a central pentagon. Sew together to form a sphere.

>> This ball is made with Berroco Comfort DK. 178yds/165m/50g, in A: True red (2751), B: Teaberry (2730), C: Seedling (2740), and D: Cornflower (2726).

Mother elephant and baby

These mother and baby elephants are worked simply in the round, the head and body in one piece and the legs, ears, and tail worked and attached separately. Turn to pages 130–131 for information about assembling your toys.

PROJECTS

For more patterns worked in the round
>> *go to pages 176 and 186*

Essential information

DIFFICULTY LEVEL Easy

SIZE Mother: approx 5¼ x 3¼in (13 x 8.5cm)
Baby: approx 4 x 2¾in (10 x 7cm)

YARN Any DK weight yarn will substitute here. Wool and acrylic fibers will work well

A x 1   **B** x 1

CROCHET HOOK G/6 US (4mm) hook

NOTIONS Black safety toy eyes, buttons, or black embroidery thread and needle
Polyfill
Yarn needle

GAUGE Exact gauge is not essential

Mother elephant

Work the stitches fairly tightly to create a firm-textured fabric and conceal the stuffing.

Head and body

ROUND 1 Work 6 sc in an adjustable ring.
ROUND 2 2 sc in each st around. (12sts)
ROUND 3 *2 sc in next st, sc in next st, repeat from * to end. (18sts)
ROUND 4 *2 sc in next st, sc in next 2 sts, repeat from * to end. (24sts)
ROUNDS 5-15 Sc in each st around.
ROUND 16 2 sc in each of the next 6 sts, sc in last 18 sts. (30sts)
ROUND 17 *2 sc in next st, sc in next st, repeat from * 5 times, sc in last 18 sts. (36sts)
ROUND 18 *2 sc in next st, sc in next 2 st, repeat from * 5 times, sc in last 18 sts. (42sts)
ROUND 19 Sc in each st around.
ROUND 20 Sc in next 24 sts, *sc2tog, sc in next 4 sts, repeat from * to end. (39sts)
ROUND 21 Sc in next 24 sts, *sc2tog, sc in next 3 sts, repeat from * to end. (36sts)
ROUND 22 Sc in next 24 sts, *sc2tog, sc in next 2 sts, repeat from * to end. (33sts)
ROUND 23 Sc in next 24 sts, *sc2tog, sc in next st, repeat from * to end. (30sts)
ROUND 24 Sc in next 24 sts, *sc2tog, repeat from * to end. (27sts)

ROUND 25 *sc2tog, sc in next 2 sts, repeat from * 5 times, 2 sc in each of next 3 sts. (24sts)
ROUND 26 *sc2tog, sc in next st, repeat from * 5 times, sc in last 6 sts. (18sts)
Begin to stuff the body firmly and attach the safety eyes, if you are using them. If you are using buttons or embroidering eyes, this is done upon completion of the toy. Continue to stuff as your work progresses. The trunk is quite small, so add stuffing little and often, and pull decreasing stitches (sc2tog) very tightly to prevent gaps.
ROUND 27 *sc2tog, repeat from * 5 times, sc in last 6 sts. (12sts)
ROUND 28 *sc2tog, sc in next 2 sts, repeat from * to end. (9sts)
ROUNDS 29-36 Sc in each st around.
ROUND 37 Sc2tog, sc in last 7 sts. (8sts)
ROUND 38 Sc2tog, sc in last 6 sts. (7sts)
ROUND 39 Sc2tog, sc in last 5 sts. (6sts)
Fasten off.

>> These toys are made with LB Collection Superwash Merino DK, 127yds/116m/50g, in A: Sky (107) for the mother and B: Denim (108) for the baby.

Add stuffing to the trunk as you work and pull stitches tight.

TOP TIP

Ears (make 2)

Work rounds 1–4 of the Head and body as on page 266. (24sts)

ROUND 5 *2 sc in next st, sc in next 3 sts, repeat from * to end. (30sts)
Fasten off.

Front legs (make 2)

Work rounds 1 and 2 of Head and body as page 266. (12sts)

ROUND 3 Sc TBL of each st around.

ROUNDS 4–12 Sc in each st around.
Fasten off.

Back legs (make 2)

Work rounds 1–3 of Front legs, as above. (12sts)

ROUNDS 4–10 Sc in each st around.
Fasten off.

The cute ears are folded and sewn closed along the turning edges, and then sewn to the baby elephant's head.

Tail

Work 9 ch.

ROW 1 Ss in fourth chain from hook, ch 3, ss in same chain, ch 3, ss in same chain.
Fasten off.

Sew legs, ears, and tail to body with a yarn needle, and weave in ends.

Baby elephant

As with the mother elephant, work the stitches tightly to create a firm-textured fabric and conceal the stuffing.

Head and body

ROUND 1 Work 6 sc in an adjustable ring.

ROUND 2 2 sc in each st around. (12sts)

ROUND 3 *2 sc in next st, sc in next st, repeat from * to end. (18sts)

ROUNDS 4–10 Sc in each st around.

ROUND 11 2 sc in next 4 sts, sc in last 14 sts. (22sts)

ROUND 12 *2 sc in next st, sc in next st, repeat from * 3 times, sc in last 14 sts. (26sts)

ROUND 13 *2 sc in next st, sc in next 2 sts, repeat from * 3 times, sc in last 14 sts. (30sts)

ROUND 14 *2 sc in next st, sc in next 3 sts, repeat from * 3 times, sc in last 14 sts. (34sts)

ROUND 15 Sc in each st around.

ROUND 16 Sc in next 19 sts, *sc2tog, sc in next 3 sts, repeat from * to end. (31sts)

ROUND 17 Sc in next 19 sts, *sc2tog, sc in next 2 sts, repeat from * to end. (28sts)

ROUND 18 Sc in next 19 sts, *sc2tog, sc in next st, repeat from * to end. (25sts)

ROUND 19 Sc in next 19 sts, *sc2tog, repeat from * to end. (22sts)

ROUND 20 *sc2tog, sc in next 4 sts, repeat from * 2 times, sc in last 4 sts. (19sts)

ROUND 21 *sc2tog, sc in next 3 sts, repeat from * 2 times, sc in last 4 sts. (16sts)

Begin to stuff the body firmly and attach the safety eyes, if you are using them. If using buttons or embroidering eyes this is done upon completion of the toy. Continue to stuff as your work progresses; as with the mother elephant, the trunk is quite small so add stuffing little and often, and pull decreasing stitches (sc2tog) quite tight to avoid gaps.

ROUND 22 *sc2tog, sc in next 2 sts, repeat from * 2 times, sc in last 4 sts. (13sts)

ROUND 23 *sc2tog, sc in next st, repeat from * 2 times, sc in last 4 sts. (10 sts)

ROUND 24 *sc2tog, sc in next 3 sts, repeat from * to end. (8sts)

ROUNDS 25–27 Sc in each st around.

ROUND 28 Sc2tog, sc in last 6 sts. (7sts)
Fasten off.

Ears (make 2)

ROUND 1 Work 6 sc in an adjustable ring, turn, ch 1.

ROUND 2 2 sc in each st, turn, ch 1. (12sts)

ROUND 3 2 sc in each st. (24sts)
Fasten off.

Fold ear in half and join along turning edges, attach to head.

Legs (make 4)

ROUND 1 Work 6 sc in an adjustable ring.

ROUND 2 *2 sc in next st, sc in next 2 sts, repeat from * to end. (8sts)

ROUNDS 3–7 Sc in each st around.
Fasten off.

Finishing

Sew legs to the body firmly with a yarn needle, secure yarn, and weave in all ends.

Tail

To make tail, after sewing on a back leg, take the end of the yarn through the elephant's bottom, make a knot about 5/8in (1.5cm) from the body and cut the yarn after this, leaving about 1/2in (1cm) to fluff out the fibers.

The elephant mom's tail is a chain with slip stitches to form a tuft. Her baby's tail is simply a knotted length of yarn.

Essential information

DIFFICULTY LEVEL Easy

SIZE 12 x 5in (30 x 12cm)

YARN You can use any DK weight yarn

A x 2 **B** x 1 **C** x 1 **D** x 1 **E** x 1

CROCHET HOOK E/4 US (3.5mm) hook

NOTIONS 2 stitch markers
Yarn needle
½in (15mm) black safety toy eyes
Black and red embroidery thread and needle
Blue ribbon
Polyfill

GAUGE Exact gauge is not essential

SPECIAL ABBREVIATIONS
ADJUSTABLE RING: See p. 132
BOBBLE STITCH: Yo, insert hook in stitch, yo, draw loop through, yo, draw through 2 loops on the hook, *yo, insert hook in same space, yo, draw loop through, yo, draw through 2 loops on hook; repeat from * 4 times, yo, draw through all 6 loops on hook.

Rag doll

This crocheted version of the traditional rag doll will soon become your child's best friend. Strands of yarn are used to make her hair, while her stockings, pretty dress, and matching shoes are all integral parts of the toy.

PROJECTS

For more single crochet projects
>> *go to pages 36 and 170*

Pattern

The head and body are worked together in one piece.

Head and body

With yarn A, make an adjustable ring and work 6 sc into the ring. (6sts)

ROUND 1 2 sc into each st to the end. (12sts)

ROUND 2 *1 sc, 2 sc in next st; repeat from * to end. (18sts)

ROUND 3 *2 sc, 2 sc in next st; repeat from * to end. (24sts)

ROUND 4 *3 sc, 2 sc in next st; repeat from * to end. (30sts)

ROUND 5 *9 sc, 2 sc in next st; repeat from * to end. (33sts)

ROUND 6 *10 sc, 2 sc in next st; repeat from * to end. (36sts)

ROUND 7 *11 sc, 2 sc in next st; repeat from * to end. (39sts)

ROUND 8 *12 sc, 2 sc in next st; repeat from * to end. (42sts)

ROUND 9 *13 sc, 2 sc in next st; repeat from * to end. (45sts)

ROUND 10 *14 sc, 2 sc in next st; repeat from * to end. (48sts)

<< This doll is made with Berroco Comfort, 178yds/163m/50g, in A: Barley (2703), B: Teaberry (2730), C: Sunshine (2719), D: Cornflower (2726), and E: Brown (2727).

ROUND 11 *15 sc, 2 sc in next st; repeat from * to end. (51sts)

ROUND 12 *16 sc, 2 sc in next st; repeat from * to end. (54sts)

Place 2 stitch markers on the next row, 12 sts apart, to mark where you will put the toy eyes.

ROUNDS 13–14 Sc in each st to the end.

ROUND 15 *sc2tog, 7 sc; repeat from * to end. (48sts)

ROUND 16 *sc2tog, 6 sc; repeat from * to end. (42sts)

ROUND 17 *sc2tog, 5 sc ; repeat from * to end. (36sts)

ROUND 18 *sc2tog, 4 sc; repeat from * to end. (30sts)

ROUND 19 *sc2tog; repeat from * to end. (15sts)

Put your working loop on a stitch holder and attach the toy eyes to your head in the places you marked on round 13. Stuff the head with polyfill. Put your working loop back on the hook and continue.

ROUND 20 *4 sc, 2 sc in next st; repeat from * to end. (18sts)

ROUND 21 Sc in each st to end.

ROUND 22 *5 sc, 2 sc in next st; repeat from * to end. (21sts)

ROUND 23 Sc in each st to end.

ROUND 24 *6 sc, 2 sc in next st; repeat from * to end. (24sts)

ROUND 25 Sc in each st to end.

ROUND 26 *7 sc, 2 sc in next st; repeat from * to end. (27sts)

ROUND 27 Sc in each st to end.

ROUND 28 *8 sc, 2 sc in next st; repeat from * to end. (30sts)

ROUND 29 Sc in each st to end.

Playing with dolls is a huge part of growing up, and having the perfect "friend" can make playtime special. Alter the color of your doll's skin, hair, and garments to please your child, and turn to pages 130–131 for information about how to assemble and stuff a crocheted toy.

ROUND 30 *9 sc, 2 sc in next st; repeat from * to end. (33sts)

ROUND 31 Sc in each st to end.

ROUND 32 *10 sc, 2 sc in next st; repeat from * to end. (36sts)

ROUND 33 Sc in each st to end.

Change to yarn D at the end of this round.

ROUND 34 *sc2tog, 10 sc; repeat from * to end. (33sts)

ROUND 35 *sc2tog, 9 sc; repeat from * to end. (30sts)

ROUND 36 *sc2tog, 3 sc; repeat from * to end. (24sts)

ROUND 37 *sc2tog, 2 sc; repeat from * to end. (18sts)

ROUND 38 *sc2tog, 1 sc; repeat from * to end. (12sts)

ROUND 39 *sc2tog; repeat from * to end. (6sts)
Cut the yarn, leaving a long tail, and pull through loop to secure.
Do not stuff the body of the doll yet.

Arms (make 2)

NOTE Stuff the arms as you go along.
With yarn A, make an adjustable ring and work 6 sc into the ring. (6sts)

ROUND 1 2 sc into each st to end. (12sts)

ROUND 2 *1 sc, 2 sc in next st; repeat from * to end. (18sts)

ROUND 3 *5 sc, 2 sc in next st; repeat from * to end. (21sts)

ROUND 4 Sc in each st to end. (21sts)

ROUND 5 *sc2tog, 5 sc; repeat from * to end. (18sts)

ROUND 6 Bobble stitch in first st, sc in each st to end.

ROUND 7 *sc2tog, 4 sc; repeat from * to end. (15sts)

ROUND 8 *sc2tog, 3 sc; repeat from * to end. (12sts)

ROUNDS 9–18 Sc in each st to end.

ROUND 19 Sc2tog, sc in each st to end. (11sts)

ROUNDS 20–24 Sc in each st to end.

ROUND 25 Sc2tog, sc in each st to end. (10sts)

ROUNDS 26–30 Sc in each st to the end. (10sts)
Cut the yarn, leaving a long tail, and pull through loop to secure.
Finish stuffing the arm firmly.
Thread the cut yarn onto a yarn needle and weave through the last 10 sts, pull the yarn to close the hole at the top of the arm, weave in yarn to secure.

Legs (make 2)

NOTE Stuff the legs as you go along.
With yarn B, make an adjustable ring and work 6 sc into the ring. (6sts)

ROUND 1 2 sc into each st to the end. (12sts)

ROUND 2 2 sc, 2 sc in the next st, 2 sc, 3 hdc in the next st, 2 hdc, 3 hdc in the next st, 2 sc, 2 sc in the last st. (18sts)

ROUND 3 3 sc, 2 sc in the next st, 2 sc, 1 hdc, 2 hdc in the next st, 4 hdc, 2 hdc in the next st, 1 hdc, 1 sc, 2 sc in the next st, sc in the last 2 sts. (22sts)

ROUND 4 2 sc in the first st, 8 sc, 3 hdc in the next st, 5 hdc, 3 hdc in the next st, sc in the last 6 sts. (27sts)

ROUND 5 Sc in each st to the end.

ROUND 6 1 sc, sc2tog, 8 sc, sc2tog, 6 sc, sc2tog, sc in the last 6 sts. (24sts)

ROUND 7 11 sc, hdc3tog, 3 hdc, hdc3tog, sc in the last 4 sts. (20sts)

ROUND 8 3 sc, sc2tog, 4 sc, sc2tog, 1 sc, sc2tog, 1 sc, sc2tog, sc in the last 3 sts. (16sts)

ROUND 9 8 sc, sc2tog, 1 sc, sc2tog, sc in the last 3 sts. (14sts)

ROUND 10 Sc in each st to the end.

ROUND 11 Sc2tog, sc in each st to end. (13sts)
Change to yarn D at the end of the row and start stripe pattern. Work two rounds D and two rounds C; repeat to round 33 and work last round in D.

ROUNDS 12–16 Sc in each st to the end.

ROUND 17 Sc2tog, sc in each st to the end. (12sts)

ROUNDS 18–22 Sc in each st to the end.

ROUND 23 Sc2tog, sc in each st to the end. (11sts)

ROUNDS 24–28 Sc in each st to the end.

ROUND 29 Sc2tog, sc in each st to the end. (10sts)

ROUNDS 30–34 Sc in each st to the end.
Cut the yarn, leaving a long tail, and pull through loop to secure.
Finish stuffing the leg firmly.
Thread the cut yarn onto a yarn needle and weave through the last 10 sts, pull the yarn to close the hole at the top of the leg. Leave the tail of yarn in place to sew onto the body later.

Dress

With yarn B, ch 21, ss into start of chain to form a loop. (21sts)

ROUND 1 *6 sc, 2 sc in next st; repeat from * to end. (24sts)

ROUND 2 Sc in each st to end.

ROUND 3 *7 sc, 2 sc in next st; repeat from * to end. (27sts)

ROUND 4 Sc in each st to end.

Thread the ribbon through the eyelet spaces created in the crochet fabric that forms the doll's skirt. A satin ribbon will give a pretty sheen, while a matte ribbon will be more muted. Tie a double bow if your doll is being made for a child under 36 months.

The doll's hair is created by first cutting same-sized lengths of yarn and attaching them to her crocheted head (see opposite). Use yarn A for her nose and give her a sweet smile. Safety toy eyes are available from craft stores or online.

ROUND 5 *8 sc, 2 sc in next st; repeat from * to end. (30sts)

ROUND 6 Sc in each st to end.

ROUND 7 *9 sc, 2 sc in next st; repeat from * to end. (33sts)

ROUNDS 8–9 Sc in each st to end.

ROUND 10 *10 sc, 2 sc in next st; repeat from * to end. (36sts)

ROUND 11 Sc in each st to end.

The next two rounds create the holes for the ribbon to go through.

ROUND 12 *ch 2, skip 1 st, sc in next st; repeat from * to end.

ROUND 13 *sc in the ch sp, sc in next st; repeat from * to end.

ROUND 14 *5 sc, 2 sc in next st; repeat from * to end. (42sts)

ROUND 15 *6 sc, 2 sc in next st; repeat from * to end. (48sts)

ROUND 16 *3 sc, 2 sc in next st; repeat from * to end. (60sts)

Cut the yarn, leaving a long tail, and pull through loop to secure.

Place the dress over the body of the doll so that the top of it sits on the third round at the top of the body.

Stuff the body of the doll now.

Thread the cut yarn from the body of the doll onto a yarn needle and weave through the last 6 stitches at the base, pull the yarn to close the hole. Weave in yarn to secure and cut off any loose ends.

Dress sleeves (make 2)

With yarn B, make an adjustable ring and work 6 sc into the ring. (6sts)

ROUND 1 *1 sc, 2 sc in next st; repeat from * to end. (9sts)

ROUND 2 *2 sc, 2 sc in next st; repeat from * to end. (12sts)

ROUNDS 3–6 Sc in each st to end.

Cut the yarn, leaving a long tail, and pull through loop to secure.

Place over the top of the arms, sew in place. Then sew the arms to the body using the photo as a guide. Weave in yarn to secure and cut off any loose ends.

Boot cuff (make 2)

With yarn B, ch 16.

ROW 1 Sc in the second ch from hook, sc in each st to the end.

Ch 1, turn. (15sts)

Cut the yarn, leaving a long tail, and pull through loop to secure.

Sew in place around the top of the boots.

Then sew the legs onto the base of the body.

Weave in yarn to secure and cut off any loose ends.

Embroidering the facial details

With yarn A, embroider nose by working 4 or 5 long stitches in the middle of the round where you placed the eyes.

Use black embroidery thread to sew on eyebrows and red embroidery thread to create a V stitch a couple of rounds under the nose to form the mouth. Catch any loose ends to the back of the head (where they won't show), weave in to secure, and cut off.

Creating the hair

Use an letter-sized piece of cardboard and wrap yarn E around the width lengthwise several times. Cut the strands of yarn in half down the middle of the cardboard. This will give you plenty of pieces of yarn the same length.

To attach to the head, start at the crown, put your crochet hook through one of the stitches on the doll's head, fold a piece of yarn in half, and pick up the loop end of the folded yarn with your hook, and pull part way through your stitch. Thread the cut ends of yarn through the loop you have just created and pull the cut ends to close the knot and attach to the head.

Repeat this process, going round in circles until you have a good covering of hair.

Finish off by threading a blue ribbon through the loops on the bottom of the dress and tie with a bow.

See left to work the two cuffs on the doll's booties. The main part of each shoe is crocheted as one piece by joining the pink shoe yarn (B) with the skin yarn (A) and continuing in single crochet stitches.

Polar bear with scarf

See a child's face light up when given this adorably cute bear. His scarf is detachable, so if giving the bear to a child under 36 months, work a couple of holding stitches through the scarf and bear in order to secure it safely.

PROJECTS

For more amigurumi patterns
>> go to pages 266, 270, and 278

Essential information

DIFFICULTY LEVEL Intermediate

SIZE Approx 9¼ x 6½in (23.5 x 16.5cm)

YARN You can use DK-weight yarn for this project

A x 1   **B** x 1

CROCHET HOOK E/4 US (3.5mm) hook

NOTIONS Stitch markers
Yarn needle
⅜in (9mm) black safety toy eyes
Polyfill
Scrap of black DK yarn

GAUGE Exact gauge is not essential

SPECIAL ABBREVIATIONS
ADJUSTABLE RING: See p. 132

Pattern

The head and body are worked together in one piece. Stuff the head and body as you go along.

Head and body

With yarn A, make an adjustable ring and work 6 sc into the ring. (6sts)

ROUND 1 *1 sc, 2 sc in next st; repeat from * to end. (9sts)

ROUND 2 *2 sc, 2 sc in next st; repeat from * to end. (12sts)

ROUND 3 *3 sc, 2 sc in next st; repeat from * to end. (15sts)

ROUND 4 *4 sc, 2 sc in next st; repeat from * to end. (18sts)

ROUND 5 *5 sc, 2 sc in next st; repeat from * to end. (21sts)

ROUND 6 *6 sc, 2 sc in next st; repeat from * to end. (24 sts) Mark this round with a stitch marker.

ROUND 7 *5 sc, 2 sc in next st; repeat from * to end. (28sts)

ROUND 8 *6 sc, 2 sc in next st; repeat from * to end. (32sts)

ROUND 9 *7 sc, 2 sc in next st; repeat from * to end. (36sts)

ROUND 10 *8 sc, 2 sc in next st; repeat from * to end. (40sts)

ROUNDS 11–13 Sc in each st to end.

ROUND 14 *sc2tog, 6 sc; repeat from * to end. (35sts)

ROUND 15 *sc2tog, 5 sc; repeat from * to end. (30sts)

The next two rounds create the bend in the neck.

ROUNDS 16-17 13 Sc, ss in the next 4 sts, 13 sc.

ROUND 18 Sc in each st to end.

ROUND 19 *9 sc, 2 sc in next st; repeat from * to end. (33sts)

ROUND 20 Sc in each st to end.
Put your working loop on a stitch holder and attach the toy eyes to the head.
Place the eyes at the top of the head, nine stitches apart on the marked round 6.
Stuff the head with polyfill.
Put your working loop back on the hook and continue:

ROUND 21 *10 sc, 2 sc in next st; repeat from * to end. (36sts)

ROUND 22 Sc in each st to end.

ROUND 23 *11 sc, 2 sc in next st; repeat from * to end. (39sts)

ROUND 24 Sc in each st to end.

ROUND 25 *12 sc, 2 sc in next st; repeat from * to end. (42sts)

ROUND 26 Sc in each st to end.

ROUND 27 *13 sc, 2 sc in next st; repeat from * to end. (45sts)

ROUND 28 Sc in each st to end.

ROUND 29 *14 sc, 2 sc in next st; repeat from * to end. (48sts)

ROUND 30 Sc in each st to end.

ROUND 31 *15 sc, 2 sc in next st; repeat from * to end. (51sts)

ROUND 32 sc in each st to end.

ROUND 33 *16 sc, 2 sc in next st; repeat from * to end. (54sts)

ROUND 34 Sc in each st to end.

ROUND 35 *17 sc, 2 sc in next st; repeat from * to end. (57sts)

>> This polar bear is made with Rowan Handknit Cotton, 93yds/85m/50g, in A: Ecru (251) and B: Atlantic (346).

Safety toy eyes usually have two parts—the eye and the washer, or backing part, to fix it onto your polar bear. For the sake of safety, the washer, or backing part, must join firmly with the eye to keep it from being pulled out by a child. Embroider the bear's nose and mouth using small snippets of black yarn.

ROUND 36 *18 sc, 2 sc in the next st; repeat from * to end. (60sts)

ROUNDS 37-39 Sc in each st to the end.

ROUND 40 *sc2tog, 18 sc; repeat from * to end. (57sts)

ROUND 41 *sc2tog, 17 sc; repeat from * to end. (54sts)

ROUND 42 *sc2tog, 7 sc; repeat from * to end. (48sts)

ROUND 43 *sc2tog, 6 sc; repeat from * to end. (42sts)

ROUND 44 *sc2tog, 5 sc; repeat from * to end. (36sts)

ROUND 45 *sc2tog, 4 sc; repeat from * to end. (30sts)

ROUND 46 *sc2tog, 3 sc; repeat from * to end. (24sts)

ROUND 47 *sc2tog, 2 sc; repeat from * to end. (18sts)

ROUND 48 *sc2tog, 1 sc; repeat from * to end. (12sts)

ROUND 49 *sc2tog; repeat from * to end. (6sts)
Cut the yarn, leaving a long tail, and pull through loop to secure.
Stuff the body firmly with polyfill.
Thread the cut yarn onto a yarn needle and weave through the last 6 sts, pull the yarn to close the hole at the base of the body, weave in yarn to secure, and cut off any loose ends.

Legs (make 4)

With yarn A, make an adjustable ring and work 6 sc into the ring. (6sts)

ROUND 1 2 sc into each st to end. (12sts)

ROUND 2 *1 sc, 2 sc in next st; repeat from * to end. (18sts)

ROUND 3 5 sc TBL, sc2tog, 4 sc, sc2tog, 5 sc. (16sts)

ROUND 4 4 sc, sc2tog, 4 sc, sc2tog, 4 sc. (14sts)

ROUNDS 5-7 Sc in each st to end.

ROUND 8 Sc2tog, sc in each st to end. (13sts)

ROUNDS 9-10 Sc in each st to end.

ROUND 11 Sc2tog, sc in each st to end. (12sts)

ROUNDS 12-14 Sc in each st to end.
Cut the yarn, leaving a long tail, and pull through loop to secure.
Finish stuffing the legs firmly with polyfill.
Using the photo as a guide, sew in place on

the polar bear body. Weave in yarn to secure and cut off any loose ends.

Ears (make 2)

With yarn A, make an adjustable ring and work 6 sc into the ring. (6sts)

ROUND 1 *1 sc, 2 sc in the next st; repeat from * to end. (9sts)

ROUNDS 2-3 Sc in each st to the end.
Cut the yarn, leaving a long tail, and pull through loop to secure.
Press flat and use a strand of yarn A to sew a V shape in the middle. Using the photo as a guide sew in place on the polar bear body. Weave in yarn to secure and cut off loose ends.
Use a scrap of black yarn to embroider a triangle nose and backstitches for the mouth.

Tail end

With yarn A, make an adjustable ring and work 4 sc into the ring. (4sts)

ROUND 1 *1 sc, 2 sc in the next st; repeat from * to end. (6sts)

ROUND 2 *2 sc, 2 sc in the next st; repeat from * to end. (8sts)

ROUNDS 3-5 Sc in each st to the end.
Cut the yarn, leaving a long tail, and pull through loop to secure.
Using the photo as a guide, above right, sew in place on the polar bear body. Weave in yarn to secure and cut off any loose ends.

Scarf

This is not worked in a spiral. Turn your work at the end of each row.
With yarn B, work 4 ch.

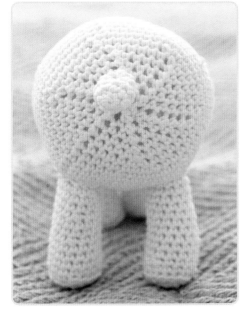

The tail end of the bear is formed by making an adjustable ring. Turn to page 57 for more information about this technique, which is really useful for making a neat round with a tidy central hole. Refer to pages 130–131 for more information about assembling your crocheted toy.

ROW 1 Starting in second ch from hook, sc in each st, ch 1, turn.

ROW 2 Sc in each st, ch 1, turn.
Repeat the last row until scarf is 13³/₄in (35cm).
Cut the yarn, leaving a long tail, and pull through loop to secure.
Knot short lengths of yarn B onto the ends of the scarf to form tassels and cut to length.
Tie the scarf around the polar bear's neck.

Floppy-eared bunny

This fun little rabbit will be at home sitting in a stroller or nursery, or being cuddled by a toddler. It is a great project for practicing your color changes on the bunny's body, legs, and arms; turn to page 39 if you need more information.

PROJECTS
For more animal patterns
>> go to pages 132 and 156

Essential information

DIFFICULTY LEVEL Intermediate

SIZE Approx 8¾ x 4in (22 x 10cm)

YARN You can use any DK-weight yarn for this project; cotton or acrylic are best for toys

A x 1   **B** x 1   **C** x 1

CROCHET HOOK E/4 US (3.5mm) hook

NOTIONS Stitch markers
Yarn needle
½in (12mm) black safety toy eyes
Black and yellow embroidery thread and needle
White felt
Polyfill

GAUGE Exact gauge is not essential

SPECIAL ABBREVIATIONS
ADJUSTABLE RING: See p. 132

<< This bunny is made with Rowan Sienna 4 Ply, 170yds/155m/50g. in A: Madras (675), B: Vindaloo (678), and C: White (651).

Stripe pattern
Stripes are worked on the body, arms, and legs. Begin with yarn B and work as follows:
2 rows blue (B)
2 rows white (C)
2 rows yellow (A)
Keep color changes at the back of your work.

Body and head
The head and body are worked together in one piece.
With yarn A, make an adjustable ring and work 6 sc into the ring. (6sts)
ROUND 1 2 sc into each st to the end. (12sts)
ROUND 2 *1 sc, 2 sc in next st; repeat from * to end. (18sts)
ROUND 3 *2 sc, 2 sc in next st; repeat from * to end. (24sts)
ROUND 4 *3 sc, 2 sc in next st; repeat from * to end. (30sts)
ROUND 5 *9 sc, 2 sc in next st; repeat from * to end. (33sts)
ROUND 6 *10 sc, 2 sc in next st; repeat from * to end. (36sts)
ROUND 7 *11 sc, 2 sc in next st; repeat from * to end. (39sts)
ROUND 8 *12 sc, 2 sc in next st; repeat from * to end. (42sts)
ROUND 9 *13 sc, 2 sc in next st; repeat from * to end. (45sts)
ROUND 10 *14 sc, 2 sc in next st; repeat from * to end. (48sts)
ROUND 11 *15 sc, 2 sc in next st; repeat from * to end. (51sts)
ROUND 12 *16 sc, 2 sc in next st; repeat from * to end. (54sts)

Place 2 stitch markers on the next row, 12 sts apart, to mark where you will put the toy eyes.
ROUND 13–14 Sc in each st to the end.
ROUND 15 *sc2tog, 7 sc; repeat from * to end. (48sts)
ROUND 16 *sc2tog, 6 sc; repeat from * to end. (42sts)
ROUND 17 *sc2tog, 5 sc; repeat from * to end. (36sts)
ROUND 18 *sc2tog, 4 sc; repeat from * to end. (30sts)
ROUND 19 *sc2tog; repeat from * to end. (15sts)
Put your working loop on a stitch holder and attach the toy eyes to the head in the places you marked on round 13.
Stuff the head with polyfill.
Put your working loop back on your hook and continue.
Starting with yarn B, begin stripe pattern:
ROUND 20 *4 sc, 2 sc in the next st; repeat from * to end. (18sts)
ROUND 21 Sc in each st to end.
ROUND 22 *5 sc, 2 sc in next st; repeat from * to end. (21sts)
ROUND 23 Sc in each st to end.
ROUND 24 *6 sc, 2 sc in next st; repeat from * to end. (24sts)
ROUND 25 Sc in each st to end.
ROUND 26 *7 sc, 2 sc in next st; repeat from * to end. (27sts)
ROUND 27 Sc in each st to end.
ROUND 28 *8 sc, 2 sc in next st; repeat from * to end. (30sts)
ROUND 29 Sc in each st to end.
ROUND 30 *9 sc, 2 sc in next st; repeat from * to end. (33sts)

ROUND 31 Sc in each st to end.

ROUND 32 *10 sc, 2 sc in next st; repeat from * to end. (36sts)

ROUND 33 Sc in each st to end.

ROUND 34 *sc2tog, 10 sc; repeat from * to end. (33sts)

ROUND 35 *sc2tog, 9 sc; repeat from * to end. (30sts)

ROUND 36 *sc2tog, 3 sc; repeat from * to end. (24sts)

ROUND 37 *sc2tog, 2 sc; repeat from * to end. (18sts)

ROUND 38 *sc2tog, 1 sc; repeat from * to end. (12sts)

ROUND 39 *sc2tog; repeat from * to end. (6 sts)

Cut the yarn, leaving a long tail, and pull through loop to secure.

Stuff the body firmly. Thread the cut yarn onto a yarn needle and weave through the last 6 stitches, pull the yarn to close the hole at the base of the body, weave in yarn to secure, and cut off any loose ends.

Arms (make 2)

Stuff the arms as you go along.

With yarn A, make an adjustable ring and work 6 sc into the ring. (6sts)

ROUND 1 2 sc into each st to end. (12sts)

ROUND 2 *1 sc, 2 sc in next st; repeat from * to end. (18sts)

ROUND 3 *2 sc, 2 sc in next st; repeat from * to end. (24sts)

ROUNDS 4–6 Sc in each st to end.

ROUND 7 *sc2tog, 2 sc; repeat from * to end. (18sts)

ROUND 8 *sc2tog, 4 sc; repeat from * to end. (15sts)

ROUND 9 *sc2tog, 3 sc; repeat from * to end. (12sts)

Starting with yarn B, begin stripe pattern:

ROUNDS 10–19 Sc in each st to end.

ROUND 20 Sc2tog, sc in each st to end. (11sts)

ROUNDS 21–25 Sc in each st to end.

ROUND 26 Sc2tog, sc in each st to end. (10sts)

ROUNDS 27–31 Sc in each st to end.

Cut the yarn, leaving a long tail, and pull through loop to secure.

Finish stuffing the arm firmly.

Thread the cut yarn onto a yarn needle and weave through the last 10 sts, pull the yarn to close the hole at the top of the arm, weave in yarn to secure.

Legs (make 2)

With yarn A, make an adjustable ring and work 6 sc into the ring. (6sts)

ROUND 1 2 sc into each st to end. (12sts)

ROUND 2 2 sc, 2 sc in next st, 2 sc, 3 hdc in next st, 2 hdc, 3 hdc in next st, 2 sc, 2 sc in last st. (18sts)

ROUND 3 3 sc, 2 sc in next st, 2 sc, 1 hdc, 2 hdc in next st, 4 hdc, 2 hdc in next st, 1 hdc, 1 sc, 2 sc in next st, sc in last 2 sts. (22sts)

ROUND 4 2 sc in first st, 8 sc, 3 hdc in next st, 5 hdc, 3 hdc in next st, sc in the last 6 sts. (27sts)

ROUND 5 Sc in each st to end.

ROUND 6 1 sc, sc2tog, 8 sc, sc2tog, 6 sc, sc2tog, sc in the last 6 sts. (24sts)

ROUND 7 11 sc, hdc3tog, 3 hdc, hdc3tog, sc in the last 4 sts. (20sts)

ROUND 8 3 sc, sc2tog, 4 sc, sc2tog, 1 sc, sc2tog, 1 sc, sc2tog, sc in last 3 sts. (16sts)

ROUND 9 8 sc, sc2tog, 1 sc, sc2tog, sc in last 3 sts. (14sts)

Starting with yarn B, begin stripe pattern:

ROUND 10 Sc in each st to end.

ROUND 11 Sc2tog, sc in each st to end. (13sts)

ROUNDS 12–16 Sc in each st to end.

ROUND 17 Sc2tog, sc in each st to end. (12sts)

ROUNDS 18–22 Sc in each st to end.

ROUND 23 Sc2tog, sc in each st to end. (11sts)

ROUNDS 24–28 Sc in each st to end.

ROUND 29 Sc2tog, sc in each st to end. (10sts)

ROUNDS 30–33 Sc in each st to the end.

Cut the yarn, leaving a long tail, and pull through loop to secure.

Finish stuffing the leg firmly.

Thread the cut yarn onto a yarn needle and weave through the last 10 sts, pull the yarn to close the hole at the top of the leg, weave in yarn to secure.

Give your bunny a friendly smile using six strands of embroidery thread or a length of black yarn. Sew the nose by making a series of increasingly smaller stitches to form a triangle, and use backstitches for the mouth.

For a neat rabbit's foot, make an adjustable ring using six single crochet stitches (see p. 57). This will create a tidy circle underneath his padded paw from which the crochet stitches will circulate out.

Bunny ears (make 2)

With yarn A, make an adjustable ring and work 6 sc into the ring. (6sts)

ROUND 1 2 sc into each st to end. (12sts)

ROUND 2 *1 sc, 2 sc in next st; repeat from * to end. (18sts)

ROUND 3 Sc in each st to end.

ROUND 4 *2 sc, 2 sc in next st; repeat from * to end. (24sts)

ROUND 5 Sc in each st to end.

ROUND 6 *3 sc, 2 sc in next st; repeat from * to end. (30sts)

ROUNDS 7–8 Sc in each st to end.

ROUND 9 Sc2tog, sc in each st to end. (29sts)

ROUND 10 Sc in each st to end.

ROUNDS 11–45 Repeat the last two rounds 17 times. (12 sts at the end of round 45)

Cut the yarn, leaving a long tail, and pull through loop to secure. Press flat and sew the opening at the top of the ear closed. Cut felt to fit inside ear and sew in place with yellow embroidery thread.

Tail

With yarn B, make an adjustable ring and work 6 sc into the ring. (6sts)

ROUND 1 2 sc into each st to end. (12sts)

ROUND 2 Sc in each st to end.

ROUND 3 Sc in each st to end.

ROUND 4 Sc2tog 6 times. (6sts)

Cut the yarn, leaving a long tail, and pull through loop to secure.

Stuff firmly with polyfill.

Thread the cut yarn onto a yarn needle and weave through the last 6 sts, pull the yarn to close the hole, weave in yarn to secure but do not cut the yarn off.

Finishing

Sew the arms, legs, ears, and tail in place with matching yarn. Weave in any loose ends and cut off. Embroider face detail using black embroidery thread.

Cut two pieces of white felt, approximately ½in (1cm) smaller all around than the finished crocheted ears. Attach them using small running stitches, cross-stitches, or blanket stitch (see p. 87). Place your stitches close to the edge of the felt and secure with a knot at the end.

Jungle finger puppets

Give your child hours of fun making up stories of animals living in the wild. These little puppets are suited to a reasonably experienced crocheter.

PROJECTS
For more animal patterns
>> go to pages 132 and 156

Essential information

DIFFICULTY Intermediate

SIZE Approx 3 x 1½in (8 x 4cm)

YARN You can use any yarn for this project

A x 1   B x 1   C x 1   D x 1   E x 1

F x 1   G x 1   H x 1   I x 1

CROCHET HOOK E/4 US (3.5mm) hook

NOTIONS Yarn needle
Polyfill
Black embroidery thread and needle
Pipe cleaner
White felt
Fabric glue

GAUGE Exact gauge is not essential

<< These puppets are made with Rowan Siena 4 Ply,
179yds/155m/50g, in A: Sorbet (683), B: Madras
(675), C: Frost (653), D: Beacon (668), E: Cream (652),
F: Chilli (666), G: Topaz (689), H: White (651) and I:
Greengage (661).

SPECIAL ABBREVIATIONS
ADJUSTABLE RING: See p. 132
LOOP STITCH: Wrap the yarn from front to back over the index finger of your yarn hand. Insert the hook in the next stitch, grab the strand of yarn from behind your index finger and draw the yarn through the stitch. The yarn on your finger becomes the loop. With the yarn loop still on your index finger, yarn over the hook and draw the yarn through the 2 loops on your hook.

Pattern

The "basic" pattern relates to all puppets. Refer to individual patterns for specific details.

Basic body
Make an adjustable ring and work 6 sc into the ring. (6sts)
ROUND 1 *1 sc, 2 sc in next st; repeat from * to end. (9sts)
ROUND 2 *2 sc, 2 sc in next st; repeat from * to end. (12sts)
ROUNDS 3–10 Sc in each st to end. (12sts)
Cut the yarn and pull through loop to secure. Sew in loose end and cut off.

Basic head
Make an adjustable ring and work 6 sc into the ring. (6sts)
ROUND 1 2 sc into each st to end. (12sts)
ROUND 2 *sc, 2 sc in next st; repeat from * to end. (18sts)
ROUND 3 *2 sc, 2 sc in next st; repeat from * to end. (24sts)
ROUNDS 4–6 Sc in each st to end. (24sts)
ROUND 7 *sc2tog, 2 sc; repeat from * to end. (18sts)

ROUND 8 *sc2tog, sc; repeat from * to end. (12sts)
ROUND 9 *sc2tog; repeat from * to end. (6sts)
Cut yarn, leaving a long tail, and pull through to secure. Stuff firmly.
Weave the yarn through the last 6 sts, pull to close at the base of head. Sew onto body and weave in loose end.

Basic arm
Make an adjustable ring and work 4 sc into the ring. (4sts)
ROUNDS 1–3 Sc in each st to the end. (4sts)
Cut and secure the yarn leaving a long tail. Stuff the arms, then weave the yarn end through the last 4 sts. Pull to close at top of arm. Sew in place and weave in loose ends.

Lion
Make one Basic body, one Basic head, and two Basic arms in yarn A.
MANE
With yarn B, ch 26, ss to join and form a loop. (26sts)
ROUNDS 1–2 Loop stitch in each stitch. (26sts)
Cut yarn, leaving long tail, and secure. Sew in place on head. Weave in loose ends.
TAIL
With yarn A, ch 12, ss in second ch from hook, ss along ch. (11sts)
Cut yarn and secure. Sew in place and weave in loose ends. Cut two strands of yarn B, fold in half and sew to end of tail to form tassel.
FINISHING
With black embroidery thread, add the facial details. Make two French knots for the eyes, a small triangle for the nose, and lines to form the mouth. Weave in loose ends.

For the lion's mane, refer to the Special stitches panel on page 283 to form the loop stitches. Make even loops by wrapping the yarn around your fingers.

Elephant

Make one Basic body, one Basic head, and two Basic arms in yarn C.

EARS (MAKE 2)

This is not worked in a spiral. Turn your work at the end of each row to form a semi circle. With yarn C, make an adjustable ring and work 4 sc into the ring. (4sts)

ROW 1 *sc, 2 sc in next st; repeat from * to end, ch 1, turn. (6sts)

ROW 2 2 sc, 2 sc in next st, 1 sc, 1 hdc, 2 hdc in last st. (8sts)

Cut yarn, leaving a long tail, and secure. Sew in place and weave in loose ends.

TRUNK

With yarn C, make an adjustable ring and work 4 sc into the ring. (4sts)

ROUNDS 1–8 Sc in each st to the end. (4sts)

Cut yarn, leaving a long tail, and secure. Cut a pipe cleaner to the length of the trunk and place inside. Weave yarn end through last 4 sts; pull to close at base of trunk. Sew in place and weave in loose ends.

TAIL

With yarn C, ch 8, ss in second ch from hook, ss along ch. (7sts)

Cut yarn and secure. Sew in place and weave in loose ends.

Use bright colors, such as blue, green, and yellow as shown above, for the parrot, for a tropical bird. Alternatively, try green, orange, and yellow, or blue, yellow, and red.

With black embroidery thread, add the facial details. Make two French knots for the eyes.

Monkey

Make one Basic body, one Basic head, and two Basic arms in yarn D.

MUZZLE

With yarn E, make an adjustable ring and work 6 sc into the ring. (6sts)

ROUND 1 Sc in each st to the end. (6sts)

Cut yarn, leaving a long tail, and secure. Weave yarn through last 6 sts and pull to close at base of body. Sew onto head and weave in loose ends.

EARS (MAKE 2)

With yarn D, make an adjustable ring and work 8 sc into the ring, ss to join ring. (8sts)

Cut yarn and pull through to secure. Sew in place and weave in loose ends.

EYE PATCHES

With yarn E, make an adjustable ring and work 8 sc into the ring, ss to join ring. (8sts)

Cut yarn and pull through to secure. Sew in place and weave in loose ends.

TAIL

With yarn D, ch 12, ss in second ch from hook, ss along ch 11sts.

Cut yarn and secure. Sew in place and weave

in yarn and cut off any loose ends. With black embroidery thread, add the facial details. Make two French knots in the center of the eye patches for the eyes.

Parrot

Make one Basic body using yarn F.

Make head pattern up to round 8 using yarn F. Cut yarn, leaving a long tail, and secure. Stuff the head firmly and sew onto body. Weave in loose ends.

LOWER BEAK

With yarn B, make an adjustable ring and work 4 sc into the ring. (4sts)

ROUND 1 Sc in each st to the end. (4sts)

Cut yarn, leaving a long tail, and secure. Stuff.

TOP BEAK

With yarn B, make an adjustable ring and work 6 sc into the ring. (6sts)

ROUNDS 1–2 Sc in each st to the end. (6sts)

Cut yarn, leaving a long tail, and secure. Stuff and sew the top and lower beak in place. Weave in loose ends.

WINGS

With yarn F, make an adjustable ring, and work 6 sc into the ring. (6sts)

ROUND 1 2 sc into each st to the end. (12sts)

ROUND 2 *3 sc, 2 sc in the next st; repeat from * to end. (15sts)

ROUND 3 Sc in each st to the end.

ROUND 4 *sc2tog, 3 sc; repeat from * to end. Change to yarn G at end of this row. (12 sts)

ROUND 5 Working through the back loop of the stitch only, sc in each st to end.

ROUND 6 *sc2tog, 4 sc; repeat from * to end. (10sts)

ROUND 7 Working through the back loop of the stitch only, sc in each st to end.

ROUND 8 *sc2tog, 3 sc; repeat from * to end. (8sts)

ROUND 9 Sc in each st to end.

ROUND 10 *sc2tog, 2 sc; repeat from * to end. (6sts)

ROUND 11 Sc in each st to end.

ROUND 12 Sc in the first stitch, ch 4, sc in the next st, ch 4, sc to end.

Cut yarn, leaving a long tail, and secure. Sew closed the hole at the base of the wing. Rejoin yarn F to first round of loops left by back loop only rounds and work as follows:

ROUND 1 *ss in first loop, sc in next, tr in next; repeat to end.

Rejoin yarn G to second round of loops left by back loop only rounds and work as follows:

ROUND 2 *ss in first loop, sc in next, tr in next; repeat to last st, ss in last st.

Cut yarn and secure. Sew the wings onto the body. Weave in loose ends.

TAIL

This is not worked in a spiral. Turn your work at the end of each row.

With yarn G, ch 7.

ROW 1 Starting in second ch from hook, 3 sc, 3 hdc, 2 ch, turn. (6sts)

ROW 2 Starting at first hdc of prev row, 3 hdc, 3 sc, 1 ch, turn. (6sts)

ROW 3 Starting at the first sc of prev row, 3 sc, 3 hdc. (6sts)

Cut yarn and pull through loop to secure.

TAIL TOP

This is not worked in a spiral. Turn your work at end of each row.

With yarn F, ch 4.

ROW 1 Starting in second ch from hook, 2 sc, hdc in last ch, ch 2, turn. (4sts)

ROW 2 1 hdc into hdc from prev row, 2 sc, ch 1, turn.

ROW 3 2 sc, hdc in the last st.

Cut yarn and secure. Sew top of tail onto bottom, then sew in place on the body. Weave in loose ends.

EYE PATCHES

With yarn H, make an adjustable ring and work 8 sc into the ring, ss to join ring. (8sts) Cut yarn and secure. Sew in place and weave in loose ends. With black embroidery thread, add the facial detail.

Crocodile

Make one Basic body, one Basic head, and two Basic arms in yarn I.

MOUTH (MAKE 2)

With yarn I, make an adjustable ring and work 6 sc into the ring. (6sts)

ROUND 1 *1 sc, 2 sc in the next st; repeat from * to end. (9sts)

ROUND 2 2 sc in the first sts, sc in each sts to end. (10sts)

ROUND 3 Sc in each st to the end. (10sts)

ROUND 4 2 sc in the first sts, sc in each st to end. (11sts)

ROUND 5 Sc in each st to the end. (11sts)

ROUND 6 2 sc in the first sts, sc in each st to end. (12sts)

ROUND 7 Sc in each st to end. (12sts)

Cut yarn and secure. Cut a felt zigzag and attach with fabric glue as teeth. Sew head in place and weave in loose ends.

EYES (MAKE 2)

With yarn H, make an adjustable ring and work 4 sc into the ring.

ROUND 1 Sc in each st to the end. (4sts)

Cut the yarn and weave it through the 4 sts, pull to close the hole and form the eyeball. Weave in loose ends.

EYE SOCKETS (MAKE 2)

With yarn I, make an adjustable ring and work 5 sc into the ring.

ROUNDS 1-2 Sc in each st to the end. (5sts)

Cut yarn and secure. Place around the eyeball. It should be a tight fit. Sew in place and weave in loose ends. With black embroidery thread, add the facial details. Sew a line down the center of each eye. With yarn I, work two French knots at the end of the top of the mouth to form the nostrils.

The elephant's trunk is made from a "tube" of eight chain stitches with a pipe cleaner inserted inside to make it stick out.

To work the French knot eyes, wrap black embroidery thread around your needle once or twice before inserting the needle back through the stitching.

White felt makes a great set of teeth for this crocodile. Use one long piece or two pieces, as used here, to create the right expression.

Bags

Granny square bag

A stylish twist on a classic crochet motif, this simple granny square shoulder bag relies on bright color combinations to give it the "wow" factor. Turn to page 102 for more information about creating a granny square.

PROJECTS

For more bag patterns
>> go to pages 292, 294, and 296

Essential information

DIFFICULTY LEVEL Easy

SIZE 12½ x 12½in (32 x 32cm)

YARN You can substitute any DK weight, wool-blend yarn for this project

A x 3   **B** x 1   **C** x 1   **D** x 1

CROCHET HOOK F/5 US (3.75mm) hook

NOTIONS Yarn needle
Cotton material for lining, measuring 24½ x 12¼in (62 x 31cm), plus seam allowance
Sewing needle and matching thread

GAUGE Rounds 1–3 measure 3in (8cm)

Pattern (make 2)

With yarn A, work 4 ch, ss in first ch to form a ring.

ROUND 1 Ch 4 (counts as 1 dc and 1 ch), *3 dc into ring, 1 ch, rep from * twice, 2 dc into ring, join with a ss to third of 4 ch. Fasten off A.

ROUND 2 Join B into any ch sp, 3 ch (counts as first dc), (2 dc, 2 ch, 3 dc) in same ch sp, 1 ch, *(3 dc, 2 ch, 3 dc) in next ch sp, 1 ch, rep from * twice, join with a ss in top of initial 3 ch. Fasten off B.

ROUND 3 Join C into any corner ch sp, 3 ch (counts as first dc), (2 dc, 2 ch, 3 dc) in same ch sp, 1 ch, 3 dc in next ch sp, 1 ch, *(3 dc, 2 ch, 3 dc) in next ch sp, 1 ch, 3 dc in next ch sp, 1 ch rep from * twice, join with a ss in top of initial 3 ch. Fasten off C.

ROUND 4 Join A into any corner ch sp, 3 ch (counts as first dc), (2 dc, 2 ch, 3 dc) in same ch sp, 1 ch, 3 dc in next ch sp, 1 ch, 3 dc in next ch sp, 1 ch, *(3 dc, 2 ch, 3 dc) in next ch sp, 1 ch, 3 dc in next ch sp, 1 ch, 3 dc in next ch sp, 1 ch, rep from * twice, join with a ss in top of initial 3 ch. Fasten off A.
Continue working each round in color sequence as follows, working as round 4. Each round will have 1 extra 3 dc in ch sp and 1 ch, worked on each side of the square; corners remain the same.

ROUND 5 Yarn D.
ROUND 6 Yarn B.
ROUND 7 Yarn A.
ROUND 8 Yarn B.
ROUND 9 Yarn C.
ROUND 10 Yarn A.
ROUND 11 Yarn D.
ROUND 12 Yarn A.

Making the strap

Work 121 ch.

ROW 1 1 sc into second ch from hook, 1 sc in each ch to end, turn. (120sts)

ROW 2 1 sc in each sc, turn.

Repeat row 2 four more times. Fasten off yarn.

Finishing

Press the front and back pieces according to ball-band instructions.
Place front and back with WS together, rejoin yarn A to top left corner space and working through front and back join on three sides as follows, 1 sc in ch sp, *1 sc in top of each of next 3 dc, 1 sc in ch sp, rep from * to corner, 3 sc in corner ch sp, rep from * to next corner sp, 3 sc in corner ch sp, rep from * to top right-hand corner, leaving top of bag open. Work 1 row of sc evenly along top edges of front and back.
Sew shoulder strap to sides of bag.
Weave in all ends.
Fold lining material in half with RS together, sew around three sides. Place lining in bag and fold over top edge. Sew top seam of lining to crochet bag.

>> This bag is made with Sublime Extra Fine Merino DK, 127yds/116m/50g, in A: Grey (18), B: Julep (307), C: Red currant (17), and D: Gem (361).

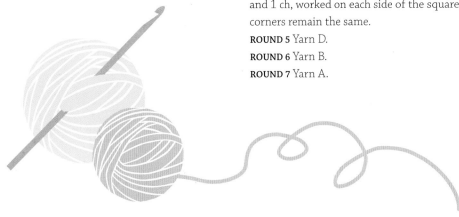

Straw beach bag

The bottom of this eye-catching yet practical bag is worked in rows, and then the rest of the bag is worked in the round, to the desired height.

PROJECTS
For more half double patterns
>> *go to pages 230 and 246*

Essential information

DIFFICULTY LEVEL Easy

SIZE 12½ x 22in (32 x 56cm)

YARN Any aran-weight, durable yarn (held double) such as cotton, linen, or string will work

A x 7   **B** x 6

CROCHET HOOK H/8 US (5mm) hook

NOTIONS Yarn needle
¾in (2cm) button

GAUGE Exact gauge is not essential

NOTE Ch 2 at the beginning of each hdc row or round is classed as the first st worked in the first st of previous row.
Ch 1 at the beginning of each sc row or round is classed as the first st worked in the first st of previous row.
Hold yarn double for extra strength.

Pattern

FOUNDATION ROW With yarn A, work 47 ch.

ROW 1 Hdc in third ch from hook and in each ch across, turn. (46sts)

ROW 2 Ch 2, hdc in each stitch across, turn. (46sts)

ROWS 3–11 Repeat row 2.
Now working in rounds.

ROUND 1 Ch 1, sc in each st to end of row, 2 sc in each row end, 1 sc in back of each foundation ch, 2 sc in each row end, join with a ss. (136sts)

ROUND 2 Ch 2, hdc in each st around, join with a ss.

ROUNDS 3–16 Repeat round 2.

ROUNDS 17–28 With yarn B, repeat round 2.

Handles

ROUND 29 Ch 2, hdc in next 12 sts, 60 ch, skip next 20 sts, hdc in next 48 sts, 60 ch, skip next 20 sts, hdc in next 35 sts, join with a ss.

ROUND 30 Hdc in each stitch and ch around, join with a ss.

ROUNDS 31–32 Hdc in each stitch around. Fasten off.

Fastening flap

With yarn B, work 11 ch.

ROW 1 Sc in second ch from hook and in each ch across, turn. (10sts)

ROW 2 Ch 1, sc in each st across, turn. (10sts)

This bag has a very sturdy base, achieved by working in straight rows. The hemp yarn used here makes for a summery feel, but for a slightly more rigid bag use raffia.

ROWS 3–4 Repeat row 2.

ROW 5 Ch 1, sc in first 4 sts, 2 ch, skip next 2 sts, sc in last 4 sts, turn.

ROW 6 Ch 1, sc in first 4 sts, sc in each of the 2 chs, sc in last 4 sts, turn.

ROWS 7–20 Repeat row 2.
Sc evenly around entire flap to neaten.
Fasten off. Sew flap and button onto bag.

>> This bag is made with Expressions hand-colored hemp, 4-ply, 93yds/85m/93yds, in A: Wow (orange) and B: Yippi (green).

Super-stretchy shopper

This handy shopping bag is made in the round, with a solid base and a mesh body. Worked in single crochet, the fabric is strong and flexible, and so the bag will expand to fit lots of shopping inside.

PROJECTS

For more single crochet patterns
>> go to pages 36 and 170

Essential information

DIFFICULTY LEVEL Easy

SIZE Approx 10 x 13in (25.5 x 33cm), with 19in (48.5cm) handles

YARN You can use any DK cotton or cotton mix yarn here to get a similar effect

x 5

CROCHET HOOK 7 US (4.5mm) hook

NOTIONS Stitch marker
Yarn needle

GAUGE Exact gauge is not essential

NOTE Mark the first stitch of each round.

Pattern

Work 2 ch.

ROUND 1 8 sc in second chain from hook.

ROUND 2 2 sc in first st, and in each st around. (16 sc). Do not join with a ss. Continue to work in a spiral, remembering to mark the first st of each round.

ROUND 3 *2 sc in next st, 1 sc in next st, rep from * around. (24sts)

ROUND 4 *2 sc in next st, 1 sc in next 2 sts, rep from * around. (32sts)

ROUND 5 *2 sc in next st, 1 sc in next 3 sts, rep from * around. (40sts)

ROUND 6 *2 sc in next st, 1 sc in next 4 sts, rep from * around. (48sts)

ROUND 7 *2 sc in next st, 1 sc in next 5 sts, rep from * around. (56sts)

ROUND 8 *2 sc in next st, 1 sc in next 6 sts, rep from * around. (64sts)

ROUND 9 *2 sc in next st, 1 sc in next 7 sts, rep from * around. (72sts)

ROUND 10 *2 sc in next st, 1 sc in next 8 sts, rep from * around. (80sts)

ROUND 11 *2 sc in next st, 1 sc in next 9 sts, rep from * around. (88sts)

ROUND 12 *2 sc in next st, 1 sc in next 10 sts, rep from * around. (96sts)

ROUND 13 *2 sc in next st, 1 sc in next 11 sts, rep from * around. (104sts)

ROUND 14 *2 sc in next st, 1 sc in next 12 sts, rep from * around. (112sts)

ROUND 15 *2 sc in next st, 1 sc in next 13 sts, rep from * around. (120sts)

ROUND 16 *2 sc in next st, 1 sc in next 14 sts, rep from * around. (128sts)

ROUND 17 *2 sc in next st, 1 sc in next 15 sts, rep from * around. (136sts)

ROUND 18 *2 sc in next st, 1 sc in next 16 sts, rep from * around. (144sts)

ROUND 19 Sc in each st around.

ROUNDS 20–23 Repeat round 19.

Mesh rounds

Now mark the first 4-ch sp (see p.76) at the beginning of each round.

ROUND 24 *Ch 4, skip 2 sts, sc in next, rep from * around, ending with a 4 ch.

ROUND 25 Sc in first 4-ch sp, *4 ch, sc in next 4-ch sp, rep from * around, ending with a 4 ch.

ROUNDS 26–65 Repeat round 25.

ROUND 66 Sc in next sc (mark this stitch), *2 sc in next 4-ch sp, sc in next st, rep from * around.

ROUND 67 Sc in first st (mark this stitch), and in each st around.

ROUNDS 68–70 Repeat round 67. Fasten off.

Handles (make 2)

Work 13 ch.

ROW 1 Sc in second chain from hook and in each ch across, turn. (12sts)

ROW 2 Ch 1, sc in each st across, turn. (12sts)

ROWS 3–46 Repeat row 2. Fasten off.
Sew the handles on the bag and weave in ends.

>> This bag is made with Rowan Softknit Cotton, 115yds/105m/50g, in Sunset red (582).

Crocheting in the round is easy to achieve and allows you to be more versatile with your stitches. Turn to page 126 if you want to try something new, such as making this bag from string.

Essential information

DIFFICULTY LEVEL Easy

SIZE Approx 12 x 9¾in (30 x 25cm) with 9½in (24cm) straps

YARN You can use any 100 percent cotton 4-ply weight yarn for this project

x 3

CROCHET HOOK E/4 US (3.5mm) hook

NOTIONS Yarn needle

TENSION 18 hdc x 16 rows per 4in (10cm)

SPECIAL ABBREVIATIONS

BEG HDC: begin half double stitch. Ch 2, insert hook in second ch from hook, yo, pull up a loop, insert hook in next stitch, yo, pull up a loop, yo and draw hook through all 3 loops.

HDC2TOG: work 2 half double stitches together. (Yo and insert hook in next st, yo and draw a loop through) twice, yo and draw through all 5 loops on hook—1 st decreased.

Everyday bag

This useful everyday bag is worked in the round, increasing until you reach the desired width, then working straight to desired height. The bag is then divided for the handles, which are broad, making them very comfortable to hold.

PROJECTS
For more bag patterns
>> *go to pages 288, 290, and 292*

Pattern

Work 4 ch, ss in first chain to form a ring.

ROUND 1 Ch 2, insert hook in second chain from hook, yo, pull up a loop, insert hook in next stitch, yo, pull up a loop, yo, draw hook through all 3 loops on hook (beg hdc made), work 7 hdc into loop, join with a ss to beg hdc. (8sts)

ROUND 2 Work beg hdc, work another hdc in same st, *2 hdc in next st, repeat from * to end, join with a ss to beg hdc. (16sts)

ROUND 3 Work beg hdc, work another hdc in same st, * hdc in next st, 2 hdc in next, repeat from * to end, join with a ss to beg hdc. (24sts)

ROUND 4 Work beg hdc, work another hdc in same st, *hdc in next 2 sts, 2 hdc in next, repeat from * to end, join with a ss to beg hdc. (32sts)

ROUND 5 Work beg hdc, work another hdc in same st, *hdc in next 3 sts, 2 hdc in next, repeat from * to end, join with a ss to beg hdc. (40sts)

ROUND 6 Work beg hdc, work another hdc in same st, *hdc in next 4 sts, 2 hdc in next, repeat from * to end, join with a ss to beg hdc. (48sts)

ROUND 7 Work beg hdc, work another hdc in same st, *hdc in next 5 sts, 2 hdc in next, repeat from * to end, join with a ss to beg hdc. (56sts)

ROUND 8 Work beg hdc, work another hdc in same st, *hdc in next 6 sts, 2 hdc in next, repeat from * to end, join with a ss to beg hdc. (64sts)

ROUND 9 Beg hdc in next st, hdc in each st to end, join with a ss to beg hdc. (64sts)

ROUNDS 10–12 Repeat round 9.

ROUND 13 Work beg hdc, hdc in same st, *hdc in next 7 sts, 2 hdc in next, repeat from * to end, join with a ss to beg hdc. (72sts)

ROUNDS 14–16 Repeat round 9. (72sts)

ROUND 17 Work beg hdc, hdc in same st, *hdc in next 8 sts, 2 hdc in next st, repeat from * to end, join with a ss to beg hdc. (80sts)

ROUNDS 18–20 Repeat round 9.

ROUND 21 Work beg hdc, hdc in same st, *hdc in next 9 sts, 2 hdc in next st, repeat from * to end, join with a ss to beg hdc. (88sts)

ROUNDS 22–24 Repeat round 9.

ROUND 25 Work beg hdc, hdc in same st, *hdc in next 10 sts, 2 in next, repeat from * to end, join with a ss to beg hdc. (96sts)

ROUNDS 26–42 Repeat round 9. At the end of round 42, do not fasten off. (96sts)

Handles (working in rows)

ROW 1 Beg hdc, hdc in next 10 sts, hdc2tog, hdc in next 24 sts, hdc2tog, turn, leaving remaining 58 sts unworked.

ROW 2 Ch 2, hdc2tog, hdc in next 22 sts, hdc2tog, turn.

ROW 3 Ch 2, hdc2tog, hdc in next 20 sts, hdc2tog, turn.

ROW 4 Ch 2, hdc2tog, hdc in next 18 sts, hdc2tog, turn.

ROW 5 Ch 2, hdc2tog, hdc in next 16 sts, hdc2tog, turn.

ROW 6 Ch 2, hdc2tog, hdc in next 14 sts, hdc2tog, turn.

ROW 7 Beg hdc in first st, hdc in next 15 sts, turn.

ROWS 8–34 Repeat row 7. At the end of row 34 fasten off.

Join yarn with a ss in beg hdc of row 1, and work as follows:

Hdc in next 10 sts, hdc2tog, hdc in next 24 sts, hdc2tog, turn leaving remaining 20 sts unworked.

Repeat rows 2–34. At the end of row 34, do not fasten off.

With wrong sides of handles held together, hdc ends of handles together to join.

Fasten off.

Edging for handles

Join yarn with a sc in row end where handles are joined, sc in each row end of handle, sc in next 20 sts of bag, and sc in each row end of other side of handle; join with a ss to first sc. Fasten off, weave in ends.

Diamond granny bag

Textured granny squares crocheted together ensure this fully lined bag will be a joy to crochet and to use. This bright and cheerful project has an attractive, striped strap and button closure.

PROJECTS

For more granny square patterns
>> go to pages 148, 154, and 302

Essential information

DIFFICULTY LEVEL Intermediate

SIZE 14 x 12in (35 x 30cm), strap measures 27in (68cm) long

YARN Any DK weight yarn will be suitable

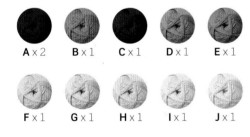

A x 2   B x 1   C x 1   D x 1   E x 1

F x 1   G x 1   H x 1   I x 1   J x 1

CROCHET HOOK G/6 US (4mm) hook

NOTIONS Stitch marker
Yarn needle
2 bag rings, 2½in (6cm) wide
Button, 1¼in (3cm) diameter
Cotton material for lining, measuring 24½ x 12¼in (62 x 31cm), plus seam allowance

GAUGE Exact gauge is not essential

Pattern

Each completed granny square should measure approx 5 x 5in (12 x 12cm).

Granny square

With first color, work 4 ch. Join with ss in last ch from hook to form loop.

ROUND 1 Ch 3 (always counts as 1 dc), (2 dc, 2 ch) into the ring, *(3 dc, 2 ch) into the ring, repeat from * twice, ending with a ss into the second ch at the beginning of the round, changing to second color on the pull through, turn work.

ROUND 2 (3 ch, 2 dc, 2 ch, 3 dc) into the 2-ch sp, *1 ch, (3 dc, 2 ch, 3 dc), into the corner 2-ch sp, repeat from * twice, ending with 1 ch, ss into the second ch at beginning of round, changing to third color on the pull through, turn work.

ROUND 3 (3 ch, 2 dc, 1 ch), into the 1-ch sp, *(3 dc, 2 ch, 3 dc) into the corner 2-ch sp, (1 ch, 3 dc, 1 ch) into the following 1-ch sp, repeat from * twice, (3 dc, 2 ch, 3 dc) into the 2-ch sp, 1 ch, ss into the second ch at beginning of round, changing to fourth color on the pull through, turn work.

ROUND 4 (3 ch, 2 dc, 1 ch), into the ch sp, *(3 dc, 2 ch, 3 dc) into the corner 2-ch sp, ([1 ch, 3 dc, 1 ch] into the following 1-ch sp) twice, 1 ch, repeat from * twice, (3 dc, 2 ch, 3 dc) into the corner 2-ch sp, (1 ch, 3 dc, 1 ch) into the following ch sp, ending with a ss into the second ch at beginning of round, changing to fifth color on the pull through, turn work.

ROUND 5 (3 ch, 2 dc, 1 ch) into the ch sp, (3 dc, 1 ch) into next 1-ch sp *(3dc, 2 ch, 3 dc) into

the corner 2-ch sp, ([1 ch, 3 dc] into the following 1-ch sp) 3 times, 1 ch, repeat from * twice, (3 dc, 2 ch, 3 dc) into the corner 2-ch sp, (1 ch, 3 dc, 1 ch) into the following 1-ch sp, ss into the second ch at beginning of round. Fasten off.

Work 12 more squares.
The colors used for each granny square and their corresponding numbers for assembly (shown below) can simply be used as a guide for substituting any color of choice:

SQUARE	PARTS	YARN USED
1	Folded (strap)	C, D, J, H, A
2	Front	B, J, F, H, A
3	Folded (side)	H, G, C, I, A
4	Folded (base)	F, C, J, B, A
5	Front	J, B, H, D, A
6	Front	C, J, I, E, A
7	Folded (base)	C, I, J, F, A
8	Folded (strap)	J, D, F, H, A
9	Folded (side)	C, J, B, F, A
10	Back	B, H, F, J, A
11	Back	J, B, D, H, A
12	Back	J, H, E, I, A
Flap	Attach to 10 and 12	H, J, B, C, A

>> This bag is made with Berroco Vintage DK, 252yds/230m/100g, in A: Cast iron (2145), B: Bubble (21106), C: Dark denim (2143), D: Delphinium (2155), E: Pool party (21107), F: Envy (2162), G: Breezeway (2194), H: Fondant (2110), I: Minty (2112), and J: Mushroom (2104).

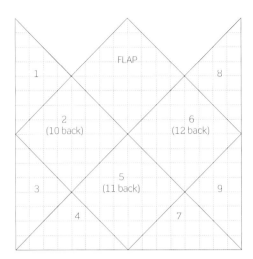

the outer (back loop) only, sc to the last st, fasten off, leaving a long end for weaving in.

ROW 2 Starting back at the first st, and using yarn B, ss into the first ch, 1 ch, sc in back loop only to end of row, fasten off, leaving a long end for weaving in.

Repeat row 2 for five more rows, changing color for each row to D, H, J, F, I.

NEXT ROW With yarn A, ss along edge of last row, in back loop only. Fasten off, leaving a long end for weaving in.

Edging for bag opening

With yarn A and RS of the back of bag facing, join with a ss at the point where square number 8 is joined to the flap.

Ch 1, sc around the top of bag opening, ending with a ss back into the first ch. Turn work, do not fasten off.

Flap edging

ROW 1 Work 39 sc along the edge of flap, place a marker, turn work.

ROW 2 Join in yarn D with a ss and working in outer loop only, work 39 sc to end of flap, fasten off.

ROW 3 Beginning at marker, repeat row 2 using yarn H.

ROW 4 Repeat row 3 using yarn B.

ROW 5 Repeat row 3 using yarn A.

ROW 6 With yarn A, begin at marker, 1 ch, sc along side edges of flap to neaten, work 19 sc, ch 6 to make buttonhole, do not work the next st, sc to end, working up the side edge of flap to neaten, turn work.

ROW 7 Ch 1, sc to 6-ch loop, work 10 sc into the 6-ch loop, sc to end of flap, ending with a ss into last st.

Joining squares

Follow the chart given for placement of each square, above.

To join the squares, place two squares WS together, and with yarn A, join with a ss at the corner, into 1 loop from each square, 1 ch, sc along the edges into 2 loops only (thus creating a ridge on the right side of work).

Bag loops

With yarn A, work 16 ch.

ROW 1 Sc into the second ch from the hook and sc to end. (15sts)

ROW 2 1 ch, sc to end of row.

Repeat row 2 for 8 rows. Fasten off, leaving a long end for weaving in.

Strap

With yarn A, work 112 ch, fasten off, leaving a long end for weaving in.

ROW 1 Starting back at the first ch and with yarn G, ss into the first ch, 1 ch, working into

O-rings and D-rings make it easy to attach straps to a handmade bag. They are available in metal, plastic, and wood, and come in a variety of sizes. We've chosen black plastic to coordinate with the yarn. Fold the edges of your crocheted straps around the bars of each O-ring and sew in place to secure.

Finishing

Fold bag loop in half, lengthwise, insert plastic loop, and sew onto topmost granny square. Repeat for other side.

Neaten strap edges and sew onto bag loops. Weave in all ends.

Cut the cotton lining material to shape using the bag as a template. Make a small hem and sew the lining inside the bag. Sew on a button.

TOP TIP *Use a 50 percent cotton yarn, or a wool mix, for a matte finish.*

Clutch bag

This bag is worked in rows, with two different stitches on different parts of the bag. It is then folded and sewn, to turn it into a clutch bag. Turn to pages 42–43 for more information about double crochet.

PROJECTS
For more double crochet patterns
>> *go to pages 44 and 234*

Essential information

DIFFICULTY LEVEL Easy

SIZE 8$\frac{1}{4}$ x 4$\frac{1}{2}$in (21 x 11.5cm)

YARN You can use any cotton or cotton-blend DK yarn; try adding Lurex® to get a similar effect

x 2

CROCHET HOOK G/6 US (4mm) hook

NOTIONS Yarn needle
$\frac{3}{8}$in (1cm) pearl button

GAUGE Exact gauge is not essential

Pattern
Work 37 ch.
ROW 1 Sc in second chain from hook and in each chain across, turn. (36sts)
ROW 2 Ch 1, sc in each st across, turn. (36sts)
Repeat row 2 until piece measures approx 9$\frac{1}{2}$in (24cm) from beginning.
NEXT ROW Ch 3, dc decrease next 2 sts tog, skip sc directly below 3 ch, and the next sc, (dc, 1 ch, dc) all in next sc, 1 ch, * skip next sc, (dc, 1 ch, dc) all in next sc, 1 ch, rep from * to last 3 sts, dc decrease last 3 sts tog, turn.
NEXT ROW Ch 1, sc in first dc, and in each 1-ch sp across to last st, sc in third of ch 3 of previous row, turn.
Ch 3, skip next st, *dc, ch 1, dc in next st, ch 1, skip next st, rep from * to last st, dc in last st. Repeat last two rows until lacy section measures approx 2$\frac{1}{2}$in (6cm) from the start of doubles row, ending with a *sc* row.

Finishing
Fold bottom of bag up 4$\frac{3}{4}$in (12cm) and sew side seams. Line up top of bag to sew on button. Weave in all ends.

The yarn used for this evening clutch has a silver thread running through it for a party finish. Alternatively, crochet your bag in a dark, matte yarn and apply one or two small rhinestones.

>> This clutch is made with Sirdar Ella Summer Luxe Cotton Blend DK, 138yds/126m/50g, in Peppermint (0007).

TOP TIP
Insert a piece of folded cardboard to keep the clutch rigid.

Child's turtle backpack

This animal-themed bag is a great, fun way for children to carry around their odds and ends. The turtle's belly is made with single crochet stitch worked in the round, while his shell is formed from seven granny hexagons.

PROJECTS

For more granny motif patterns
>> *go to pages 104–106*

Essential information

DIFFICULTY Intermediate

SIZE Approx 15¼ x 14¼in (39 x 36cm)

YARN You can use any DK yarn for this project

A x 2   **B** x 1   **C** x 1   **D** x 1   **E** x 1

CROCHET HOOK E/4 US (3.5mm) and G/6 US (4mm) hooks

NOTIONS Stitch marker
Yarn needle
2 x 1¾in (4.5cm) buckles
½in (12mm) black safety toy eyes
12in (30cm) zipper
Fabric for lining: 2 circles 13in (33cm) diameter
Polyfill
Strong cotton tape for straps, optional

GAUGE 19 sts x 14 rows per 4in (10cm)

<< This bag is made with Rowan Handknit Cotton, 93yds/85m/50g, in A: Gooseberry (219), B: Rosso (215), C: Blue John (365) D: Yacht (357), and E: Ecru (251).

SPECIAL ABBREVIATIONS

ADJUSTABLE RING: See p. 57

BEGINNING BOBBLE ST: Ch 2, yo, insert hook in stitch, yo, draw loop through, yo, draw through 2 loops on the hook, yo, insert hook in same space, yo, draw loop through, yo, draw through 2 loops on hook, yo, draw through all 3 loops on hook.

BOBBLE STITCH: See p. 198

HTR: half treble stitch. This is a simple variation on the treble stitch (see p. 48). Yo twice, insert hook in next stitch and draw up a loop (4 loops on hook), yo and draw through two loops (3 loops on hook), yo and draw through all 3 loops (1 loop on hook).

Bag front

HEXAGON MOTIFS PATTERN

With yarn A (color 1) and E/4 US (3.5mm) hook, make an adjustable ring and work 6 sc into the ring, ss to join ring. (6sts)

ROUND 1 Work beginning bobble st in first st, (2 ch, bobble st) in remaining 5 sts, ss into top of first bobble to join round. (6 bobbles, 6-ch sp)

Cut yarn, leaving a long tail, and pull through. Join second yarn (color 2) at any ch sp.

ROUND 2 Work beginning bobble st in ch sp, 2 ch, bobble st in same ch sp, 2 ch, (bobble st, 2 ch, bobble st, 2 ch) in remaining 5-ch sp. Ss into top of first bobble to join round. (12 bobbles, 12-ch sp)

Cut yarn, leaving a long tail, and pull through. Join third yarn (color 3) at any ch sp.

ROUND 3 (2 ch, 2 dc, 2 ch, 3 dc) in first ch sp, 3 dc in next ch sp, *(3 dc, 2 ch, 3 dc) in next

ch sp, 3 dc in next ch sp; rep from * to end, ss to join the round. (54 dc, 6-ch sp)

HEXAGON MOTIFS

Motif 1: Color 1 A, color 2 E, color 3 D.
Motifs 2, 3, and 4: Color 1 A, color 2 E, color 3 B.
Motifs 5, 6, and 7: Color 1 D, color 2 E, color 3 C.

Joining motifs

Use yarn E to join motifs together. Put motifs 1 and 2 together with the wrong side facing. Work stitches over both of the motifs to join together. Join yarn at a ch sp, sc in ch sp, along next 9 sts, sc in ch space. Motif 2 is now attached. Next attach motif 5 to the next side of motif 1 in the same way. Then working counterclockwise around all the sides of motif 1, add the next four motifs as shown in the diagram below.

Hexagon motifs diagram

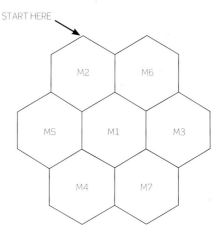

Complete by joining the sides of the motifs together in the same way.

Join yarn E to the ch sp marked by the arrow in the Hexagon motifs diagram on page 303. Work in rounds around the edges of the joined-up hexagons.

ROUND 1 Dc in every st and every outer ch sp around. (174sts)

Change to yarn A and use a stitch marker to mark the first stitch of each new round.

ROUND 2 *10 sc, 2 hdc, 2 dc, 2 htr, 5 dtr, 2 htr, 2 dc, 2 hdc, 2 sc; rep from * to end.

ROUND 3 Dc in each st to end.

ROUND 4 *27 sc, sc2tog; rep from * to end. (168sts)

ROUND 5 Dc in each st to end.

ROUND 6 *26 sc, sc2tog; rep from * to end. (162sts)

ROUND 7 Dc in each st to end.

ROUND 8 *25 sc, sc2tog; rep from * to end. (156sts)

ROUND 9 Dc in each st to end.

Cut the yarn, leaving a long tail, and secure.

Bag back

With yarn A and E/4 US (3.5mm) hook, make an adjustable ring and work 6 sc into ring. (6sts)

ROUND 1 2 sc into each st to end, place marker. (12sts)

ROUND 2 *1 sc, 2 sc in next st; rep from * to end. (18sts)

ROUND 3 *2 sc, 2 sc in next st; rep from * to end. (24sts)

ROUND 4 *3 sc, 2 sc in next st; rep from * to end. (30sts)

ROUND 5 *4 sc, 2 sc in next st; rep from * to end. (36sts)

ROUND 6 *5 sc, 2 sc in next st; rep from * to end. (42sts)

ROUND 7 *6 sc, 2 sc in next st; rep from * to end. (48sts)

ROUND 8 *7 sc, 2 sc in next st; rep from * to end. (54sts)

ROUND 9 *8 sc, 2 sc in next st; rep from * to end. (60sts)

ROUND 10 *9 sc, 2 sc in next st; rep from * to end. (66sts)

ROUND 11 *10 sc, 2 sc in next st; rep from * to end. (72sts)

ROUND 12 *11 sc, 2 sc in next st; rep from * to end. (78sts)

ROUND 13 *12 sc, 2 sc in next st; rep from * to end. (84sts)

ROUND 14 *13 sc, 2 sc in next st; rep from * to end. (90sts)

ROUND 15 *14 sc, 2 sc in next st; rep from * to end. (96sts)

ROUND 16 *15 sc, 2 sc in next st; rep from * to end. (102sts)

ROUND 17 *16 sc, 2 sc in next st; rep from * to end. (108sts)

ROUND 18 *17 sc, 2 sc in next st; rep from * to end. (114sts)

ROUND 19 *18 sc, 2 sc in next st; rep from * to end. (120sts)

ROUND 20 *19 sc, 2 sc in next st; rep from * to end. (126sts)

ROUND 21 *20 sc, 2 sc in next st; rep from * to end. (132sts)

ROUND 22 *21 sc, 2 sc in next st; rep from * to end. (138sts)

ROUND 23 *22 sc, 2 sc in next st; rep from * to end. (144sts)

ROUND 24 *23 sc, 2 sc in next st; rep from * to end. (150sts)

ROUND 25 *24 sc, 2 sc in next st; rep from * to end. (156sts)

ROUNDS 26–29 Dc in each st to end. Cut the yarn, leaving a long tail, and secure. Sew the front and back together leaving a 12in (30cm) gap at one end.

Cut two pieces of lining fabric slightly larger than the entire bag. Sew the pieces together, leaving a 12in (30cm) gap at one end. Turn RS out and pin in place inside the bag. Pin a 12in (30cm) zipper into the opening. Sew zipper and lining in place.

Turtle head

With yarn A and E/4 US (3.5mm) hook, make an adjustable ring and work 6 sc into ring. (6 sts)

ROUND 1 2 sc into each st to end, place marker. (12sts)

ROUND 2 *1 sc, 2 sc in next st; rep from * to end. (18sts)

Give your turtle a happy smile using two large backstitches. Use safety eyes to prevent little fingers from pulling them out and attach them when stated within the pattern.

An adjustable buckle is really useful, since it will allow the straps to be as long or short as you like. Plastic and metal buckles are available at most fabric stores. Choose a contrasting color to stand out or a coordinating shade of green to blend in.

A white zipper and lining fabric work well for this project, but since they will not be visible for most of the time, you can use whatever color you prefer. Attach the zipper using a long strand of matching yarn or thread.

ROUND 3 *2 sc, 2 sc in next st; rep from * to end. (24sts)

ROUND 4 *3 sc, 2 sc in next st; rep from * to end. (30sts)

ROUND 5 *9 sc, 2 sc in next st; rep from * to end. (33sts)

ROUND 6 *10 sc, 2 sc in next st; rep from * to end. (36sts)

ROUND 7 *11 sc, 2 sc in next st; rep from * to end. (39sts) Mark this round with a stitch marker.

ROUND 8 *12 sc, 2 sc in next st; rep from * to end. (42sts)

ROUNDS 9–12 Dc in each st to end.

ROUND 13 *12 sc, sc2tog; rep from * to end. (39sts)

ROUND 14 *11 sc, sc2tog; rep from * to end. (36sts)

ROUNDS 15–16 Dc in each st to end.

ROUND 17 *sc2tog, 4 sc; rep from * to end. (30sts)

ROUND 18 *sc2tog, 3 sc; rep from * to end. (24sts)

Cut the yarn and secure. Put eyes on the marked round 12 sts apart. Stuff the head.

Legs (make 4)

With yarn A and E/4 US (3.5mm) hook, make an adjustable ring and work 6 sc into ring. (6sts)

ROUND 1 2 sc into each st to the end, place marker. (12sts)

ROUND 2 *1 sc, 2 sc in next st; rep from * to end. (18sts)

ROUND 3 *2 sc, 2 sc in next st; rep from * to end. (24sts)

ROUNDS 4–6 Dc in each st to end.

ROUND 7 *sc2tog, 6 sc; rep from * to end. (21sts)

ROUNDS 8–9 Dc in each st to end.

ROUND 10 *sc2tog, 5 sc; rep from * to end. (18sts)

ROUNDS 11–12 Dc in each st to the end. Cut the yarn, leaving a long tail, and secure. Stuff.

Tail

With yarn A and E/4 US (3.5mm) hook, make an adjustable ring and work 4 sc into ring. (4sts)

ROUND 1 *1 sc, 2 sc in next st; rep from * to end, place marker. (6sts)

ROUND 2 *2 sc, 2 sc in next st; rep from * to end. (8sts)

ROUND 3 *3 sc, 2 sc in next st; rep from * to end. (10sts)

ROUND 4 *4 sc, 2 sc in next st; rep from * to end. (12sts)

ROUNDS 5–6 sc in each st to end. (15sts)

Cut the yarn, leaving a long tail, and secure. Stuff the tail. Sew the head, legs, and tail onto the body of the backpack. Weave in loose ends.

Straps (make 4)

These are worked straight. Turn your work at the end of each row.

With yarn A and G/6 US (4mm) hook, ch 7.

ROW 1 Starting in second ch from hook, sc in each st, ch 1, turn.

ROW 2 Dc in each st, ch 1, turn.

Repeat the last row until the strap is 14in (35cm) long. Cut the yarn and secure. Strengthen the straps with strong cotton tape, if desired. Sew the end of two straps onto the middle bar of the buckles. Sew the straps in place on the bag. Thread the other end of the straps through the buckle to finish.

Change purses

These tiny projects are ideal for getting children into crochet. They are both worked in the round, in two different ways, to create small pouches for change.

PROJECTS

For more single crochet patterns
>> go to pages 64, 218, and 266

Essential information

DIFFICULTY LEVEL Easy

SIZE Round purse: approx 4in (10cm) diameter
Rectangular purses: approx 3½ x 2¾in (9 x 7cm)

YARN Any fine crochet thread will work

A x 6   **B** x 2   **C** x 2   **D** x 2   **E** x 6

CROCHET HOOK B/1 US (2.5mm) hook

NOTIONS Stitch marker
Yarn needle
3½in (9cm) zipper for each change purse
Bead (optional)

GAUGE Exact gauge is not essential

NOTE Change purses are worked in spirals. Do not join rounds, but place a marker at first stitch of the round, moving it each round to mark the beginning of the next round.

Round purse

Make 2 ch and work 6 sc into second ch from hook, join round with a ss to first st.
ROUND 1 1 ch, work 2 sc in each sc around, do not join round, place marker. (12sts)
ROUND 2 (2 sc in next sc, 1 sc in next 1 sc) around. (18sts)
ROUND 3 (2 sc in next sc, 1 sc in next 2 sc) around. (24sts)
ROUND 4 (2 sc in next sc, 1 sc in next 3 sc) around. (30sts)
ROUND 5 (2 sc in next sc, 1 sc in next 4 sc) around. (36sts)
ROUND 6 (2 sc in next sc, 1 sc in next 5 sc) around. (42sts)
Continue in this way, working one extra st between increases in each round until you have worked 9 rounds and have 60 sts.
Work straight on these 60 sts for 7 rounds.
ROUND 17 (sc2tog, 1 sc in next 8 sc) around. (54sts)
Work 2 rounds straight.
ROUND 20 (sc2tog, 1 sc in next 7 sc) around. (48sts)
Work one round straight.
ROUND 22 (sc2tog, 1 sc in next 6 sc) around. (42sts)
Work two rounds straight.
Fasten off yarn and weave in ends.

Rectangular purse

Work 31 ch.
ROUND 1 3 sc into second ch from hook, 1 sc in each ch to last ch, 3 sc in last ch, turn work 180 degrees and work along other side of ch, working 1 sc into the bottom of each ch, do not join round.
ROUND 2 1 sc into each sc around.
Rep last round for desired height of purse, sample shown is 2¾in (7cm), changing colors for striping where desired.
Fasten off yarn and weave in ends.

Finishing

Sew zipper into top of each purse. Make a tassel (see p. 74) and attach it by inserting the strands through the zipper hole, securing as normal and adding a bead, if desired.

When choosing a bead to attach to your zipper, make sure that it's central hole is sufficiently large enough to thread the strands of yarn through. Tie a knot right up close to the bead to secure.

>> These change purses are made with Rowan Siena 4-ply, 306yds/280m/100g, in A: White (651). B: Topaz (689), C: Tandoori (676), D: Greengage (661), and E: Mariner (672).

Tablet sleeve

This practical, crocheted tablet cover is quick to work both in the round and in rows, and it will protect your tablet from knocks and scratches. It closes with a button-and-loop fastening for easy access.

PROJECTS
For more half double patterns
>> *go to pages 40 and 294*

Essential information

DIFFICULTY LEVEL Easy

SIZE Approx 10 x 8in (25 x 20cm)

YARN You can use any chunky weight yarn to complete this project; some synthetic fiber is preferable, for durability

x 2

CROCHET HOOK I/9 US (5.5mm) hook

NOTIONS Yarn needle
1¼in (3cm) button, in tonal color

GAUGE 14 sts x 14 rows per 4in (10cm) square

Half double crochet, worked in a chunky yarn, creates a dense fabric that is ideal for protecting your tablet screen from getting scratched or knocked. A stylish button adds a decorative feature and gives this case a modern look.

Pattern

Work 30 ch.
ROW 1 Work 1 hdc in second ch from hook (2 ch count as a st), work 1 hdc in each st to end. (29sts)
Continue to work 1 hdc in each st on the back side of the foundation chain to end. (58sts)
Begin working in rounds. Do not turn or join.
ROUND 1–31 1 hdc in each st.
ROUND 32 1 hdc in each st, ch 1, turn.
Begin working in rows.
ROW 1 1 hdc in next 29 sts, ch 1, turn. (29sts)
ROW 2 1 hdc in each st, ch 1, turn.
ROWS 3–9 Repeat row 2.
ROW 10 1 hdc in first 13 st, ch 3, miss 3 st, 1 hdc in last 13 sts, ch 1, turn.
ROW 11 1 sc in first 13 st, 3 sc in ch loop, 1 sc in last 13 st.
Fasten off, weave in ends.

Finishing

Place a tablet in the cover and close the flap to mark the position of the button. Attach the button securely with a strand of yarn.

>> This sleeve is made with Lion Brand Jiffy Solid, 135yds/123m/85g, in Apple green (132).

Choose a synthetic yarn to protect your screen.

TOP
TIP

Glossary

Adjustable ring A method of beginning crochet in the round that allows you to pull the ring tightly closed after the first round, thus eliminating the unsightly central hole (see p. 57).

Afghan stitch See Tunisian stitch. Afghan stitches are shaped like little squares with two horizontal strands of yarn and a vertical bar on top.

Afghan square An alternative name for the granny square.

Amigurumi A Japanese style of crocheting, or knitting, small animals and other objects, often with anthropomorphic features.

Back and front posts Vertical segments of a crochet stitch.

Ball band The wrapper around a ball of yarn that usually details fiber content, weight, length, hook size, gauge, and washing instructions.

Ball-winder A device for winding hanks of yarn into balls; also used to wind two or more strands together to make a double-stranded yarn. Often used in conjunction with a swift.

Blocking Manipulating the finished piece into the correct shape by wetting and pinning it out, or pinning it out and steam-pressing it.

Broomstick lace A lacy stitch made using both a crochet hook and knitting needle.

Button loop An alternative to a buttonhole, a chain loop is crocheted into the last two rows, or edging, on a piece of crocheted fabric (see p. 89).

Chain loop, chain space A length of chain stitches worked between basic stitches to create a space in the fabric.

Colorwork Any method of incorporating color into crochet, including stripes, jacquard, and intarsia.

Darning in ends The process of completing a piece of crochet by weaving in the yarn ends using a blunt-ended yarn needle to disguise them.

Decrease Removing a stitch or stitches to reduce the number of working stitches and shape the fabric.

Single crochet join An invisible way of joining in new yarn, using single crochet stitches, when at the end of the current row or round.

Dye lot A record taking during the dyeing of yarn to identify it. Use yarn from one dye lot for each project and do not mix the dye batches or your crochet fabric may change in tone.

Fibers Yarn is made up of fibers, such as the hair from an animal, man-made (synthetic) fibers, or fibers derived from a plant. The fibers are processed and spun into a yarn.

Filet crochet A form of openwork crochet created by working a combination of squares or rectangles of open mesh and solid blocks.

Foundation chain The base of chain stitches that the first row of crochet is worked onto.

Front and back loop only A crochet instruction to indicate that the hook should be inserted into either the front or back loop only of a stitch.

Gauge The number of stitches and rows over a given area, usually 4in (10cm) square. Also, the relative tightness used by the crocheter. Changing hook size can help achieve correct gauge.

Hank A twisted ring of yarn that needs to be wound into one or more balls before it can be used.

Increase Adding a stitch or stitches to increase the number of working stitches and shape the fabric.

Intarsia A technique in which a color appears only in a section of a row and is not needed across the whole row. Unlike jacquard crochet, more than two colors may be worked in a row. A separate ball or length of yarn is used for each area of color and carried vertically up to the next row when it is needed again.

Jacquard crochet A type of colorwork crochet worked in single crochet stitch, with no more than two colors in each row, in which the color not in use is carried across the top of the row below and covered with the stitches of the other color so that it is hidden from view. This results in a thicker-than-normal fabric, so it is best worked in a fine yarn.

Medallion (or motif) A flat-shaped piece of crochet worked from the center outward.

Möebius strip Also called a twisted cylinder, this shape is a loop with a half-twist in it. Often used as a shape for crocheted cowls.

Notions Items other than fabric or yarn needed to complete a project, such as a button, zipper, or elastic. Notions are normally listed in the pattern.

Openwork crochet A lacelike effect created by working chain spaces and/or loops between the basic stitches.

Plying This is a process used to create a strong, balanced yarn. All yarns are made from more than one strand of spun fiber, so 4-ply is four strands plied together. Plying prevents the yarn from twisting.

Raised stitches Three-dimensional crochet stitches, such as bobbles and puffs, that create texture. Great for hats and blankets.

Right side (RS) The front of a piece of fabric, the side that will normally be in view when the piece is finished.

Round A row worked in a circle, with the last stitch of a row being joined to the first to complete the circle.

Roving A long and narrow bundle of unspun fiber, produced during the process of making spun yarn from wool fleeces. Rovings are used mainly for spinning, but can also be used for making many kinds of felted items and other specialty textiles.

Row Working back and forth in rows to create a piece of crocheted fabric. Turn the work at the end of each row, making a turning chain, and start back across the next row.

Seam The join formed when two pieces of fabric are sewn or crocheted together.

Slipknot A knot that is formed when placing the first loop on a crochet hook.

Slip stitch The shortest of all the crochet stitches. Although slip stitches can be worked in rows, the resulting fabric is very dense and suitable only for bag handles. Slip stitches are frequently used to join new yarn, to work invisibly along the top of a row to move to a new position, and to join rounds.

Skein Yarn wound into an oblong shape that is ready to crochet.

Stitch marker A device used to mark locations on a work in progress (see p. 20). Often used in circular crochet to mark the start and end of a round.

Swift An umbrellalike tool used to hold a hank of yarn while it is being wound off into a ball.

Tension Another term for gauge.

Tunisian crochet Also known as afghan crochet, a style of crochet that takes elements from both knitting and crochet, creating a fusion of techniques. A Tunisian hook looks similar to a knitting needle but either has a hook at both ends, or a hook at one end and a stopper at the other. The resulting fabric is slightly less elastic than normal crochet.

Turning chain A length of stitches worked at the start of a row in order to bring the hook up to the necessary height to work the first stitch of that row (see p. 68).

T-shirt yarn A unique, super bulky yarn produced from stretchy jersey fabric as a by-product of garment manufacturing. This type of yarn is becoming popular in crochet for making sturdy items (see p. 164). Because the material is recycled, every colorway is a limited edition.

Velcro™ Two-part fabric fastening consisting of two layers, a "hook" side and a "loop" side; when pressed together the two pieces cling together.

Wool A natural animal fiber, available in a range of weights, weaves, and textures. It is warm, comfortable to wear, and crease-resistant.

Wrong side (WS) The reverse of a piece of fabric, the side that will normally be hidden from view when the piece is finished.

Yarn Fibers that have been spun into a long strand. Yarns may be made of natural fibers, man-made fibers, a blend of the two, or even non-standard materials.

Yarn bobbin Small plastic shape for holding yarn when doing intarsia work, where there are many yarns in different colors (see p. 20).

Crochet terminology

The following terms are commonly used in crochet patterns. Many crochet terms are the same in the US and the UK, but where they differ, the UK equivalent is given in parentheses. Turn to the pages indicated for how to work the various increases, decreases, or stitch techniques listed.

bobble: A cluster stitch generally made up of double crochet, where several half-finished stitches are worked into the same stitch from the row below and then joined at the top (see p. 79).

cluster: A group of stitches worked into the same stitch, but only equaling one stitch in total. They are usually decreased, or left half-finished, and then finished at once to produce one stitch (see p. 79).

crab stitch: A reverse single crochet stitch. Instead of working from right to left, it is worked from left to right, creating a twisted edge.

dc2tog (work 2 dc together): See p. 53. (UK tr2tog)

dc3tog (work 3 dc together): (Yo and insert hook in next st, yo and draw a loop through, yo and draw through first 2 loops on hook) 3 times, yo and draw through all 4 loops on hook—2 sts decreased. (UK tr3tog)

fasten off: Cut the yarn and draw it through the remaining loop on the hook to secure (see p. 25).

foundation row: The first row of a piece of crochet (the row worked onto the foundation chain) is sometimes called the foundation row.

hdc2tog (work 2 hdc together): (Yo and insert hook in next st, yo and draw a loop through) twice, yo and draw through all 5 loops on hook— 1 st decreased. (UK htr2tog)

hdc3tog (work 3 hdc together): (Yo and insert hook in next st, yo and draw a loop through) 3 times, yo and draw through all 7 loops on hook— 2 sts decreased. (UK htr3tog)

popcorn: A bobble made with complete stitches, generally double crochet, then drawn together at the top (see p. 79).

puff stitch: A bobble made with half doubles; also called a pineapple stitch.

sc2tog (work 2 sc together): See p. 52. (UK dc2tog)

sc3tog (work 3 sc together): [Insert hook in next st, yo and draw a loop through] 3 times, yo and draw through all 4 loops on hook—2 sts decreased. (UK dc3tog).

shell: Several stitches worked into the same stitch in the previous row or into the same chain space (see p. 78).

skip a stitch: Do not work into the stitch, but go on to the next stitch. (UK "miss" a stitch)

Index

Acknowledgments

Dorling Kindersley would like to thank the following people for their hard work and contributions toward *Crochet*:

Crochet designers

Lesley Arnold-Hopkins: Child's hat with earflaps p. 196, Tweed cowl p. 204, Child's hoodie p. 240; **Vicki Brown:** Men's beanie hat p. 194, Men's chunky scarf p. 206, Ladies' ankle socks p. 224, Men's chunky socks p. 226, Striped sweater p. 236, Cropped sweater p. 250, Summer tunic dress p. 246; **Ali Campbell:** Baby blanket p. 148, Fish and starfish garland p. 180; **May Corfield:** Desktop storage pots p. 162, Cat basket p. 174; **Simone Francis:** Intarsia pillow p. 122, Ladies' textured cardigan p. 254; Diamond granny bag p. 296, **Melanie Galloway:** Straw beach bag p. 290, Super-stretchy shopper p. 292, Everyday bag p. 294, Clutch bag p. 300; **Shelley Gould:** Fabric pillows p. 98; **Helen Jordan:** Broomstick lace shawl p. 202; **Claire Montgomerie:** Beaded necklace p. 28, Chunky bracelet p. 30, Cell phone cover p. 36, Pretty headbands p. 46, Party bunting p. 54, Circular pillow p. 64, Flower garland p. 80, Crochet-edged pillows p. 98, Flower blanket p. 142, Lap blanket p. 144, Colorful granny blanket p. 146, Chevron pillow p. 152, Structured baskets p. 164, Fruit bowl p. 176, Filigree bookmarks p. 178, Flower pin cushion p. 184, Baby bonnet p. 190, Child's hat with ears p. 192, Lacy scarf p. 200, Ladies' wrist warmers p. 214, Giant play ball p. 264, Change purses p. 306; **Margaret O'Mara:** Owl pillow p. 156, Baby's crossover cardigan p. 230, Child's poncho p. 234; **Wendy Rainthorpe:** Shell mesh scarf p. 116, Mother elephant and baby p. 266, Tablet sleeve p. 308; **Irene Strange:** Baby girl's booties p. 216, Baby boy's booties p. 218; **Tracey Todhunter:** Striped washcloths p. 34, self-fringing scarf p. 40, Textured pillow p. 44, Coaster set p. 58, Pot holders p. 60, Granny pillow p. 154, Hanging toy basket p. 166, Round stool cover p. 168, Rustic ottomans p. 170, Chunky rug p. 186, Child's wrist warmers p. 210, Child's mittens with string p. 212, Child's edged slippers p. 220, Ladies' soft slippers p. 222, Granny square bag p. 288; **Emma Varnam:** Women's beret p. 198, Baby rattles p. 260; **Liz Ward:** Teddy bear p. 132, Rag doll p. 270, Polar bear with scarf p. 274, Floppy-eared bunny p. 278, Jungle finger puppets p. 282, Child's turtle backpack p. 302.

Pattern checker Carol Ibbetson
Proofreaders Angela Baynham, Erica Sanders-Foege
Indexer Marie Lorimer
Design assistance Elaine Hewson, Hannah Moore, and Navidita Thapa
Editorial assistance Christine Stroyan
Photography assistant Julie Stewart
Props Backgrounds Prop Hire
Location for photography 1st Option
Models Estelle Abberley, Georgia Abberley, Celia Arn, Liz Boyd, Joshua Caulfield, Maria Clancy, Clare Cross, Maria Elston, Marco Elston, Lucas Goldstein, Saskia Janssen, Martha Jenkinson, Bodhi Nair, Tulsi Nair, Clara Proctor, Martha Rhodes, Julie Stewart, Eden White, Mia White, and Oscar the cat

The following yarn manufacturers and distributors for supplying yarn for some projects by:

Coats Craft UK, DMC Creative World, Rico Design, Artesano Ltd., Designer Yarns Ltd., King Cole Ltd, Sirdar Spinning Ltd, Texere Yarns Ltd, Thomas B. Ramsden & Co.

About the consultant

Claire Montgomerie is a textiles designer who specializes in crochet and knitting, constructing fabrics, garments, creatures, and accessories that are fun, quirky, and modern. Her main goal is to reinvent the products of ancient and traditional needlecraft processes, while retaining all their intricacies and comforting charm. Claire has written many crochet and knitting books and also edits the UK craft magazine, *Inside Crochet*.